Perspectives on Rethinking and Reforming Education

Series Editors

Zhongying Shi, Faculty of Education, Beijing Normal University, Beijing, China
Shengquan Yu, Faculty of Education, Beijing Normal University, Beijing, China

This book series brings together the latest insights and work regarding the future of education from a group of highly regarded scholars around the world. It is the first collection of interpretations from around the globe and contributes to the interdisciplinary and international discussions on possible future demands on our education system. It serves as a global forum for scholarly and professional debate on all aspects of future education. The book series proposes a total rethinking of how the whole education process can be reformed and restructured, including the main drivers and principles for reinventing schools in the global knowledge economy, models for designing smart learning environments at the institutional level, a new pedagogy and related curriculums for the 21st century, the transition to digital and situated learning resources, open educational resources and MOOCs, new approaches to cognition and neuroscience as well as the disruption of education sectors. The series provides an opportunity to publish reviews, issues of general significance to theory development, empirical data-intensive research and critical analysis innovation in educational practice. It provides a global perspective on the strengths and weaknesses inherent in the implementation of certain approaches to the future of education. It not only publishes empirical studies but also stimulates theoretical discussions and addresses practical implications. The volumes in this series are interdisciplinary in orientation, and provide a multiplicity of theoretical and practical perspectives. Each volume is dedicated to a specific theme in education and innovation, examining areas that are at the cutting edge of the field and are groundbreaking in nature. Written in an accessible style, this book series will appeal to researchers, policy-makers, scholars, professionals and practitioners working in the field of education.

More information about this series at http://www.springer.com/series/14177

Xudong Zhu · Jian Li

Faculty Development in Chinese Higher Education

Concepts, Practices, and Strategies

 Springer

Xudong Zhu
Faculty of Education
Beijing Normal University
Beijing, China

Jian Li
Faculty of Education
Beijing Normal University
Beijing, China

Research on the Institutional Guarantee of Teacher Education Quality in China (ID:17JJD880003)

ISSN 2366-1658   ISSN 2366-1666 (electronic)
Perspectives on Rethinking and Reforming Education
ISBN 978-981-13-7766-2   ISBN 978-981-13-7767-9 (eBook)
https://doi.org/10.1007/978-981-13-7767-9

© Springer Nature Singapore Pte Ltd. 2019
This work is subject to copyright. All rights are reserved by the Publisher, whether the whole or part of the material is concerned, specifically the rights of translation, reprinting, reuse of illustrations, recitation, broadcasting, reproduction on microfilms or in any other physical way, and transmission or information storage and retrieval, electronic adaptation, computer software, or by similar or dissimilar methodology now known or hereafter developed.
The use of general descriptive names, registered names, trademarks, service marks, etc. in this publication does not imply, even in the absence of a specific statement, that such names are exempt from the relevant protective laws and regulations and therefore free for general use.
The publisher, the authors and the editors are safe to assume that the advice and information in this book are believed to be true and accurate at the date of publication. Neither the publisher nor the authors or the editors give a warranty, expressed or implied, with respect to the material contained herein or for any errors or omissions that may have been made. The publisher remains neutral with regard to jurisdictional claims in published maps and institutional affiliations.

This Springer imprint is published by the registered company Springer Nature Singapore Pte Ltd.
The registered company address is: 152 Beach Road, #21-01/04 Gateway East, Singapore 189721, Singapore

Foreword

The model of faculty development with Chinese characteristics is initially constructed and epitomized in the book from Chinese political, cultural, and social dimensions. This book concentrates on investigating faculty development model at the Chinese context in conceptual, practical, and strategic domains. It is expected to satisfy the widespread craving for an in-depth understanding of the currently vivid historical landscape insightfully in contemporary Chinese higher education system. In addition, this book also offers a critical reflection on constructing the model of faculty development with Chinese characteristics.

The detail on each chapter is illustrated as follows:
The introductory chapter involves clarifying the context of the research on faculty development at Chinese universities and colleges. The study on faculty development is subjected to a systematic and in-depth study of the nature and internal logic of the development of faculty member in contemporary China. Specifically, the term faculty development is considered as an important academic and scientific research profession. In addition, the study on faculty development is conducive to promoting the overall comprehensive development of universities and colleges in the Chinese context. As an important academic research profession, the study on faculty development is conducive for promoting the development of faculty members. Since 1959, Chinese scholars did lots of research on faculty development in order to examine the overall landscape of faculty development in the current Chinese context. Therefore, this chapter involves reviewing and analyzing the general situation of faculty development at Chinese universities and colleges. In addition, the "subject-object" clustering model is proposed to analyze the study on faculty development at Chinese context.

Chapter 2 concentrates on offering the overview of research on Western faculty development from historical, theoretical, and practical perspectives. Specifically, a historical review of Western faculty development research involves examining the academic research ability, teaching ability, and social service ability of faculty at universities and colleges. The history of faculty development can be traced back to Socrates and Plato in ancient Greece. In addition, the theoretical study on faculty development focuses on introducing and investigating the theoretical origin and theoretical development of faculty in Western developed countries. The practical research on faculty development concentrates on two aspects: one is to study the current situation and existing problems of faculty development in recent years; the other is to draw lessons from and introduce the problems and contents of the research on faculty development in Western countries.

Chapter 3 involves conceptualizing faculty development model from Chinese context. Faculty development model at Chinese context involves Chinese-specific educational, historical, and cultural elements historically and contextually. Therefore, this chapter is mainly divided into three parts: in the first part, the introduction on faculty development model is discussed to offer an overview of the landscape of faculty development. The second part involves exploring and constructing a faculty development model with Chinese characteristics. The faculty development model with Chinese characteristics is synthesized as "M-RTS" ("M" represents faculty professional morality; "R" represents research; "T" represents teaching; "S" represents service). In conclusion, faculty development model with Chinese characteristics offers a specific insight to examine the rationale of faculty development model from Chinese contextual perspective.

Chapter 4 explores the rationale of Chinese faculty professional morality through historical comparisons of the elements of faculty professional morality between Western and Eastern. First, the study synthesizes Western faculty professional morality as deontology, utilitarianism and egoism-focused ethics, reasoning competencies, civic-dominated moral and modern faculty morality, and identity-oriented professional ethics-oriented contemporary faculty morality. Second, the interior–exterior inherited model is initially proposed to examine the rationale of Chinese characterized faculty professional morality, including ancient Chinese faculty morality philosophy of fraternity, loyalty and selfless dedication, make faculty an example, equality, Chinese modern faculty professional morality of freedom, equality and fraternity, comprehensive personality, and Chinese contemporary faculty professional morality of political ideological-oriented mandate. In addition, the differences and similarities between Chinese and Western faculty moral model are explored to examine the paradigm of faculty professional morality contextually. The conclusion and remarks are provided at the end of the study.

Chapter 5 concentrates on introducing Chinese faculty development centers from the aim, goal, programs, platform, and politics perspectives. The Center for Faculty Development of Beijing Normal University is examined as one example to investigate the specific development of faculty development center contextually. In addition, the overview of the Center for Faculty Development of Beijing Normal University involves mission, working concept, working standards, work content, working principle, and faculty development assessment.

Chapter 6 mainly involves providing the whole landscape of Chinese faculty development from Chinese institutional perspective. A couple of experts and scholars in the field of Chinese faculty development are invited to examine the problems, difficulties, and strategies of Chinese faculty development contextually. Overall speaking, there are 40 interviews transcripts, focusing on both high-frequency words and the key points.

Chapter 7 concentrates on analyzing the previous interviews of Chinese faculty development from a qualitative approach. NVivo 12 is to be used for analyzing 40 interviews and to obtain a series of analytical results. Along with the analytical results, we can observe that the high-frequency words are generally identical, and they occurred in different interviews with different proportions, which we can get the corresponding key points of the interview. It also indicates that with different positions, it is possible that the ideas and opinions can be different toward the same question.

Chapter 8 involves exploring faculty development at Chinese context from conclusion, remark, and implication perspectives. Along with the analyses result from the previous chapter, this chapter is fundamentally subject to offer explanations and illustrations to examine the complexity of constructing faculty development at Chinese context. The conclusion, remarks, and implication are proposed to epitomize faculty development with Chinese characteristics.

Beijing, China   Jian Li

Acknowledgements

In the realization of this book, I am grateful for the generosity and positive spirit of collegiality. I would like to express my appreciation to many experts and scholars to accept interviews to share their academic viewpoints and experiences in order to enrich the study of faculty development contextually.

Warm Thanks To

Wangqian Fu is a doctoral candidate in Faculty of Education, Beijing Normal University. Her research interests include education policy, inclusive education, and special education with research and publications on internationalization of higher education; the implication of inclusive education of U.S. to China; the education equality for the children with disabilities. During her doctoral program, she works in the China Institute of Education and Social Development as a research assistant, being responsible for editing public opinion of education weekly, which is entrusted by the Ministry of Finance.

Jinhui Xu is a Ph.D. student of statistics at Arizona State University. He earned his M.S. in statistics from Indiana University. His main research areas are causal inference, Bayesian statistics, and educational statistics. Now his interest is to develop a novel model in causal inference by combining stochastic process, non- and semi parametric statistics and Bayesian Statistics and endeavor to apply it into the social science area. In educational statistics, he is now interested in cheating detection in large-scale testing. He is also interested in financial statistics and mathematics (mostly in option pricing), (Bayesian) design of experiments (to investigate causality), and actuarial science.

Contents

Part I Conceptual Faculty Development at Chinese Context

1 Overview of Chinese Faculty Development Research: Themes and Strategies 3
   1.1 A Brief Review of Study on Chinese Faculty Development 3
   1.2 Research Themes on Chinese Faculty Development 4
       1.2.1 Research on the Subjectivity of Chinese Faculty Development 4
       1.2.2 Research on the Objectivity of Chinese Faculty Development 8
   1.3 Study on Chinese Faculty Professional Development 8
       1.3.1 Research on the Values of Faculty Development 9
       1.3.2 Reflection on the Research of Faculty Development in China 9
   1.4 Strategies on Chinese Faculty Development 10
       1.4.1 Deepen the International Perspective of Faculty Development Research 10
       1.4.2 Strengthen the Research of Faculty Development 10
       1.4.3 Optimize the Research Methods of Faculty Development 11
   References 11

2 Historical, Theoretical, and Practical Dimensions on Faculty Development Research 13
   2.1 Historical Review of Faculty Development Research 13
   2.2 Theoretical Research on the Faculty Development 14
   2.3 Practical Research on the Faculty Development 17
   References (in Chinese) 20

3	**Examining Faculty Development Model: From Chinese Context**		23
	3.1	Introduction on Faculty Development Model	23
	3.2	Examining Faculty Development Model at Chinese Context	25
	3.3	Conclusion and Remarks	26
	References (All Paper in Chinese)		26
4	**Faculty Professional Morality with Chinese Characteristics: A Comparative Perspective**		27
	4.1	Introduction and Overview	27
	4.2	Elements of Western Faculty Professional Morality	28
		4.2.1 Ancient Ethical Elements: Deontology, Utilitarianism, and Egoism	29
		4.2.2 Modern Faculty Morality: Reasoning Competencies, Civic-Dominated Morality	29
		4.2.3 Contemporary Faculty Morality: Identity-Oriented Professional Ethics	30
	4.3	Elements of Chinese Faculty Professional Morality	31
		4.3.1 Elements of Ancient Chinese Faculty Morality: Fraternity, Loyalty, and Selfless Dedication, Make Faculty an Example and Equality	32
		4.3.2 Chinese Modern Faculty Professional Morality: Freedom (Meaning), Equality (Forgiveness) and Fraternity (Benevolence), Comprehensive Personality	35
		4.3.3 Chinese Contemporary Faculty Professional Morality: Political–Ideological-Oriented Mandate	36
	4.4	Comparison of Elements of Faculty Professional Morality	38
		4.4.1 Differences Between Chinese and Western Faculty Moral Model	38
		4.4.2 Similarities Between Chinese and Western Faculty Moral Model	39
	4.5	Conclusion and Remark	39
		4.5.1 Conclusion	39
		4.5.2 Remarks	40
	References		41
5	**Overview of Faculty Development Center at Chinese Context: An Example of BNU**		43
	5.1	Mission of the Center for Faculty Development	43
	5.2	Working Concept of Faculty Development Center	44
	5.3	Working Standards of Faculty Development Center	45
	5.4	Working Content of Faculty Development Center	45
	5.5	Working Principle of Faculty Development Center	46

		5.6	Faculty Development Center Assessment	47
		Bibliography		48

Part II Practical Faculty Development at Chinese Context

6 Interviews of Chinese Faculty Development: Narratives and Dialogues 53
- 6.1 Peking University—Liu 53
  - 6.1.1 High-Frequency Words 53
  - 6.1.2 Key Points of Interview 53
- 6.2 Beijing Normal University—Zhang 56
  - 6.2.1 High-Frequency Words 56
  - 6.2.2 Key Points of Interview 56
- 6.3 Northeast Normal University—Liu 58
  - 6.3.1 High-Frequency Words 58
  - 6.3.2 Key Points of Interview 58
- 6.4 Northeast Normal University—Gao 60
  - 6.4.1 High-Frequency Words 60
  - 6.4.2 Key Points of Interview 60
- 6.5 Northeast Normal University—Jin 63
  - 6.5.1 High-Frequency Words 63
  - 6.5.2 Key Points of Interview 63
- 6.6 Northeast Normal University—Ma 67
  - 6.6.1 High-Frequency Words 67
  - 6.6.2 Key Points of Interview 67
- 6.7 Northeast Normal University—Shi 68
  - 6.7.1 High-Frequency Words 68
  - 6.7.2 Key Points of Interview 68
- 6.8 Northeast Normal University—Department of Personnel: Zhang 69
  - 6.8.1 High-Frequency Words 69
- 6.9 East China Normal University—Ding 71
  - 6.9.1 High-Frequency Words 71
  - 6.9.2 Key Points of Interview 71
- 6.10 East China Normal University—Liu 75
  - 6.10.1 High-Frequency Words 75
  - 6.10.2 Key Points of Interview 76
- 6.11 East China Normal University—Pang 78
  - 6.11.1 High-Frequency Words 78
  - 6.11.2 Key Points of Interview 78
- 6.12 East China Normal University—Wu 80
  - 6.12.1 High-Frequency Words 80
  - 6.12.2 Key Points of Interview 80

6.13	East China Normal University—Yan	82
	6.13.1 High-Frequency Words	82
	6.13.2 Key Points of Interview	82
6.14	East China Normal University—Ye	84
	6.14.1 High-Frequency Words	84
	6.14.2 Key Points of Interview	84
6.15	East China Normal University—Yu	87
	6.15.1 High-Frequency Words	87
	6.15.2 Key Points of Interview	87
6.16	Central China Normal University—Research on Higher Education: Liu	88
	6.16.1 High-Frequency Words	88
	6.16.2 Key Points of Interview	89
6.17	Huazhong University of Science and Technology—Institute of Higher Education: Zhang	90
	6.17.1 High-Frequency Words	90
	6.17.2 Key Point of Interview	90
6.18	Huazhong University of Science and Technology—Education and Economy: Fan	92
	6.18.1 High-Frequency Words	92
	6.18.2 Key Points of Interview	92
6.19	Huazhong University of Science and Technology—Li	94
	6.19.1 High-Frequency Words	94
	6.19.2 Key Points of Interview	94
6.20	Huazhong University of Science and Technology—Department of Personnel: Ren	96
	6.20.1 High-Frequency Words	96
	6.20.2 Key Points of Interview	96
6.21	Central China Normal University—Social Sciences Department: Shi	97
	6.21.1 High-Frequency Words	97
	6.21.2 Key Points of Interview	98
6.22	Central China Normal University—School of Education: Tu	99
	6.22.1 High-Frequency Words	99
	6.22.2 Key Points of Interview	100
6.23	Shaanxi Normal University—School of Education: Hao	102
	6.23.1 High-Frequency Words	102
	6.23.2 Key Points of Interview	102
6.24	Shaanxi Normal University—School of Education: Chen	105
	6.24.1 High-Frequency Words	105
	6.24.2 Key Points of Interview	106

6.25	Shaanxi Normal University–School of Education: Fang		108
	6.25.1	High-Frequency Words	108
	6.25.2	Key Points of Interview	109
6.26	Shaanxi Normal University–School of Education: Huo		110
	6.26.1	High-Frequency Words	110
	6.26.2	Key Points of Interview	111
6.27	Shaanxi Normal University—School of Literature: Li		113
	6.27.1	High-Frequency Words	113
	6.27.2	Key Points of Interview	113
6.28	Shaanxi Normal University—Social Sciences Administration Department: Ma		115
	6.28.1	High-Frequency Words	115
	6.28.2	Key Points of Interview	115
6.29	Shaanxi Normal University—Wang		118
	6.29.1	High-Frequency Words	118
	6.29.2	Key Points of Interview	118
6.30	Shaanxi Normal University—School of Psychology: You		120
	6.30.1	High-Frequency Words	120
	6.30.2	Key Points of Interview	121
6.31	Shanghai Jiaotong University (SJTU)—Institute of Higher Education: Liu		122
	6.31.1	High-Frequency Words	122
	6.31.2	Key Points of Interview	123
6.32	Southwest University—Chen		125
	6.32.1	High-Frequency Words	125
	6.32.2	Key Points of Interview	125
6.33	Southwest University—Huang		128
	6.33.1	High-Frequency Words	128
	6.33.2	Key Points of Interview	128
6.34	Southwest University—Jin		131
	6.34.1	High-Frequency Words	131
	6.34.2	Key Points of Interview	131
6.35	Southwest University—Human Resource Office: Liu		133
	6.35.1	High-Frequency Words	133
	6.35.2	Key Points of Interview	134
6.36	Southwest University Faculty of Arts–Liu		136
	6.36.1	High-Frequency Words	136
	6.36.2	Key Points of Interview	136
6.37	Southwest University—Song		139
	6.37.1	High-Frequency Words	139
	6.37.2	Key Points of Interview	139

	6.38	Southwest University—Institute of Psychology: Zhang	141
		6.38.1 High-Frequency Words	141
		6.38.2 Key Points of Interview	141
	6.39	Southwest University Office of Academic Affairs—Zhou	144
		6.39.1 High-Frequency Words	144
		6.39.2 Key Points of Interview	144
	6.40	Southwest University—Zhu	146
		6.40.1 High-Frequency Words	146
		6.40.2 Key Points of Interview	147
7	**Analysis of Interviews of Chinese Faculty Development**		151
	7.1	Introduction and Summary	151
	7.2	Comprehensive Analysis	151
		7.2.1 Basic Information	151
		7.2.2 High-Frequency Word Analysis	152
	7.3	Correlation Analysis for High-Frequency Words	159
	7.4	Analysis by Universities	167
		7.4.1 For Central China Normal University (CCNU)	175
		7.4.2 For East China Normal University (ECNU)	180
		7.4.3 For Northeast Normal University (NENU)	185
		7.4.4 For Shaanxi Normal University (SSNU)	190
		7.4.5 For Southwest University (SWU)	198
		7.4.6 For Other Universities (PKU, BNU, SJTU, and HUST)	203
		7.4.7 Conclusion of Group Analysis	204
8	**Faculty Development at Chinese Context: Conclusion, Strategies, and Implications**		207
	8.1	Conclusions on Faculty Development at Chinese Context	207
		8.1.1 Resource Allocation Mechanism	207
		8.1.2 Obstacles of Resource Allocation Mechanism	208
	8.2	Strategies on Faculty Development at Chinese Context: Resource Allocation Mechanism	209
		8.2.1 Flexible Management	209
		8.2.2 Faculty Selection and Recruitment Mechanism	211
		8.2.3 Strategies on Faculty Selection and Recruitment Mechanism	213
	References		220

The Details About the Contribution

The project manager: Prof. Zhu Xudong in the specific implementation and coordination: Li Yuyu and Kang Xiaowei

Preliminary research project formulation: Prof. Zhu Xudong and all the students of Reading Club

Field interviewers: Kang Xiaowei, Zhang Wenwen, Li Na, Cui Yingying, Xiang Jun, Wu Mengyin, Li Aixia

Interviews: Kang Xiaowei, Zhang Shufang, Wang Yaqin, Guan Tinge, Zhu Menghua, Li Xianqi, Zhao Jing

Research Paper Writing (Issue 7 of Comparative Education Research, 2011): Zhu Xudong, Li Yuqiu, Li Qiong, Wu Mengyin, Song Huan, Kang Xiaowei, Luo Xin, Li Aixia, Zhao Ping, Liao Wei, Cui Yingying, Ye Zhixiong, Li Na

Writing research reports: Zhu Xudong, Li Yuyu, Kang Xiaowei, Zhang Wenwenwen, Zhao Jing, Li Xianqi, Cui Yingying, Wu Mengyin, Li Na, Liao Wei, Li Aixia

Reporting Presidential Draft: Kang Xiaowei
This study is the research result of the subproject of the National Social Science Foundation's major project "Research on the Major Issues of Educational Innovation and Innovative National Construction under the Guidance of the Scientific Outlook on Development," "Research on the Construction of Innovative Teachers—Perspective of Teachers' Innovative Ability." The project is implemented by Prof. Zhu Xudong, who is responsible for the planning, design, implementation, and writing of the project. Ph.D. and graduate students led by Prof. Zhu Xudong participated in the project as team members. Among them, Dr. Li Yuqiu and Dr. Kang Xiaowei assisted in the specific liaison and implementation work. Participating in specific field research are Kang Xiaowei, Zhang Wenwenwen, Li Na, Cui Yingying, Xiang Jun, Wu Mengyin, and Li Aixia. Participants included Kang Xiaowei, Zhang Shufang, Wang Yaqin, Guan Tinge, Zhu Menghua, Li Xianqi, and Zhao Jing. The research papers were written by

Zhu Xudong, Li Yuqiu, Li Qiong, Wu Mengyin, Song Huan, Kang Xiaowei, Luo Xin, Li Aixia, Zhao Ping, Liao Wei, Cui Yingying, Ye Zhixiong, and Li Na. Participated in the writing of research reports are Zhu Xudong, Li Yuqiu, Kang Xiaowei, Zhang Wenwenwen, Zhao Jing, Li Xianqi, Cui Yingying, Wu Mengyin, Li Na, Liao Wei, and Li Aixia. Kang Xiaowei assisted Prof. Zhu Xudong in drafting the research report.

About the Authors

Jian Li and Xudong Zhu serve as co-first author to contribute this book.

Xudong Zhu is the Dean of Faculty of Education and Professor in the Institute of Teacher Education of Beijing Normal University. His work focuses on teacher education, comparative education, and history of education, with an emphasis on the system transformation of teacher education in China, comparative study on the national development and education, the history of ideas of education in the West. Much of his work has involved the policy, practice of teacher education and teacher professional development, supported by research in China, World Bank, UNESCO, Intel, etc. He is the Secretary of National Expert Committee of Teacher Education of MOE in China, the Director of the Center for Teacher Education Research among the Key Research Institutes of Humanities and Social Sciences in the University of MOE. He is Director of Institute of Teacher Education of Beijing Normal University, and an Editor-in-Chief of the Journal of Teacher Education Research, China. He was the Fulbright Senior Visiting Scholar of U.S. State Department during the year of 2002–2003.

Jian Li is Assistant Professor in China Institute of Education and Social Development, Faculty of Education, Beijing Normal University. She received her Ph.D. in Educational Leadership and Policy Studies (ELPS), School of Education, Indiana University Bloomington. Her research interests focus on Global Learning, Global Competence, Global Citizenship, Globalization and Internationalization of Higher Education.

Dr. Li currently also serves as think tanker at China Institute of Education and Social Development, Beijing Normal University. China Institute of Education and Social Development (CIESD) was co-founded by the China Association for Promoting Democracy and Beijing Normal University. It was founded on the base of the China Institute of Education Policy and China Academy of Social Management of Beijing Normal University. Beijing Normal University integrated internal resources and giving solid supports to the foundation of CIESD. Its mission is to advance the modernization of education and social construction with Chinese characteristics. And it is committed to building a new type of high-end-oriented think tank with the characteristics of the education reform and development and the social governance innovation. Over the past decade, hundreds of the research papers have been undertaken by CIESD members, more than 530 of which obtained important instructions from party and state leaders at various levels, CIESD has drafted a number of the national education standards, and made great influence on the decision-making and the revision of the education law for the party and government. CIESD has held different classes and high-level series of the forums, which has played positive roles in influencing public opinion. CIESD has created a new mechanism within the international exchange and cooperation filed for the institution's foundation of public diplomacy. CIESD will continue to adhere to the high standard, and build a professional high-end-oriented think tank with the international visionary and significant influence in educational and social fields.

Part I
Conceptual Faculty Development at Chinese Context

Chapter 1
Overview of Chinese Faculty Development Research: Themes and Strategies

This chapter involves clarifying the context of the research on faculty development at Chinese universities and colleges. The study on faculty development is subjected to a systematic and in-depth study of the nature and internal logic of the development of faculty member in contemporary China. Specifically, the term faculty development is considered as an important academic and scientific research profession. In addition, the study on faculty development is conducive to promoting the overall comprehensive development of universities and colleges in Chinese context. As an important academic research profession, the study on faculty development is conducive for promoting the development of faculty members. Since 1959, Chinese scholars did lots of research on faculty development in order to examine the overall landscape of faculty development in current Chinese context. Therefore, this chapter involves reviewing and analyzing the general situation of faculty development at Chinese universities and colleges. In addition, the "subject-object" clustering model is proposed to analyze the study on faculty development at Chinese context.

1.1 A Brief Review of Study on Chinese Faculty Development

From 1959 to 2017, Chinese scholars have published about 12,065 academic papers and dissertations of the study on Chinese faculty development. In the past 40 years, the research on faculty development in current China can be roughly divided into two stages: the initial stage of the research on faculty development (from 1959 to 1990) and the development stage (from 1959 to 1990). The annual number of publications about the research on faculty development in contemporary China is units digit, the median number of publications is 5. The initial stage of study on faculty development from 1991 to 2005 is relatively high. From 2006 to 2011, the number of publications and the median number of publications were 100 and 496, respectively. From 2012 to 2017, the number of publications and the median number of publications were

© Springer Nature Singapore Pte Ltd. 2019
X. Zhu and J. Li, *Faculty Development in Chinese Higher Education*, Perspectives on Rethinking and Reforming Education, https://doi.org/10.1007/978-981-13-7767-9_1

1,000 and 1,382, respectively. In the stage of all-round development, from 1959 to 2017, there were 11,354 educational journals, 532 academic journals and general journals, 130 master's papers, and 49 doctoral dissertations. The number of faculty development publications will continue to increase. Generally speaking, the research on faculty development in China is increasing year by year from the overall number to the number and scale of researchers participating in the research.

1.2 Research Themes on Chinese Faculty Development

The research topics of faculty development in China can be roughly divided into two categories: the subjectivity of faculty development and the objectivity of faculty development. Based on the age distribution of academic subjects, the specialty of subjects, and the types of colleges and universities, the research on the subject of faculty in Chinese colleges and universities has drawn four major themes: the research on young faculty in colleges and universities, the research on science and engineering faculty in colleges and universities, the research on teachers in private colleges, and the research on faculty in local colleges and universities. The research on the object of faculty development mainly includes three main research subjects and fields: the research on the professional development of faculty, the research on the career of faculty, and the research on the values of faculty. There are interaction and coincidence between the subjectivity study and the objectivity study in different perspectives.

1.2.1 Research on the Subjectivity of Chinese Faculty Development

"Subjectivity" research refers to the study of the subject part of things, philosophically, which refers to the ability to understand and act on the object (Bergquist and Phillips, 1975; Centra, 1976, 1978). The subject includes the perception, judgment, and action of subjectivism on objects (Batt, 2009; Bird & Morgan, 2003; Boice, 1992; Gaff, 1975). The study of faculty's subjectivity mainly focuses on the characteristics, types, and behavior patterns of universities' faculty as research subjects (Brayboy, 2003; Brookfield, 1995; Calder & McCollum, 1998; Casper & Buffardi, 2004; Costa & Garmston, 2002). The research on the subjectivity of faculty is mainly concerned with the differences within the main body of faculty member (Dawson, 2014). According to the search of academic journal papers, postgraduate papers, and educational or related publications published from 1959 to 2017 in the research literature on the subject attributes of faculty, four main considerations are proposed: subject attention, duration of research, total number of published papers, and topic influence and attention. In other words, the research on the subjectivity of faculty

1.2 Research Themes on Chinese Faculty Development

development involves the four main dimensions of the age distribution of academic subjects, the specialty of subjects, the types of colleges and universities, and the regions of colleges and universities (Costa & Garmston, 2013, 2016; Dawson, 2014; Driscoll et al., 2009; Furco, 2007; Foote & Solem, 2009; Glassdoor, 2014; Holland, 2001). It also extracts the four main themes of the research on the subject attributes of faculty: the research on young faculty member, the research on university science and engineering faculty, the research on private university faculty, and the research on local university faculty.

In terms of academic age, the research on faculty in Chinese colleges and universities has become a hot topic in recent years. From 1989 to 2018, 539 articles on psychological problems of young faculty were published, and 70 articles were published in 2014, reaching the annual peak of psychological problems of young college faculty. The major publications focus on the three major disciplines of higher education, education theory and education management, and psychology. Specifically, He et al. (2015) conducted a mental health survey on young faculty in 25 colleges and universities in Zhejiang Province. The results showed that the scores of somatization, obsessive–compulsive symptoms, depression, anxiety, phobia, paranoia, and psychotic factors of young faculty in colleges and universities were significantly higher than the national norm. There are significant differences in mental health status among young college faculty with different professional titles, teaching age, marital status, and children's status.

The mental health of young faculty in colleges and universities should be highly concerned by individuals, schools, and society. Zhang (2014) argued that, in order to solve the practical difficulties of young faculty, we should also actively build and improve the mental health education system of young faculty, and truly promote the healthy development of young faculty. Chen and Wang (2016) found that the psychological resilience of young college faculty consists of five core dimensions: teaching efficacy, pursuit of scientific research, job confidence and satisfaction, love of education, and professional belief. The study suggests that the development of young college faculty's psychological resilience needs to rebuild their professional beliefs and work confidence, provide more professional guidance for their scientific research development, and create a good organizational culture. Zheng (2014) analyzes the problems existing in the psychological quality and vocational adaptation of young faculty in colleges and universities, and constructs a system to improve the psychological quality of young faculty in colleges and universities, which is of great significance to the construction of young faculty in colleges and universities. Jiang (2015) believes that strengthening the ideological and political work of young faculty will inevitably require doing a good job in their stress management, seeking to alleviate and eliminate the pressure of scientific countermeasures. Ni (2015) reveals the basic elements of the motivation of the young faculty in colleges and universities by using the method of system theory. In other words, the motivation of young faculty involves the elements of accomplishment, the elements of goal, the elements of need, the elements of attitude, and the elements of behavior. Talent goal is the leader of the formation of talent motivation, talent need is the drive of the formation of talent motivation, talent attitude is the key to the formation of talent motivation, talent behavior is the means of the formation of talent motivation, and talent motivation environment is analyzed.

From the perspective of the subject particularity of university faculty, the research on science and engineering faculty has become the main content of the research in the past 10 years. From 2005 to 2017, a total of 44 articles were published on the issue of faculty of higher science and engineering, reaching an annual peak on the psychological problems of young university faculty. Sun (2016) chose the development of local universities' faculty in the field of engineering as the research object. Following the idea of "putting forward problems—analyzing the causes—establishing models—putting forward solutions", she made a thorough analysis and research on how to promote the development of local universities' faculty in the field of engineering. The study shows that faculty's professional identity is relatively high, comparing to a lower professional identity. Faculty development orientation is also relatively high and it is not balanced. The implementation process of faculty development projects is rigid, which is lack of pertinence and specialty. From 1991 to 2017, a total of 1,620 papers, postgraduate papers and educational or related journals, were published on the issue of faculty development in private colleges and universities, reaching the level of research on young faculty in private colleges and universities in 2016. In other words, the research on faculty in Chinese private colleges and universities mainly focuses on the salary and treatment, incentive system, and team loss of faculty in private colleges and universities. Xu and Zhang (2017) show that different types of incentives in the incentive mechanism of private colleges and universities have different effects on faculty's teaching. Zhou and Liu (2016) believe that the government should not only play an active role in market research and respect the law of the market but also pay attention to the incentive policies for faculty in private colleges and universities. Yang and Liu (2015) pointed out that different measures should be taken to improve faculty's abilities, according to different individual characteristics of faculty groups, which will be conducive to the professional development of applied talents. From 1991 to 2017, a total of 1,542 papers on the issue of faculty in private colleges and universities were published. The total number of postgraduate papers and educational or related journals was about 1,542, which reach the annual peak value of research on local university faculty. The research on local university faculty in China mainly focuses on the improvement of teaching level, the cultivation of teaching ability, the development of professional survival, and professional ecological environment of local university faculty (Ferguson & Wijekumar, 2000; Flaherty, 2007; Saltmarsh & Hartley, 2011; Morgan & O'Reilly, 1999; Mathews, 2003; McCormack & West, 2006; Merriam, 2009).

In recent years, in the field of higher education organization and practice in China, the trend of thought of academic differentiation in universities has been raised, which mainly includes academic and applied educational practice systems. Local university faculty prefers the practice of applied educational activities. Wen (2017) believes that local colleges and universities need to focus on teaching standards, establish an ecological environment conducive to teaching and learning, establish and improve the system conducive to the development of teaching and learning, and further enhance the teaching and academic level of teachers in local colleges and universities. Li

1.2 Research Themes on Chinese Faculty Development 7

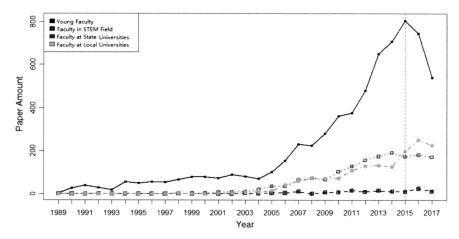

Fig. 1.1 University faculty's subjectivity research: focusing on content, quantity, and trend comparison

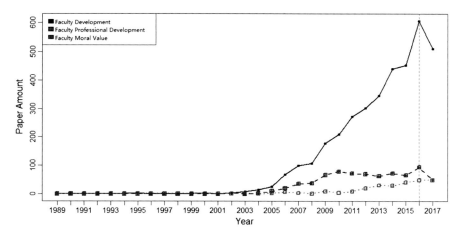

Fig. 1.2 University faculty objectivity research focuses: content, quantity, and trend comparison

(2016) suggested that academic organization should be the two basic principles to cope with the academic profession differentiation of university faculty in the context of the transformation and development of local undergraduate universities (Figs. 1.1 and 1.2).

1.2.2 Research on the Objectivity of Chinese Faculty Development

"Objectivity" research refers to the characteristics and contents of the object of study. Object includes not only the things that exist objectively and can be perceived subjectively but also the things that are exploited by thinking (Palloff & Pratt, 2000; Parr, 1996; Pattie et al. 2006). The object is relative to the subject. The research on objectivity of university faculty is mainly the sum of the research individuals, who study the objectivity of university faculty as research subjects and the corresponding things that exist. In other words, the study of faculty's objectivity focuses on the differences and diversity of the corresponding objects within the subject of university faculty.

According to the searches for academic journal papers, postgraduate papers, and educational or related publications published on the objectivity research literature of university faculty between 1959 and 2017, four main considerations are proposed: subject attention, duration of research, total number of published papers, and topic influence and attention. The research of faculty professional development, faculty career, and faculty values have become the three main research subjects in the field of objectivity of faculty development. It is worth noting that the research on the professional development of university faculty and the career of university faculty are closely related but differentiated from each other from the research dimension. The professional development of university faculty lays more emphasis on the internal development law of university teachers as the subject of academic research in the three major functions of teaching, scientific research, and social service. The traditional and comprehensive study of mode and mechanism and the study of university faculty's career take university faculty as a human capital group of academic productive nature, and faculty's job burnout, incentive, evaluation, and promotion from the perspective of management and psychology. The former studies put university faculty in the traditional paradigm of academic knowledge research to consider the path and law of faculty's professional development; the latter studies focus on the relationship between university faculty's organization and management from the perspective of human capital and psychological capital theory.

1.3 Study on Chinese Faculty Professional Development

From 1989 to 2017, a total of 3642 journal papers, postgraduate papers, and educational or related journals were published, reaching the annual peak of research on the professional development of university faculty. Since 2008, the research on the professional development of university faculty in China has been flourishing day by day, increasing steadily in a hundred figures every year. The research on the professional development of university faculty is a broad concept category, including the professional development of university faculty as academic subjects in teaching, scientific research, and social services. The research on faculty's professional development in China focuses on the theory of knowledge construction of university faculty, the empirical case analysis between "teaching center", "teaching ability", and "professional development" of faculty. The exploration of professional development of university faculty in China is inherently imbedded in the construction of the policy-oriented mechanism and faculty professional development. In the research on the professional development of faculty member, the research on the group differences of university faculty has been increasing year by year in recent years, especially the research on the professional development of private university faculty, the reform of teaching contents, and teaching methods of university faculty applying the Internet and other educational technologies.

1.3.1 Research on the Values of Faculty Development

From 1996 to 2018, 263 articles were published on the values of young faculty in colleges and universities. The frequency of publication and the number of publications increased steadily year by year. The peak value of publication in 2017 and 2016 was parallel. The research on the values of college faculty in China mainly focuses on the influence and change of the world outlook, outlook on life, and values of young college teachers on their professional outlook and moral outlook. Gai (2016) focuses on the values of young teachers in colleges and universities. The research indicated that the values of young faculty in colleges and universities are characterized by attaching importance to material values while neglecting spiritual values, attaching importance to scientific and technological values over humanistic values, attaching importance to immediate values over long-term values, and attaching importance to personal utility over social welfare. She also points out that the culture is characterized by a simultaneous superposition of historical changes, a shift from elite culture to mass culture, and a shift from political to economic orientation. The change of interest structure, the transfer of social power, the pluralism of value evaluation, and the change of social development have profound influence on the values of college teachers. Yang (2006) studied the values of young college faculty and analyzed the values of young faculty from the perspectives of life, morality, society, occupation, and life. Zhang (2016) analyzed the four-dimensional structure of Marx's belief education of young faculty in colleges and universities.

1.3.2 Reflection on the Research of Faculty Development in China

The study on faculty development in China has a history of 58 years from 1959 to 2017. From the perspective of faculty development, the overall level of research on faculty development is not high and the influence of university faculty has not yet formed. The research on faculty development in China needs to further deepen the international vision of faculty development, strengthen the research contents of university faculty, and optimize the research methods of faculty.

1.4 Strategies on Chinese Faculty Development

This section focuses on examining the strategies on Chinese faculty from different perspectives, which including depending the international perspective of faculty development research, the research of faculty development, and optimizing the research methods of faculty development.

1.4.1 Deepen the International Perspective of Faculty Development Research

The international vision of faculty research in China needs to be further deepened. Our country's research on faculty development has paid too much attention to the construction of domestic faculty ranks and professional development of faculty, and lacks long-term systematic links between China's university faculty and international developed countries' research on faculty. For example, for the comparative research field of university teachers in China and the United States, the research topics in China are scattered, and the research contents are mostly focused on introducing the research status and development of American teachers, lacking in-depth and lasting comparative study of international faculty development. In addition, the distribution of core research institutions in China's university faculty research field is uneven, the core author group is still not formed, there is no long-term international exchange platform and mechanism for university faculty, and there is also a lack of cooperative application and research projects for university faculty abroad. Therefore, China's research on faculty needs to deepen the international perspective of research, deepen the internal and external links between China's research on faculty and foreign research on faculty, and expand the academic influence and authority of China's research on faculty in international universities.

1.4.2 Strengthen the Research of Faculty Development

The research contents and themes of university teachers in China are scattered, and there is no systematic research category of university teachers, and there is no clear research context and School of University teachers. Therefore, strengthening the research of faculty development in China should mainly include several components: strengthening the theoretical research of faculty development is pivotal to improve the overall quality of faculty development. At present, the research on faculty development in China mostly adopts the theory of psychology and management, and has not formed the core theory research and development of faculty professional development. Therefore, it is necessary to strengthen the theoretical research of faculty and integrate the core concepts and important theories of the research of faculty in China. It is necessary to strengthen the practical research of faculty development. It is worth noting that it is necessary to strengthen the cross-section research and pay attention to the changing laws and problems of faculty scientific research, teaching and social services under the background of internet, information technology, and artificail intelligence.

1.4.3 Optimize the Research Methods of Faculty Development

Most of the research methods of faculty development in China remain in speculative research. In recent years, both qualitative interviews and quantitative research have been gradually concerned. Most of the quantitative research mainly focuses on case analysis, transplanting, and applying the research methods of foreign university teachers. On the basis of the theory and practice of foreign faculty research, China should design a theoretical and practical model suitable for the development of university teachers in China, and form a systematic research paradigm of faculty. The introduction of diversified research methods for university teachers does not adhere to the traditional qualitative and quantitative research models of social sciences. Taking university teachers as the research object of demographic significance, anthropological research methods, and historical research methods can be incorporated into the research methods for university teachers.

References

Batt, E. (2009). Cognitive coaching: A critical phase in professional development to implement sheltered instruction. *Teaching and Teacher Education, 26*(4), 997–1005.
Bergquist, W. H., & Phillips, S. R. (1975). Components of an effective faculty development program. *Journal of Higher Education, 46,* 177–211.
Bird, J., & Morgan, C. (2003). Adults contemplating university study at a distance: Issues, themes, and concerns. *The International Review of Research in Open and Disturbed Learning, 4*(1).
Boice, R. (1992). Lessons learned about mentoring. In M. D. Sorcinelli & A. E. Austin (Eds.), *Developing new and junior faculty* (pp. 51–61). San Francisco: Jossey-Bass.
Brayboy, B. (2003). The implementation of diversity in predominantly White colleges and universities. *Journal of Black Studies, 34*(1), 72–86.
Brookfield, S. (1995). *Becoming a critically reflective teacher*. San Francisco: Jossey-Bass.
Calder, J., & McCollum, A. (1998). *Open and flexible learning in vocational education and training*. London: Kogan Page.

Casper, W. J., & Buffardi, L. C. (2004). Work-life benefits and job pursuit intentions: The role of anticipated organizational support. *Journal of Vocational Behavior, 65*(3), 391–410.

Centra, J. A. (1976). *Faculty development practices in U.S. colleges and universities* (p. PR-76-30.). Princeton, N.J: Educational Testing Service.

Centra, J. A. (1978). Types of faculty development programs. *The Journal of Higher Education, 49*(2), 151–162.

Costa, A., & Garmston, R. (2002). *Cognitive coaching. A foundation for renaissance schools syllabus*. Norwood, MA: Christopher-Gordon.

Costa, A., & Garmston, R. (2013). *Cognitive coaching seminars. Foundation training learning guide*. Highlands Ranch, CO: Thinking Collaborative.

Costa, A., & Garmston, R. (2016). *Cognitive coaching: Developing selfdirected leaders and learners*. Lanham, MD: Roman & Littlefield.

Dawson, P. (2014). Beyond a definition: Toward a framework for designing and specifying mentoring models. *Educational Researcher, 43*(3), 137–145.

Driscoll, L. G., Parks, A. K., Tilley-Lubbs, G. A., Brill, J. M., & Bannister, V. R. (2009). Navigating the lonely sea: Peer mentoring and collaboration among aspiring women scholars. *Mentoring and Tutoring: Partnership Learning, 17*(1), 5–21.

Ferguson, L., & Wijekumar, K. (2000). Effective design and use of web-based distance learning environments. *Professional Safety, 45*(12), 28–33.

Flaherty, C. N. (2007). *The effect of tuition reimbursement on turnover: A case study analysis*. Stanford University, Stanford Institute for Economic Policy Research. Stanford: Stanford University.

Foote, M., & Solem, M. N. (2009). Towards better mentoring for early career faculty: Results of a study of US geographers. *International Journal of Academic Development, 14*(1), 47–58.

Furco, A. (2007). Institutionalising service learning in higher education. In L. McIlrath & I. MacLabhrainn (Eds.), *Higher education and civic engagement: International perspectives* (pp. 65–82). Burlington, VT: Ashgate Publishing.

Gaff, J. G. (1975). *Toward faculty renewal*. San Francisco: Jossey-Bass.

Glassdoor. (2014). Employment confidence survey. Retrieved from Glassdoor Press Center: https://www.glassdoor.com/press/surveys/.

Holland, B. A. (2001). Toward a definition and characterization of the engaged campus: Six cases. *Metropolitan Universities, 12*(3), 20.

Li (2016). A Study on the Professional Development of English Theory Teachers in Applied Universities. *Journal of Huaqiao Foreign Languages College*, Jilin, (02): 109–112.

Mathews, P. (2003). Academic monitoring. Enhancing the use of scarce resources. *Educational Management and Administration, 31*(3), 313–334.

McCormack, C., & West, D. (2006). Facilitated group mentoring develops key career competencies for university women: A case study. *Mentoring & Tutoring: Partnership in Learning, 14*(4), 409–431.

Merriam, S. B. (2009). *Qualitative research: A guide to design and implementation*. San Francisco, CA: Jossey-Bass.

Morgan, C., & O'Reilly, M. (1999). *Assessing open and distance learners*. London: Kogan Page.

Palloff, R., & Pratt, K. (2000). Making the transition: Helping teachers teach online. EDUCAUSE 2000: Thinking IT through. Nashville: EDUCAUSE.

Parr, E. (1996). *Dropping in and dropping out: An alternative view of attrition Lismore*. Lismore: Southern Cross University.

Pattie, M., Benson, G. S., & Baruch, Y. (2006). Tuition reimbursement, perceived organizational support, and turnover intention among graduate business school students. *Human Resource Development Quarterly, 17*(4), 423–442.

Saltmarsh, J., & Hartley, M. (Eds.). (2011). *"To serve a larger purpose": Engagement for democracy and the transformation of higher education*. Philadelphia: Temple University Press.

Zhang (2014) Compliance and anomie of professional ethics mechanism of young university teachers. *Education and occupation*, (35): 89–90.

Chapter 2
Historical, Theoretical, and Practical Dimensions on Faculty Development Research

This chapter concentrates on offering the overview of research on Western faculty development from historical, theoretical, and practical perspectives. Specifically, historical review of Western faculty development research involves examining the academic research ability, teaching ability, and social service ability of faculty at universities and colleges. The history of faculty development can be traced back to Socrates and Plato in ancient Greece. In addition, the theoretical study on the faculty development focuses on introducing and investigating the theoretical origin and theoretical development of faculty in Western developed countries. The practical research on faculty development concentrates on two aspects: one is to study the current situation and existing problems of faculty development in recent years; the other is to draw lessons from and introduce the problems and contents of the research on faculty development in Western countries.

2.1 Historical Review of Faculty Development Research

The core issues of faculty development research mainly focus on the academic research ability, teaching ability, and social service ability of faculty at universities and colleges. The history of faculty development can be traced back to Socrates and Plato in ancient Greece. Socrates put forward "maternity" as the essence of faculty's teaching. Historically speaking, the study on faculty development was originated in the United States since the 1960s. In 1965, American psychologist Wilbert founded the first real university faculty development project in the United States occurred at the University of Michigan. He reinterpreted the faculty development from the perspective of teaching ability, thus disseminate to the United States. In 1991, the American Federation of Education (NEA) published the report "University Faculty Development: Enhancing National Strength", formally put forward the concept of faculty all-round development. It is pointed out that the development of university faculty should focus on four goals: personal development, professional development, organizational development, and teaching development. Specifically, professional development refers to the acquisition or improvement of professional knowledge and ability; teaching development includes the preparation of learning materials, curriculum content. and teaching mode updating. In addition, Boyer, the former chairman of the Carnegie Foundation for the Promotion of Teaching in the United States, put forward the concept of "university teaching academy" in 1990, which had a great influence on the teaching philosophy and practice of universities in Western countries. Boyer put forward his scholarship of faculty professions. It can be divided into four categories: scholarship of discovery, scholarship of application, scholarship of integration, and scholarship of teaching. It should have an academic, applied academic, integrated academic, and teaching scholarship. We can find that Boyer's research on the development of university faculty pays more attention to the importance of academic teaching in the professional development of University faculty. From the perspective of historical development, the research on the development of university teachers has a long history in Western countries, forming more research and Practice on the professional development of faculty. As far as the development of faculty in China is concerned, the research on the development of faculty in China is still in the preliminary exploration period. The main research focuses on two aspects: one is to analyze the theory and practice of the research on the development of faculty in Europe and the United States; the other is to actively explore the current situation, difficulties, and challenges of faculty development in China. And combined with the existing survival situation of Chinese universities, this chapter analyzes the practical path and operational guidelines of Chinese faculty to guide the practice of professional development of Chinese faculty. In recent years, the research on the development of faculty in China mainly focuses on theoretical research and practical research (He et al., 2015; Lin & Li, 2007; Qin, 2012; Zhang, 2014; Zheng, 2014; Zhou & Ma, 2013).

2.2 Theoretical Research on the Faculty Development

The theoretical research on the faculty development in China mainly focuses on introducing and researching the theoretical origin and theoretical development of faculty in Western developed countries, mainly in the United States. Specifically, there mainly existed three theoretical models of faculty development in the United States. William H. Bergquist and Steven R. Phillips initially proposed the first model of faculty development in 1975. The faculty development model is an integral part of an effective university faculty development program. Teaching Development (Process), Organizational Development (Structure), and Personal Development (Attitude) are three intercorrelated activities. Jerry Gaff proposes the second model of faculty development in the same year. The Faculty Renewal Model is initially constructed by Jerry Gaff to serve as the foundational work of faculty development. Geoff ingeniously used "faculty renewal" as the title of the book, meaning that "faculty development" is a broader term and a global concept. In 1977, while editing the Handbook on Faculty Development, he revised the theoretical model and proposed a new outline.

2.2 Theoretical Research on the Faculty Development

Overall speaking, we can find that in the model of faculty development proposed by William H. Bergquist and Steven R. Phillips, we mainly focus on the three key dimensions of faculty personal development, teaching development, and organizational development. The fundamental goal is to cultivate faculty academic values, academic attitudes, and organizational development. Both academic profession and teaching abilities are pivotal to consolidating the organizational effectiveness of faculty. Faculty is expected to improve the professional development by establishing life planning, strengthening interpersonal communication, adopting diverse teaching methods, forming teams, and improving management training. Jerry Gaff, on the basis of his research on William H. Bergquist and Steven R. Phillips, has further deepened the theoretical model of university teacher development and further expounded the internal relationship among personal development, teaching development, and organizational development. In 1977, William H. Bergquist and Steven R. Phillips further revised the former model of faculty development and put forward three dimensions: individual, group, institution, and macro-system of University teachers, and the three dimensions of the structure, process, and attitude of the development of faculty into three dimensions. We can find that the research on the development of American faculty involves the characteristics of speculation. According to the different types of universities and the characteristics of faculty, we can formulate the development model and types of faculty with humanistic characteristics (Cai, 2018; He & Wang, 2015; Jiang & Lin, 2011; Li, 2018; Pang, 2012; Wu & Chen, 2014).

Especially, there existed a couple of arguments of Chinese scholars towards the Study of Faculty Development. For example, Liu and Wang (2011) summarized the experience and enlightenment of the development of American faculty and put forward that the development of American faculty mainly includes the period of scholars, teachers, developers, learners, network, and other major faculty development, and combined with the development period of American faculty. The development of faculty in China should strengthen the concept of autonomy, cooperation, specialization, lifelong development, and internationalization, and establish the development model of faculty with Chinese characteristics in line with China's national conditions. It also suggests that China should establish a research center for faculty development as soon as possible to actively promote the self-development of faculty in China. The main innovation and scientific development should attach importance to the construction of institutional environment, psychological environment, and academic community to create a good environment for faculty development, formulate various forms of development plans to promote the professional growth of faculty at different stages, reform the evaluation and promotion mechanism of faculty, and actively pay attention to the professional development of young faculty. Wang (2009) research on the attribution of the professionalization of American faculty in 2009 shows that in the course of the formation of American faculty profession, the factors promoting its development are embodied in four aspects: the high-threshold system of faculty admission; the effective guarantee of University faculty's professional organization, the implementation of peer review evaluation system; the openness and mobility. The professional growth of faculty in China can be enlightened from the following aspects: cultivating a high degree of academic community awareness; establishing a strong professional organization; establishing and improving academic-oriented evaluation system; and enhancing the mobility and international attractiveness of the academic labor market. Lin and Wei (2018) studied the competency model of faculty development workers in North American universities. The faculty development model mainly involves strategic thinking ability, political understanding ability, financial management ability, employee selection and motivation ability, and the evaluation of development items. They also pointed out that, according to the research on the professionalization of faculty in North America, we can learn from Debra Dawson, a scholar at the University of Western Ontario in Canada, who classifies faculty development workers into three categories: junior, senior, and director according to different stages of their careers, in terms of knowledge, competence and skills.

Liu (2018) concentrated on the characteristics of the reform of faculty development organizations in American research universities and proposed that the mission of reconstructing faculty development organizations should be excessive from single mission to multiple missions, so as to promote the growth of faculty learning community as a mission, adapt to the changes of university governance environment, and reconstruct faculty development organizations in universities. The important role is to cultivate faculty from resource dependence to resource supplier, expand the support of department level to the resource space of faculty development, rebuild the professional organization and development of faculty, and go from the edge of university governance to the center of university governance. Cai (2018) put forward the concept of professional academy and teaching academy in the process of faculty development in China, pointing out that the integration of professional academy and faculty academy is needed, the development of faculty should be based on the integration of science and education, and the evaluation method of combining teaching academy with professional academy should be established in China. The interactive development mechanism of faculty and institutional environment needs to pay attention to the effective evaluation of faculty development projects. Qu (2018) analyzed the environment, process and organizational characteristics of the University of Michigan's Faculty Development Center. Specifically, Qu (2018) analyzed that the University of Michigan established the first faculty development center in the United States, namely the Center for Research on Learning and Teaching (CRLT). Pays close attention to the American model of university faculty development and its significance for reference. He points out that the formation of the American model of faculty development has gone through the stages of spontaneity and germination, theoretical clarification and project promotion, and the organizational stage of faculty development. The development model of American faculty has several remarkable characteristics: it has obvious empiricism orientation; it carries out phased projects according to the development needs of different groups of teachers; it pays attention to the role of faculty development and learning community; and it implements school-centered power management model. Referring to the American model, we should attach importance to the cultivation of faculty practical knowledge, strengthen the construction and function promotion of faculty development organizations, and adopt diversified, lifelong, and independent faculty development strategies. Jiang and Lin (2011) studied the concept and practice of faculty development in Japan, and analyzed that in the late 1940s, Japan began to pay more and more attention to the study of university teacher development, and carried out some kinds of surveys, which laid a foundation for the development of university parity teachers and played a historical significance. Taking the faculty development of Kyoto University as the main case, they make a detailed and comprehensive analysis of the concept and practice of faculty development of Kyoto university in Japan, which can be used as a reference for the future development of faculty in China. Lin and Wei (2016) studied the international trend of faculty development. Based on the perspective of comparative education, the goal of faculty development needs to be upgraded, the mode of faculty development needs to be informationized, and the resources of faculty development need to be integrated at Chinese universities and colleges.

2.3 Practical Research on the Faculty Development

The practical research on faculty development in China mainly concentrates on two aspects: one is to study the current situation and existing problems of faculty development in recent years; the other is to draw lessons from and introduce the problems and contents of the research on faculty development in Western countries. Specifically, Pang (2012) studied the operation mechanism of China's faculty development through the mixed research methods. The study shows that since the 1980s, the international higher education has mainly begun to pay attention to the individual survival and faculty development. It is a historical and realistic necessity for China to begin attaching importance to study on faculty development. We should concentrate on the national and institutional conditions, properly orientating its function and nature, handling the relationship with relevant functional departments, and establishing a sound operating mechanism. He and Wang (2015) pointed out that university teaching culture is closely related to the development of faculty member. The faculty development has the characteristics of relevance, dynamic, synergy, balance, and so on. At the same time, they also face the problems of utilitarian academic ecology and psychological ecology under excessive pressure. Improving university teaching culture is conducive to promoting the ecological development of faculty member. Conversely, sustainable ecological development of faculty is conducive to the construction of university teaching culture. To construct a harmonious ecological environment for faculty development, it is necessary to establish a holistic ecological environment for faculty development, optimize the ecological environment for faculty development with teaching culture, create a good academic environment, and create a healthy psychological ecological environment.

According to the survey conducted by Shen Hong in 2016 for Chinese faculty in 2014, Chinese faculty has the characteristics of young age, short time for obtaining a degree, high proportion of doctorates, heavy academic inbreeding, many from rural villages and towns, low level of parental education and occupation, high job stress, and high satisfaction. The results show that the profession of faculty is the fairest but needs to be joined by people with diversified backgrounds.

Lu (2014) focuses on analyzing the core content and basic characteristics of Stanford University's faculty professional development system in the study of Stanford University faculty professional development. He put forward practical characteristics of Stanford University's faculty professional development, such as guided training projects and workshop management projects. In addition, Wu and Chen (2014) put forward their views and ideas on the construction of faculty development centers, taking the University of London, Royal College of London and Oxford University as examples. From the historical perspective, they traced the development of British University faculty and explored the practical process of the development of British university faculty. The functions, activities, institutional settings, and special projects of the faculty development centers of three famous British universities, namely London College, Royal College, and Oxford University are comprehensively analyzed and the organizational characteristics of faculty development centers in British universities are also summarized. Specifically, dimensional development involves the various aspects of faculty professional development, expanding the exchange platform for faculty, providing various incentives and faculty protection mechanism. In addition, Wu and Chen also put forward much enlightenment to the faculty development centers in China, and put forward that China should further improve the organizational setup, clarify the division of labor among employees, develop many different characteristics, expand the demand group and the income group, and provide for our faculty.

Li (2013) put forward some thoughts on the system logic and theoretical connotation of the construction of faculty development center in China, and proposed that the construction of faculty development center in China should focus on the supply-oriented system logic and implement the practical reform action of the teacher development under the guidance of the government power. Therefore, the leading features of Chinese government characterize the study on faculty development. Li believes that the construction of faculty development center in China marks the beginning of the university to treat faculty development as a systematic project, which integrates the national institutional arrangements, university development and faculty self-realization of the multi-demands, the fundamental is to achieve the conscious action of teacher development. Based on this, the construction of university faculty development center in China should follow the general organizational framework guided by the national system, take knowledge as the main content of development, and meet the special requirements of different university faculty development. Be and Li (2014) proposed that the construction of China's faculty teaching development center should be committed to promoting the transformation of faculty from the experience development model, focusing on the personal understanding and self-reflection. They emphasized that the construction of Chinese faculty development center should not be a purely institutional administrative institution or a purely academic research institution, but an institution with the dual characteristics of both administrative and academic institutions to guide the faculty development in order to integrate the nature of administrative and academic institutions organically. The establishment of faculty development centers with Chinese characteristics is the fundamental approach and the main basis for the construction of university faculty

2.3 Practical Research on the Faculty Development

development centers in China. In addition, they also pointed out that the main functions of the faculty development centers in China are to strengthen the cognition of teaching specialty, enhance the ethics of teaching specialty, cultivate the culture of teaching specialty, and promote the improvement of the level of running a university and the quality of personnel training. Pan (2015) pointed out that improving the quality of higher education in China is closely related to the professional faculty development in China. We should adopt new experience and new ideas to develop the research on faculty development. Generally speaking, the development and evaluation of faculty in China are not yet comprehensive, and there is no systematic practice pathway of faculty with Chinese characteristics. In addition, Chen and Zhu (2018) put forward the types of insurance for faculty development in China. They took the papers on the topic of faculty development, which published in CSSCI source journals and core journals from 2000 to 2017 as samples, and made a quantitative analysis of the overall trend of research, theme distribution, functional orientation, research methods, research subjects and institutions distribution, and the frequency of citation of the papers. Faculty development research has gone from confusion to rationality. The future research on the faculty development in China should construct a systematic concept of faculty development on the subject, strengthen the construction of crisscross research platforms on the research platform, and focus on the transformation of research function orientation to "indigenous constructivism rooted in the Chinese context". We should pay attention to the building of the institutional community. In his opinion, the demand–supply-oriented evaluation model of faculty professional development projects advocates that the needs of the organization and participants should be satisfied as the main basis for judging the effectiveness of the teaching development projects, and the supply adjustment should be used to improve and improve the demand satisfaction. A complete project design of faculty professional development should start with exploring the needs of faculty, and then go through the following steps: the serialization of organizational needs, confirmation of project needs, establishment of project objectives, presupposition of project evaluation schemes, project planning, project implementation, and establishment of project resource support system and data (or information) collection and support system. Based on the perspective of supply-side structural reform, the essentials of faculty professional development project innovation lie in requiring suppliers to guide and meet faculty professional development needs timely and effectively and gradually solve different types of problems by strengthening the ability of project design, flexibly utilizing all kinds of resources, especially high-related human resources such as trainers. Moreover, Ji (2016) carried out a review and discussion on the faculty development in China and proposed whether the faculty development should be equal to the training of faculty, whether the faculty development should copy the relevant experience of Western universities, and whether the faculty development should be carried out at the national level or not. The problems, such as the university level, whether the faculty should pay more attention to teaching or scientific research, and how the evaluation organizations of faculty development should play their roles are discussed. In addition, Pan (2017) put forward the outline of the faculty development from the perspectives of calendar year, connotation, mode, organization, and motivation in 2017, which is of guiding significance to the establishment of the basic practice of the development of university teachers in China. Wang Xia and Cui Jun's research on university teachers mainly focuses on the theoretical basis and promotion strategies of faculty teaching development and proposes that at the national and regional levels.

References (in Chinese)

Be, D., & Li, J. (2014). Nature and function of the University Teacher Development Center [J]. *Fudan Education Forum, 12*(04), 41-47.

Cai, Y. (2018). On professional academy and teaching academy in the development of university teachers [J]. *Teacher Education Research, 30*(02), 27–31.

Chen, S., & Wang, H. Research on the psychological resilience structure and influencing factors of young teachers in colleges and universities.

Chen, Z., & Zhu, D. (2018). Research on the development of university teachers: Status quo, problems and prospects [J]. *Education Exploration,* (01), 1–7.

He, Z., & Wang, R. University teaching culture and teacher development ecology [J]. *Higher Education Research, 36*(01), 57–61.

He, X., Meng, T., Lou, L., & Jia, L. (2015). Investigation and research on mental health status of young teachers in colleges and universities: A case study of 25 universities in Zhejiang province [J]. *Educational Review, 11,* 114–117.

Ji, F. (2016). Retrospect and discussion on the development of university teachers in China [J]. *Education Review,* (02), 118–121.

Jiang, Y., & Lin, J. (2011). The idea and practice of teacher development in Japanese Universities: A case study of Kyoto University [J]. *Peking University Education Review, 9*(03), 29–44 + 188–189.

Li, X. (2013). Institutional logic and theoretical connotation of the construction of teacher development center in colleges and universities [J]. *China Higher Education Research,* (12), 69–72.

Li, X. (2018). The American model of the development of university teachers and its reference significance [J]. *Jiangsu Higher Education,* (01), 52–56.

Lin, J., & Li, L. (2007). Three theoretical models of teacher development in American Universities [J]. *Modern University Education,* (01), 62–66 + 111–112.

Lin, J., & Wei, H. (2016). The international trend of university teacher development [J]. *University Education Management, 10*(01), 86–91.

Lin, J., & Wei, H. (2018). Competency model for teacher development workers at North American University [J]. *College Education Management, 12*(01), 92–98.

Liu, Z. (2018). The reform of teacher development organization in American research universities from the perspective of governance: Path and reference [J]. *Modern Education Management* (03), 58–63.

Liu, J., & Wang, Z. (2011). The experience and enlightenment of American university teacher development [J]. *Education Research, 32*(11), 104–107.

Lu, D. (2014). Research and enlightenment of teacher professional development in Stanford University [J]. *China Higher Education Research,* (03), 48–54.

Pan, M. (2015). The quality of higher education and the development of university teachers [J]. *Higher Education Research, 36* (01), 48.

Pan, M. (2017). Outline of university teacher development—Idea, connotation, mode, organization and motivation [J]. *Higher Education Research, 38*(01), 62–65.

Pang, H. (2012). Research on the function and operation mechanism of the University Teacher Development Center [J]. *Journal of the National Institute of Education Administration* (08), 60–65 + 33.

References (in Chinese)

Qin, G. (2012). The history and enlightenment of teacher development in American Universities [C]//Annual Meeting of the Comparative Education Branch of the Chinese Education Association.

Qu, L. (2018). The generation environment, establishment process and organizational characteristics of the teacher development center of the University of Michigan [J]. *China Higher Education Research,* (01), 75–80 + 86.

Shen, H. (2016). The development of university teachers in China-based on the analysis of the "2014 China University Teachers Survey" [J]. *Higher Education Research, 37*(02), 37–46.

Wang, C. (2009). Attribution of teachers' professionalization in American Universities and its enlightenment to China [J]. *Higher Education Research,* (2), 11–11.

Wu, W., & Chen, C. (2014). The characteristics and enlightenment of the faculty development center of british universities: A case study of University of London, Royal College of London and Oxford University [J]. *Exploration of Higher Education,* (03), 53–57 + 64.

Zhang, X. (2014). Mental health problems and countermeasures of young teachers in universities in China [J]. *Education Review,* (04), 44–47.

Zheng, X. (2014) Analysis and improvement strategy of young college teachers' psychological quality [J]. *Education Review,* (12), 47–49.

Zhou, G., & Ma, H. (2013). Teaching academic competence: A new framework for the development and evaluation of university teachers [J]. *Educational Research, 34*(08), 37–47.

Chapter 3
Examining Faculty Development Model: From Chinese Context

This chapter involves conceptualizing faculty development model from Chinese context. Faculty development model at Chinese context involves Chinese specific educational historical and cultural elements historically and contextually. Therefore, this chapter is mainly divided into three parts: in the first part, the introduction on faculty development model is discussed to offer an overview of the landscape of faculty development. The second part involves exploring and constructing a faculty development model with Chinese characteristics. The faculty development model with Chinese characteristics is synthesized as "M-RTS" ("M" represents faculty professional morality; "R" represents research; "T" represents teaching; "S" represents service). In conclusion, faculty development model with Chinese characteristics offers a specific insight to examine the rationale of faculty development model from Chinese contextual perspective.

3.1 Introduction on Faculty Development Model

Faculty development has become an increasingly significant concept for an increasing number of faculty and administrators in American colleges and universities. Over the past decades, numerous studies have been written about faculty development. Since 1970s, there existed various faculty development models, including some activities and different programs. Specifically, Bergquist and Philips initially offered the components of faculty development model, which include instructional development, personal development, and organizational development. The instructional development involves curriculum instructions and faculty personal training. Personal development focuses on different activities to improve faculty personal development. The organizational development is associated with accelerating institutional climate for improving the effectiveness of faculty development. In other words, the instructional development, personal development, and organizational development all contribute to shape the structure and content of faculty development. In addition, Gaff's model is similar to Bergquist and Philips's model. The faculty renewal model is a proposal by Gaff. Comparing to Bergquist and Philips's model, Gaff considered instructional development as focusing more on curriculum design and shaping faculty personal behavior. Both Gaff and Bergquist-Philips models concentrate more on heuristic domain rather than empirical domain. The significant student–faculty relations are closely associated with constructing a faculty development model. Advancing the specialized and professional knowledge is considered as main orientation of shaping faculty development model. Gaff's faculty development model involves faculty renewal. The faculty renewal is parallel to faculty development, including personal development, instructional improvement, and organizational development. All these three development components are intertwined with each other. From Gaff's perspective, establishing and operating faculty renewal programs and activities are inherently imbedded in constructing a faculty development model.

Faculty contract or identities consider the formal and informal agreement relationship between universities and faculty members. It contains three major components: rule contract, psychological contract, and social contract. Generally speaking, there existed formal and nonformal relationships between faculty and universities. The obligation and reciprocity of formal mutual commitment are universities and faculty. The basis for establishing formal and informal relations is established in past decades. In the past, the top universities in China were still in the process of higher education construction and reform. "Personal administration" is dominant and it has not been able to realize from personal relationship to contract. Generally speaking, the key issues in the construction of faculty contractual relationship involve transforming personal administration system into faculty contract. Universities and colleges have already implemented a series of education policy for preparing the implementation of the long-term appointment system. It is more urgent to rebuild contract relationship between faculty and universities. The analysis of the concept of "contract" is closely associated with the agreement on responsibility between university and faculty. The personal relationship is considered to be an important foundation for the growth of modern society and organization. The key to universities' faculty contract is to change the relationship between faculty's identity and management. The contractual relationship is also considered as a contractual obligation. In contemporary Chinese higher education system, the values, resources, environment, and organization within the universities are allocated based on the acts, responsibilities, obligations, and specific agreement clauses. In addition, when a faculty accepts a university appointment, it means that the two sides have made a specific contract. The relationship between faculty and universities will be constructed accordingly. Commitment to university commitments and participation in university development goals serves as the main task for Chinese faculty members.

Overall speaking, Chinese faculty professional morality is not only inhabited in traditional ethnic Chinese morality but also has a substantial number of aboriginal culture and value at modern society. Historically, Chinese-characterized faculty professional morality is rooted in traditional fragment-oriented fundamental ethics. In this logic, there is a lack of consistency in the use of terms, such as "faculty/teacher value" or "faculty/teacher virtue" in Chinese education history. China is the most valued ethnic nation. Faculty morality is a kind of professional ethics.

Faculty professional ethics refer to faculty ethics, as the moral norms and codes of conduct that the faculty member and all educators must abide by in their specific educational activities, as well as the corresponding moral concepts, sentiments, and qualities (Huang, 2003; Yu, 2011; Zhang & Li, 2011; Zhang & Zhou, 2003).

3.2 Examining Faculty Development Model at Chinese Context

Conceptual faculty development model at Chinese context is proposed to explore the rationale of faculty development historically, culturally, and contextually. In Chinese context, faculty development involves a complex profession, including researching, teaching, and learning. In a centralized ideological society, the nature of faculty development with Chinese characteristics is more likely to concentrate on cultivating faculty professional morality. Chinese faculty professional morality is obviously different from Western faculty professional ethics. There existed a couple of differences and similarities. In addition, the conceptual faculty development model with Chinese characteristics included four elements: research, teaching, service, and professional morality. The faculty professional morality serves as core idea of constructing faculty development model with Chinese characteristics. In other words, faculty development model with Chinese characteristics is synthesized as "M-RTS" ("M" represents faculty professional morality; "R" represents research; "T" represents teaching; "S" represents service). Research, teaching, and service should be consistent with faculty professional morality at Chinese context. Highlighting the importance of faculty professional morality is considered as a vivid feature of Chinese-characterized faculty development model. As previously illustration, the traditional faculty development models have been introduced and analyzed. Therefore, this section focuses on investigating faculty professional morality with Chinese characteristics (See Fig. 3.1).

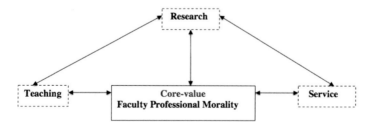

Fig. 3.1 Conceptual faculty development model at Chinese context

3.3 Conclusion and Remarks

The proposed faculty development is inherently rooted in Chinese traditional pedagogical paradigm. Faculty professional morality is considered as a fundamental core idea of faculty development model with Chinese characteristics. The synthesized faculty development model with Chinese characteristics ("M-RTS") vividly reveals the core conceptual feature of Chinese faculty development. Cultivating faculty professional ethical value plays an essential to integrate teaching, research, and service into a comprehensive faculty development paradigm. In the meanwhile, the proposal faculty development model with Chinese characteristics is nested in Chinese political, cultural, and historical development inherently. In this sense, the faculty professional morality serves as core and indisputable element to connect with faculty traditional development, including teaching, research, and service.

References (All Paper in Chinese)

Huang, J (2003). The master of the world—On confucius's teacher's view [J]. (1), 43.

Yu, Z. X. (2011). The thought of Chinese education masters [M]. Wuhan: Huazhong Normal University Publishing Club.

Zhang, Z., & Li, J. (2011). Educational wisdom of Chinese and foreign education masters. Beijing: Petroleum: M Industrial Press.

Zhang, S., & Zhou, L. The vitality of ideological education—If the idea of ideological and moral education is M. Hangzhou: Zhejiang University.

Chapter 4
Faculty Professional Morality with Chinese Characteristics: A Comparative Perspective

This chapter explores the rationale of Chinese faculty professional morality through historical comparisons of the elements of faculty professional morality between Western and Eastern. First, the study synthesizes Western faculty professional morality as deontology, utilitarianism and egoism-focused ethics, reasoning competencies, civic-dominated moral and modern faculty morality, and identity-oriented professional ethics-oriented contemporary faculty morality. Second, the interior–exterior-inherited model is initially proposed to examine the rationale of Chinese-characterized faculty professional morality, including ancient Chinese faculty morality philosophy of fraternity, loyalty, and selfless dedication, make faculty an example, equality, Chinese modern faculty professional morality of freedom, equality and fraternity, comprehensive personality, and Chinese contemporary faculty professional morality of political–ideological-oriented mandate. In addition, the differences and similarities between Chinese and Western faculty moral model are explored to examine the paradigm of faculty professional morality contextually. The conclusion and remarks are provided at the end of the study.

4.1 Introduction and Overview

Longtime observers of Chinese higher education have witnessed a series of shifting trends in mission and purpose. In the current period, the priority is to Chinese faculty with moral and value responsibility. The stated purpose of higher education reflects the political and social expectation of the era as well as the character of the institution and the branding by leadership at a particular moment in time. In the meanwhile, the faculty professional morality is inherently embedded in the mission, vision, and value statements of Chinese higher education institutions. For power, inequity is considered as a fatal ethical flaw in faculty–student romances. Therefore, the faculty professional morality has in recent years spread virtually within the contemporary higher education regime. Comparatively speaking, in the history of American history, the "ethics boom" (Davis, 1990, 1999a, 1999b, 2003a, 2003b) was initially proposed and examined by the Hastings Center in the late 1970s, which producing seminal essays and monographs about ethics education in US colleges and universities. Specifically, in U.S. higher education institutions, the ethics education for both faculty and students involve the implicit values of higher education through examining trends of ethics education. Generally speaking, in the Western higher education system, the major ethical components embrace both the behavior and functional activities of universities and colleges. The ethical behaviors include pedagogical ethics, research ethics, organizational ethics, professional ethics, nonacademic activities ethics, and ethical achievements (Davis, 2004, 2009a; 2009b, 2010, 2014; Davis et al. 2016).

However, in Chinese context, there is different understanding and illustrations to examine faculty professional morality with Chinese characteristics historically and traditionally. Chinese faculty professional morality is inherently embedded in the mission, vision, and value statements of Chinese higher education institutions. Comparing with Western faculty professional morality philosophy, there implicitly existed historical and contextual complexity and differences. However, there are few studies on investigating Chinese faculty professional morality philosophy with Chinese characteristics. Therefore, this study explores the rationale of Chinese faculty professional morality through examining the literature review of Western faculty professional morality: first, elements of Western faculty professional morality are summarized as deontology, utilitarianism and egoism-focused ethics, reasoning competencies, civic-dominated moral and modern faculty morality, and identity-oriented professional ethics-oriented contemporary faculty morality. Second, the interior–exterior-inherited model is constructed to examine the rationale of Chinese-characterized faculty professional morality. Third, the differences and similarities between Chinese and Western faculty moral model examine the paradigm of faculty professional morality contextually. Lastly, the conclusion and remarks are provided at the end of this study.

4.2 Elements of Western Faculty Professional Morality

Overall speaking, Western faculty professional morality involves ancient ethical philosophy of deontology, utilitarianism and egoism, modern faculty morality of reasoning competencies, civic-dominated morality, and contemporary faculty morality of identity-oriented professional ethics. The term faculty professional morality/ethics is initially examined and constructed by Western scholars and educators. Specifically, traditional Western ethical philosophy of faculty professional morality is epitomized as deontology, utilitarianism, and egoism. Modern Western faculty professional morality involves promoting moral reasoning competencies to teach students' civic education and moral education. Contemporary faculty professional morality is more complex and specific, concentrating on examining identity-oriented professional ethics.

4.2 Elements of Western Faculty Professional Morality

4.2.1 Ancient Ethical Elements: Deontology, Utilitarianism, and Egoism

In Western philosophy, the ethical philosophical construction involves some specific term, such as deontology, utilitarianism, and egoism. The term deontology derived from the Greek for duty (*deon*). Deontology is identified as rule-based ethics. In other words, the concept of deontology refers to certain actions, which intrinsically make a right or wrong ethical decision. The ethical egoism refers to the act or behavior to create the greatest good for individual (Aristotle, 1964, 2002; Kagan, 1997; Northouse, 2013; Plato, 1975). Ethical egoism focuses on individual's moral obligation in order to enhance his or her own good (Kagan, 1997). The idea of egoism is comprehensively based on maximizing self-interest ahead of the organization. In other words, the egoistic ethical climate indicated that individual perceives that the organization generally promotes self-interested decisions at the expense of others (Al-Omari, 2012). The idea of utilitarianism involves the greatest good for the greatest number of people, clearly the opposite of ethical egoism (Northouse, 2013; Victor & Cullen, 1987, 1988).

Within Western higher education regime, students' moral and civic capacities are inherently associated with faculty's professional morality. Specifically, both Plato's utopian dialogue, *The Republic*, and Aristotle's experimental school, *The Lyceum*, concentrate on appreciation of the importance of education in preparing promising leaders who have the character necessary to govern. Considered education as the social construction that made it possible for autonomous individuals to understand that individual happiness was dependent on the health and happiness of the community within which they lived. Therefore, the faculty server as transmitter and student is a receptor in the learning of nature of health and happiness. Throughout the Western ancient higher education history, faculty morality was subject to enhance and reinforce higher education community standards and principles. In contemporary higher education system, the profession's code of ethics is considered as a historical artifact to be investigated, appraised, defended, or condemned (Colby et al., 2003). Shared values involve promoting student learning for sustaining the environment simultaneously collaborative and competitive work of seeking new knowledge. Western faculty morality more focuses on the honesty, integrity, and self-discipline for advocating intellectual charity (Colby et al., 2003; Ebels-Duggan, 2015; Roberts, 1999; Wolff, 1994).

4.2.2 Modern Faculty Morality: Reasoning Competencies, Civic-Dominated Morality

Moral education traditionally includes the teaching of substantive content as well as the development of moral reasoning competencies. The moral education is subjected to improving the foundation of systematic moral formation in order to investigate the major historical and contemporary controversies within a specific discipline of study. Ethical reasoning involves asking faculty and students to be able to assess their own ethical values and the social context of problems, recognize ethical issues in a variety of settings, think about how different ethical perspectives might be applied to ethical dilemmas, and consider the ramifications of alternative actions (Association of American Colleges and Universities 2010). Within the campus, faculty professional morality is subjected to civic education and ethical education (Colby et al., 2003; Harris, 2009a, 2009b; Keller, 2002; Keohane, 2006; Reid, 2010; Sia, 2001). Faculty professional morality plays a pivotal role in advocating students' ethical education and informal socialization in order to facilitate their civic and moral development (Matchett, 2008; Ozar, 1977; Whitbeck, 1995). In other words, the key components of faculty professional morality are to offer ethic model to encourage students' perspective taking or provide structured opportunities to practice moral decision-making (Mayhew & King, 2008). In the Western pedagogy, since 1980, the faculty professional morality is epitomized as equity, fairness, political ideology, self-determination, and imperialism. Western faculty professional morality is in adherence to a written code, such as an "honors code" or rules of a religion as a statement of universal standards. In other words, faculty members are required to cultivate certain virtues or act in certain ways rather than follow any particular standards. In other words, the so-called virtuous conduct is subjected to satisfy moral standards. Professional ethics is parallel to professional responsibility, professionalism, professional conduct, responsible conduct, social responsibility, and integrity. The professional ethics implies moral theory. Since Socrates, the philosophy is identified as the *"pursuit of wisdom"* (Thoma & Bebeau, 2013; Thompson, 2006; Thornton & Jaeger, 2008; Tsei, 2002; Whitbeck, 1995).

4.2.3 Contemporary Faculty Morality: Identity-Oriented Professional Ethics

In addition, in contemporary education regime, the identity-oriented professional ethics is considered core value-laden attribute of contemporary faculty morality at Western cultural context. It derived from the traditional breadth of ethics, namely, as the study of free human behavior. The moral theories are too complex to serve as practical guides to conduct specific training of faculty professional morality. Hence, the starting point of contemporary faculty morality is the opposite of the present fashion of treating professional ethics as a standalone area of inquiry, as though it were independent of other moral concerns. In its modern segregated state, ethics is often understood to be the study of decision-making principles and evaluation of isolated acts, detached from the acts that led to the present circumstances and from their effect on the agent. By this logic, the contemporary moral act is specific as a disinterested judgment, which, for better or worse, aligns more closely with the conditions of the classroom and debate than with ethical practice. Lost in this framing of the ethical problem is the relationship between the agent and the act, with the corresponding separation of the telos of the act from the telos of the agent. A consequence of this division is an incoherent separation between the social good promised by a profession and the agents and their acts that constitute it. Specifically, the linguistic expression of this relationship between moral act and institutions is initially proposed in the Greek of Aristotle's period: ethos (habit) and êthos (character) are cognate (Aristotle 2002, 1103a19–23). The major task of cultivating faculty professional morality is to help stimulate students' moral imagination, recognize moral issues, analyze key moral concepts and principles, elicit the sense of responsibility, and deal with moral ambiguity and disagreement. In conclusion, in contemporary higher education system, faculty professional morality more emphasized on disseminating identity-oriented professional ethics through constructing moral education curriculum and instructions for cultivating students' civic and moral education. The teaching–learning relationship between faculty members and students is shaping and finalizing the concept of identity-oriented professional ethics inherently.

4.3 Elements of Chinese Faculty Professional Morality

Overall speaking, Chinese faculty professional morality is not only inhabited in traditional ethnic Chinese morality, but also has a substantial number of aboriginal culture and value at modern society. Historically, Chinese-characterized faculty professional morality is rooted in traditional fragment-oriented fundamental ethics. In this logic, there is lack of consistency in the use of terms, such as "faculty/teacher value" or "faculty/teacher virtue" in Chinese education history. China is the most valued ethnic nation. Faculty morality is a kind of professional ethics. Faculty professional ethics refer to faculty ethics, as the moral norms and codes of conduct that the faculty member and all educators must abide by in their specific educational activities, as well as the corresponding moral concepts, sentiments, and qualities (Huang, 2003; Yu, 2011; Zhang & Li, 2011;).

The interior–exterior nested model is initially proposed to examine the rationale of Chinese-characterized faculty professional morality. This model includes three historical components of Chinese faculty morality philosophy, such as ancient Chinese faculty morality philosophy of fraternity, loyalty, and selfless dedication, make faculty an example, equality, Chinese modern faculty professional morality of freedom, equality and fraternity, comprehensive personality, and Chinese contemporary faculty professional morality of political–ideological-oriented mandate. Specifically, Chinese faculty morality philosophy of fraternity, loyalty, and selfless dedication, make faculty an example, and equality is considered as intrinsic historical core value for advocating faculty morality; Chinese modern faculty professional morality of freedom, equality and fraternity, comprehensive personality, and Chinese contemporary faculty professional morality of political–ideological-oriented mandate are regarded as extrinsic core value. As previously illustrated, Western faculty professional value is relatively loosely inherited among Western ancient wisdom,

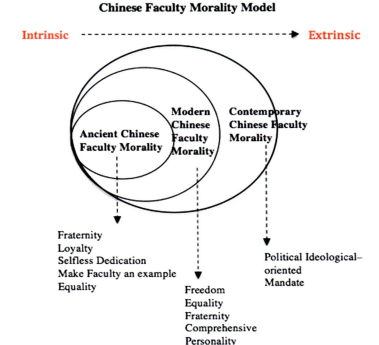

Fig. 4.1 Chinese faculty morality model

modern cultural and value reconstruction, and contemporary individualism-oriented value. To some extent, there is relatively lack of consistency, correlation, and inheritance. Comparing with Western faculty professional morality, Chinese-characterized faculty professional moral value focuses on a radiant relation between the ancient Chinese moral wisdom and modern and contemporary generalized faculty consensus and common values. By this logic, Chinese-characterized faculty professional morality follows an implicit pathway, connecting, inheriting, and integrating Chinese ancient value components to refine Chinese-characterized landscape of faculty professional morality philosophy (See Figs. 4.1 and 4.2).

4.3.1 Elements of Ancient Chinese Faculty Morality: Fraternity, Loyalty, and Selfless Dedication, Make Faculty an Example and Equality

Chinese ancient faculty morality philosophy is epitomized as the key concept of fraternity, loyalty, and selfless dedication. Specifically, Confucius's philosophy of

4.3 Elements of Chinese Faculty Professional Morality

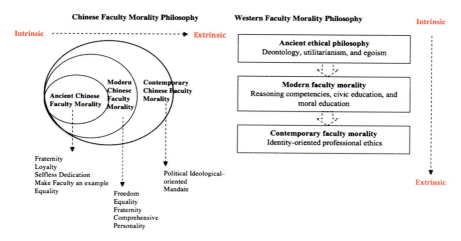

Fig. 4.2 The comparison between Chinese faculty morality philosophy and western faculty morality philosophy

faculty professional morality concentrates on "benevolence" as the core and the highest moral standard. Faculty professional morality is closely associated with students' ethical education. Confucius illustrated the relationship between faculty professional morality and student ethical cultivation. Confucius insisted that, "Before stand up and build people, you should reach them and achieve it." It is also stated that "do not impose on others what you do not want." Therefore, within Chinese traditional education regime, being a teacher must be loyal to education, love of life, learn the "tireless", and selfless dedication. It is the concrete manifestation and requirement of teachers' professional ethics. Confucius is in faculty professionalism is shown in the following aspects: loyalty education and love of life. There still existed moral disagreement and ambiguity in Chinese faculty professional morality. In addition, lifelong learning and learning without tiring are the truth of Confucius's life as a teacher. Mencius ever said that, "Sage is not mine and I am never tired of learning." While practicing and mastering and using existing knowledge, we constantly pursue new knowledge and heir. Therefore, overall speaking, the traditional faculty professional morality aims to keep the pace with the knowledge development and renewal, and the establishment of a "good learning" list for students. Specifically, to cultivate students' lifelong learning ability requires teachers to be a lifelong learner. Confucius argued that teacher should be sensitive and good learner.

Confucius argued that, "faculty morality is the exemplary behavior." Example is better than precept. Confucius's philosophy of faculty professional morality also illustrated that the teacher uses his exemplary behavior as the example of his students and work can create enormous educational strength. Confucius is also a teacher, focusing on constructing ethical reasoning and improving morality. Teachers' moral example has great influence on students' life of the apprentice. More importantly, in the domain of the Analects of Confucius, teacher should be ethical in his own right. Teachers' behavior gives students an example. Confucius suggested that, "The beauty of personality is the source of educational vitality. The educator should be magnanimity." In other words, faculty professional morality involves perceiving the rhythm of life and feeling the pain and suffering of the world. Moreover, Confucius also highlighted the importance of cultivating faculty an awareness of the harmony of teaching and receiving, harmony between emotion and reason, persisting in teaching without any kind of teaching and classes. Confucius advocated "teaching without classes," as long as we treat teachers with courtesy. In addition, teachers should have equal education, while adhering to the concept of equality. As a teacher, we should also adhere to the student viewpoints of education development. An equal and developing view of students is a positive. The affirmative outlook on students deserves teachers' good inheritance and development. Besides, teachers should establish a democratic teaching concept. On the basis of equal status, teachers were expected to strive to create a democratic and active harmony. The teaching atmosphere is the requirement of effective teaching and good teaching. Confucius advocated that "benevolence, not the teacher." This is more than a century later than ancient Greek education. Aristotle, a thinker, said, "I love my teacher, I love truth more." They encourage students to think boldly and think actively in teaching.

In conclusion, Confucius provided a fundamental understanding of faculty's virtue and value in ancient Chinese education regime. Confucius, as the great educationist in Chinese traditional society, offers valuable narratives on faculty professional idea, quality, spirit, style, attitude, cultivation, and skills the moral need of a teacher. Confucius' argument of faculty's virtue has an enduring influence on modern faculty's professional moral growth. In traditional Chinese context, faculty morality includes both faculty professional morality as a group and faculty concrete morality as a group. Traditional Western education involves individual morality. Traditionally, China has always had a high moral expectation for faculty, but because of its lack of respect for faculty. Almost rigorous moral requirements tend to weaken and neglect the privatization of faculty and the legitimate needs of life and moral pursuit. This phenomenon of selective moral injustice is a manifestation of the indiscriminate distinction between public and private in the field of faculty's morality in China. Therefore, it is necessary to distinguish the precious areas between faculty professional ethics and individual ethics in order to clarify the boundaries and links between public and private ethics in faculty's ethics. In ancient China, teacher's morality is parallel to teacher's soul. Moral standards and codes of conduct, teachers' morality determines the quality of teachers. Faculty professional morality is deeply associated with the quality and effectiveness of education.

4.3.2 Chinese Modern Faculty Professional Morality: Freedom (Meaning), Equality (Forgiveness) and Fraternity (Benevolence), Comprehensive Personality

Chinese modern faculty professional morality is mainly proposed and examined by CaiYuanpei (1868–1940), who is a well-known democratic revolutionist, great educator, and outstanding educational thinker in modern China. CaiYuanpei contributed to Chinese modern moral education. Mao Zedong endorsed him as "a great scholar and a model of the world." CaiYuanpei insightfully reflected on and reviewed Chinese traditional moral thoughts, and proposed to integrate Chinese and Western cultures to build a new morality suitable for Chinese moral education development. He was also the first person to embark on Chinese-characterized moral education practically. Moreover, the thought of moral education occupies an extremely important position in CaiYuanpei's whole educational ideological system.

CaiYuanpei's Chinese faculty professional morality education thought mainly involves the concept of freedom, equality, and charity. He said that the freedom is a kind of virtue and also high-level moral autonomy. In his moral education, equality means to individual's social status and he insisted that individual's nobleness is determined by personal character. In addition, charity is considered as the most valuable character and norm. He argued that Chinese faculty professional morality should be in accordance with the principle of subjectivity. CaiYuanpei also indicated that faculty should pay much attention to the self-learning process and practices. Faculty is expected to disseminate morality education through providing knowledge and physical exercise. In other words, CaiYuanpei's faculty professional morality involves human-centered educational concept, including respecting, understanding, caring, stimulating, educating, shaping, liberating, trusting, and depending people.

CaiYuanpei advocated that faculty professional morality is considered a pivotal role to spread civic virtues. He argued that faculty should emphasize on combining the concept of freedom, equality, and charity into current educational regime. In order to achieve accomplishment, "Comprehensive personality" is initially epitomized to highlight the importance of moral education for both faculty and students. In his moral educational ideological system, faculty professional morality is regarded as a disseminator to advocate Chinese-characterized civic moral education. CaiYuanpei argued that cultivating faculty professional morality should deal with three relationships among moral education and physical education, moral education and intellectual education, moral education, and aesthetic education. Specifically, CaiYuanpei argued that the process of sports is also a process of moral education. Therefore, faculty should develop public morality to make people understand honor of the body rather than being honest and defeated. The relationship between moral education and intellectual education is relatively implicit. Learning is the final result of moral education. Knowledge is the foundation of moral education. Therefore, CaiYuanpei emphasized that faculty professional morality focuses on expanding knowledge for pure conduct and cultivation of conduct. Understanding of the formation of human morality is associated with the establishment of criteria for good and evil. In other words, faculty moral cultivation lies in the learning and knowledge of science. The relationship between moral education and aesthetic education is illustrated by CaiYuanpei to guide faculty focusing on personal aesthetic cultivation. The aesthetic education was wrapped in moral education. CaiYuanpei argued that civic virtues and aesthetic education are all related to faculty moral cultivation. Freedom (meaning), equality (forgiveness), and fraternity (benevolence) all contribute to epitomize CaiYuanpei's morality thoughts.

4.3.3 Chinese Contemporary Faculty Professional Morality: Political–Ideological-Oriented Mandate

Chinese contemporary faculty professional morality is epitomized as political–ideological-oriented mandate in higher education system. In recent years, Chinese central government initiated a series of policies to advocate faculty professional morality. Specifically, in May 2013, the plan entitled *the Some Opinions on Strengthening and Improving the Ideological and Political Work of Young Faculty in Colleges and Universities* was issued. The plan was made to strengthen and improve the ideological and political work of young faculty in colleges and universities, and the examination archives of faculty ethics would be established. Faculty morality should be exactly faculty's morality, which is the social public morality that faculty should abide by in order to safeguard social public interests. Faculty morality is a kind of professional ethics. In addition, Prohibition of Faculty's Moral Conduct in Colleges and Universities ("Red Seven Bar") is considered another pivotal educational policy document to facilitate political–ideological-oriented mandate of Chinese contemporary faculty professional morality. Specifically, the document entitled the "Opinions of the Ministry of Education on the Establishment and Improvement of a Long-term Mechanism for the Construction of Faculty's Morality in Colleges and Universities" clearly stated the punishment mechanism for the violations of faculty's ethics should be established and perfected, and the "seven red bars" for teachers' ethical prohibition with warning educational significance should be drawn out. The details are as follows: first, acts that harm the interests of the state and harm the legitimate rights and interests of students and schools; second, in education and teaching activities, there are words and deeds that violate the party's line, guidelines, and policies; third, falsification, plagiarism, falsification and embezzlement of other people's academic achievements, illegal use of scientific research funds, and misuse of academic resources and academic influence in scientific research; fourth, part-time concurrent pay actions that affect normal education and teaching; fifth, engage in malpractices in the work of enrollment, examination, student promotion, and insurance research; sixth, requesting or receiving gifts, gifts, securities, payment vouchers, and other properties of students and parents; and seventh, sexual harassment of students or improper relations with students (other violations of the professional ethics of university teachers).

On September 29, 2014, the Ministry of Education issued *the Opinions on Establishing and Improving a Long-term Mechanism for the Construction of Faculty Morality in Colleges and Universities* on the 10th of Teachers' Day. This opinion profoundly understands the importance and urgency of establishing and perfecting the long-term mechanism for the construction of faculty professional morality in contemporary Chinese colleges and universities. The principles and requirements of establishing and perfecting the long-term mechanism are subjected to the construction of faculty morality in colleges and universities. The main measures of establishing and perfecting the long-term mechanism for the construction of faculty morality in colleges and universities involve the conscientiousness and practicality of stimulating the construction of the main body of responsibility for the construction of faculty morality in colleges and universities.

The main measures to establish and improve the long-term mechanism for the construction of faculty morality in colleges and universities, including innovating the education of faculty morality and guide teachers to set up lofty ideals, strengthening the propaganda of faculty morality and cultivate good morality, improving the examination of faculty morality and promoting faculty self-cultivation, strengthening the supervision of faculty' morality so as to effectively prevent faculty anomie behavior, and paying attention to the encouragement of faculty morality. We should guide teachers to enhance their spiritual realm, strictly punish their ethics, and give full play to the system's normative and binding role.

Suggestions on promoting faculty profession morality is proposed by the Ministry of Education as follows: First, we should have a deep understanding of the importance and urgency of establishing and perfecting a long-term mechanism for the construction of faculty' ethics in colleges and universities in the new period; second, we should establish and improve the principles and requirements of a long-term mechanism for the construction of faculty ethics in colleges and universities; third, establish and improve the main measures for the long-term mechanism of teachers' moral construction in colleges and universities; fourth, fully stimulate the consciousness of university teachers to strengthen the construction of teachers' ethics; fifth, clearly define the main body of responsibility for the construction of teachers' morality in colleges and universities. In current context, Chinese faculty morality includes faculty moral cognition, faculty moral emotion, faculty moral will, and faculty moral beliefs. Chinese faculty morality is considered as the core of faculty profession, which can be summarized as, "master love is the soul, knowledgeable person is master, integrity is the model."

4.4 Comparison of Elements of Faculty Professional Morality

Comparing the elements of faculty professional morality of Western and Eastern provides a clear pathway to explore the differences and similarities within two cultures. Both differences and similarities contribute to unveil the rational and paradigm from political, cultural, and social perspectives.

4.4.1 Differences Between Chinese and Western Faculty Moral Model

Relations, ancient logic start, and contemporary practical goal contribute to explore differences between Chinese and Western faculty moral model. Specifically, for Chinese faculty professional morality model, each historical element, constructing faculty professional morality model, follows an interior–exterior-inherited structure. Specifically, Chinese faculty professional morality inhabited in traditional ethnic Chinese morality with a substantial number of aboriginal culture and value historically. For example, the core ideas of fraternity, loyalty, and selfless dedication consistently reveal in the flow of historical development of Chinese faculty professional morality. The consistency of ancient, modern, and contemporary faculty professional morality elements is inherently rooted in Chinese traditional ideological-oriented fundamental ethics. Otherwise, comparing with the relation of elements of Chinese faculty moral model, elements of Western faculty professional morality follow a loosely top-down hierarchical structure with lack of consistency, correlation, and inheritance. In current Western faculty professional morality, the contemporary moral act is specific as a disinterested judgment, which, for better or worse, aligns more closely with the conditions of the classroom and debate than with ethical practice. In addition, from the ancient logic start perspective, Chinese faculty moral model involves fraternity, loyalty, and selfless dedication. The Western faculty moral model concentrates on deontology, utilitarianism, and egoism. From contemporary practical goal perspective, Chinese faculty moral is more likely to focus on political–ideological-oriented mandate to construct the principles and requirements of establishing and perfecting the long-term mechanism are subjected to the construction of faculty morality in colleges and universities. Comparing with Chinese contemporary practical goal, Western faculty moral model more likely to concentrate on individual identity-oriented profession to shape faculty personal ethical cognitions and behaviors at different contexts.

4.4 Comparison of Elements of Faculty Professional Morality

Table 4.1 Differences and similarities between Chinese and Western faculty moral model

	Elements of Chinese faculty moral model	Elements of Western faculty moral model
Differences		
Relations	Interior–exterior-inherited	Top-down hierarchical
Ancient logic start	Fraternity, loyalty, selfless, dedication	Deontology, utilitarianism, egoism
Contemporary practical goal	Political–ideological-oriented	Individual identity-oriented profession
	Mandate	
Similarities		
Orientation	Enhance and reinforce higher education community standards and principles	
Overlapping ideas	Fraternity, equality	

4.4.2 Similarities Between Chinese and Western Faculty Moral Model

Both the orientation and overlapping ideas of faculty professional morality model provide similar feature of enhancing and reinforcing higher education community standards and principles. The relationship among stakeholders offers a community identity-oriented professional ethics inherently. This community identity-oriented profession is gradually constructed and shaped through a series of principles, regulars, and conducts. Particularly, Western faculty professional morality is subjective to a written code, honors code, and rules of a religion for creating the universal standards. In this sense, certain specific standards are constructed to satisfy moral standards within different contexts. In Chinese context, Chinese government is more likely to make a series of political documents in order to strengthen the ideological and political goal and examine faculty ethical activities (See Table 4.1).

4.5 Conclusion and Remark

4.5.1 Conclusion

We have sought to examine how the concept of identity, understood as the iterative process of planning and action that forms a teleological quest, can orient professional ethics, instruction. In addition, this extrinsic–intrinsic teleology is robust enough to support the diverse important elements that constitute professional ethics. Specifically, Chinese faculty professional morality is associated with the mission, vision, and value of Chinese higher education conditions. Inconsistent with Western faculty professional morality philosophy, there implicitly existed historical and contextual differences between Western and Eastern culture. In this sense, investigating Chinese faculty professional morality philosophy with Chinese characteristics should apply both historical and contextual retrospect and prospect approach in order to explore the rationale of Chinese faculty professional morality. The synthesized Western faculty professional morality includes deontology, utilitarianism and egoism-focused Ancient ethical philosophy, reasoning competencies, civic education and moral education-based modern faculty morality, and identity-oriented professional ethics-oriented contemporary faculty morality. Paralleling to Western faculty professional core ideas, the proposal extrinsic–intrinsic teleological model explores the rationale of Chinese-characterized faculty professional morality, focusing on ancient Chinese faculty morality philosophy of fraternity, loyalty, and selfless dedication, make faculty an example, and equality, Chinese modern faculty professional morality of freedom, equality and fraternity, comprehensive personality, and Chinese contemporary faculty professional morality of political–ideological-oriented mandate.

4.5.2 Remarks

Chinese faculty professional morality provides the foundation, allowing propositional and practical knowledge associated with the codes of ethics, laws, and accepted practices of a profession to be integrated into an individual's identity, instead of always remaining as external dictates. It also captures the historical dimension of Chinese-characterized faculty professional ethical values and connects it to the behaviors and reactions of constructing faculty professional acts. Additionally, it also encompasses components of Chinese traditional and contemporary moral act that have been shown by social psychologists to be determinant in professional ethical behavior, including faculty professional judgment, which is reflective and requires an understanding of faculty research fields of virtue as well as their limitations; the commitment, the firmness of will that is accurately identified that can be constructed through individual practices; and a moral imagination that enables various innovative solutions to ethical problems at different contexts. Moreover, the proposed Chinese-characterized faculty professional moral model is identified as a radiant relation-based circle model between the ancient Chinese moral wisdom and modern and contemporary generalized faculty consensus and common values. In other words, Chinese-characterized faculty professional morality is subject to inheriting and integrating Chinese ancient value elements to shape Chinese contemporary faculty professional morality landscape.

References

Al-Omari, A. A. (2012). The perceived organizational ethical climate in Hashemite University. *Asia-Pacific Education Researcher, 22*(3), 273–279. https://doi.org/10.1007/s40299-012-0033-1.

Aristotle. (1964). In E. Barber (Ed.), *The politics of Aristotle*. New York: Oxford University Press.

Aristotle. (2002). *Nicomachean ethics* (trans: Sachs, J.) Newburyport, MA: Focus Publishing.

Colby, A., Ehrlich, T., Beaumont, E., & Stephens, J. (2003). *Educating citizens, preparing America's undergraduates for lives of moral and civic responsibility*. San Francisco: Jossey-Bass.

Davis, M. (1990). Who can teach workplace ethics. *Teaching Philosophy, 13*(1), 21–38.

Davis, M. (1999a). *Ethics and the university*. New York: Routledge.

Davis, M. (1999b). *Ethics and the university*. New York: Routledge.

Davis, M. (2003a). What's wrong with character education? *American Journal of Education, 110*, 32–57 (November 2003a).

Davis, M. (2003b). What can we learn by looking for the first code of professional ethics? *Theoretical Medicine and Bioethics, 24*, 433–454.

Davis, M. (2004). Five kinds of ethics across the curriculum: An introduction to four experiments with one kind. *Teaching Ethics, 4*, 1–14 (Spring 2004).

Davis, M. (2009a). The usefulness of moral theory in practical ethics: A question of comparative cost. *Teaching Ethics*, 69–78 (Fall 2009a).

Davis, M. (2009b). Is engineering a profession everywhere? *Philosophia, 37*, 211–225 (June).

Davis, M. (2010). The usefulness of moral theory in teaching practical ethics: A reply to Gert and Harris. *Teaching Ethics, 11*, 51–60 (Fall 2010).

Davis, M. (2014). Professional ethics without moral theory: A practical guide for the perplexed non-philosopher. *Journal of Applied Philosophy, 6*, 1–9.

Davis, M., Laas, K., & Hildt, E. (2016). Twenty-five years of ethics across the curriculum: An assessment. *Teaching Ethics, 16*, 55–74 (Spring 2016).

Ebels-Duggan, K. (2015). Autonomy as intellectual virtue. In H. Brighouse & M. McPherson (Eds.), *The aims of higher education, problems of morality and justice* (pp. 74–90). Chicago: The University of Chicago Press.

Harris, C. E. (2009a). Is moral theory useful in practical ethics? *Teaching Ethics, 10*(1), 51–68.

Harris, C. E. (2009b). Response to Michael Davis: The cost is minimal and worth it. *Teaching Ethics, 10*(1), 79–86.

Huang, J. (2003). The master of the world—On confucius's teacher's view [J]. (1): 43.

Kagan, S. (1997). *Normative ethics. Dimensions of philosophy series*. Boulder CO: Westview Press.

Keller, D. R. (2002). The Perils of communitarianism for teaching ethics across the curriculum. *Teaching Ethics, 3*, 49–76 (Fall 2002).

Keohane, N. O. (2006). *Higher ground: Ethics and leadership in the Modern University*. Durham, NC: Duke University Press.

Matchett, N. (2008). Ethics across the curriculum. *New Directions for Higher Education*, 25–38.

Mayhew, M. J., & King, P. (2008). How curricular content and pedagogical strategies affect moral reasoning development in college students. *Journal of Moral Education, 37*(1), 17–40.

Northouse, P. G. (2013). *Leadership: Theory and practice*. Thousand Oaks, CA: Sage.

Ozar, D. T. (1977). Teaching philosophy and teaching values. *Teaching Philosophy, 2*(3–4), 237–245.

Plato. (1975). *The trial and death of socrates* (trans: Grube, G. M. A.). Indianapolis, IN: Hackett Publishing.

Reid, T. (2010). *Essays on the active powers man*. In K. Haakonsen & J. Harris (Eds.). Edinburgh: Edinburgh University Press.

Roberts, P. (1999). A dilemma for critical educators? *Journal of Moral Education, 28*(1), 19–30.

Sia, S. (2001). Teaching ethics in a core curriculum: Some observations. *Teaching Ethics, 2*, 69–76 (Fall 2001).

Thoma, S. J., & Bebeau, M. J. (2013). Moral motivation and the four component model. In K. Heinrichs, F. Oser, & T. Lovat (Eds.), *Handbook of moral motivation: Theories, models, applications* (pp. 49–68). Rotterdam: The Netherlands, Sense Publishers.

Thompson, C. (2006). Unintended lessons: Plagiarism and the University. *Teachers College Record, 108*(12), 2439–2449.

Thornton, C. H., & Jaeger, A. J. (2008). The role of culture in institutional and individual approaches to civic responsibility at research institutions. *Journal of Higher Education, 79*(2), 160–182.

Tsei, L. (2002). Fostering critical thinking through effective pedagogy. *The Journal of Higher Education, 2*, 740.

Victor, B., & Cullen, J. B. (1987). A theory and measure of ethical climate in organizations. *Research in Corporate Social Performance and Policy, 9,* 51–57.

Victor, B., & Cullen, J. B. (1988). The organizational bases of ethical work climates. *Administrative Science Quarterly, 33,* 101–125.

Whitbeck, C. (1995). Teaching ethics to scientists and engineers: Moral agents and moral problems. *Science and Engineering Ethics Journal, 1*(3), 299–308.

Wolff, R. P. (1994). The myth of the neutral university. In R. L. Simon (Ed.), *Neutrality and the academic ethic* (pp. 103–109). Lanham, MD: Rowman & Littlefield.

Yu, Z. X. (2011). *The thought of Chinese education masters [M]*. Wuhan: Huazhong Normal University Publishing Club.

Zhang, S., & Zhou, L. The vitality of ideological education—If the idea of ideological and moral education is M. Hangzhou: Zhejiang University.

Zhang, Z., & Li, J. (2011). *Educational wisdom of Chinese and foreign education masters*. Beijing: Petroleum: M Industrial Press.

Chapter 5
Overview of Faculty Development Center at Chinese Context: An Example of BNU

In recent years, Chinese government more and more paid much attention to build faculty development center in order to improve faculty teaching and research competencies at Chinese universities and colleges. Therefore, this chapter concentrates on introducing Chinese faculty development centers from the aim, goal, programs, platform, and politics perspectives. The Center for Faculty Development of Beijing Normal University is examined as one example to investigate the specific development of faculty development center contextually. In addition, the overview of the Center for Faculty Development of Beijing Normal University involves mission, working concept, working standards, work content, working principle, and faculty development assessment.

5.1 Mission of the Center for Faculty Development

The Faculty Development Center of Beijing Normal University[1] was established on February 22, 2012 to meet the historical trend of the development of international higher education, to cope with the grim reality of the rapid popularization of higher education in China and the creation of world-class universities, and to effectively solve the long-standing problems of teaching ability in higher education. The wave of globalized university teaching innovation is surging forward. All teaching reform measures must be carried out and implemented through the frontline teachers. Therefore, faculty is in the most important position in teaching reform. However, from the past, the overall situation of faculty in China is not optimistic. For a long time, the teaching work of faculty has not been regarded as a specialized occupation. If fac-

---

[1] http://fd.bnu.edu.cn/zxgk/zxjj/73113.html.

© Springer Nature Singapore Pte Ltd. 2019
X. Zhu and J. Li, *Faculty Development in Chinese Higher Education*, Perspectives on Rethinking and Reforming Education, https://doi.org/10.1007/978-981-13-7767-9_5

ulty lacks of knowledge and research, he will not be taught. Therefore, faculty is a thoroughly specialized profession, one of the highest degrees of professionalism, not competent with knowledge. The specialization of faculty profession is mainly reflected in teaching methods. Therefore, "what to teach" and "how to teach" are both real problems. We should not oppose them. As a university faculty, we should not only teach but also teach well. We should not only teach carefully but also study hard. Those who cannot use two minds must not be teachers. At present, there are still many university teachers engaged in teaching activities, only starting from the logic of teaching content, and few in-depth studies of teaching methods. In fact, besides the logic of teaching content, there is another logic in university teaching practice, that is, the logic of teaching methods. Only when the two logics are in harmony can the teaching process bring about a good spiritual experience for teachers and students, and students can enjoy learning. The problem of how to teach and how to learn is still not effectively solved. There are a large number of phenomena in the classroom, students just sit and listen in the classroom, and communication between faculty and students is missing. Despite all faculties' efforts, students are still expressionless and unresponsive, even playing mobile phones, sleeping, chatting in class, and making great efforts to desert. All these problems make students feel disappointed in class, and their creativity, judgment, expressiveness, thinking ability, and ability to solve new problems have not been developed. Then, how can we really help university faculty to enhance their teaching execution, so that university teachers in the right track to continuously obtain professional development? This is an imminent task facing all the people who are concerned about improving the quality of university teaching all over the world.

5.2 Working Concept of Faculty Development Center

Therefore, the working concept of the faculty development center is "useful, someone will learn." Faculty should be provided with useful research projects to help faculty solve real teaching problems and confusion encountered in teaching practice, pay attention to the effectiveness of the work, and help should be to the point. How to find practical teaching problems, we must go deep into teaching practice, in-depth teaching site, and teachers are closely linked, integrated, fully understand what teachers think, difficult.

Hence, the goal of the Teacher Development Center is to enhance the teaching execution of university faculty and then to improve the teaching quality of higher education. It is universities' or colleges' responsible to promote the comprehensive development of faculty member. Specifically, first of all, we must inherit and carry forward the teaching culture of the university, pass on the centuries-old accumulation of the university from generation to generation, and absorb the essence of others, thus becoming an inexhaustible motive force. Second, help faculty to establish advanced teaching concepts, facing the new human beings, we must form new teaching concepts, new ideas, and new ways. Third, faculty should be helped to study the necessary teaching methods and skills in university teaching, and gradually sum up teaching experience and conduct teaching research. Let each faculty who wishes to get help from teaching methods can fulfill his wish. Fourth, provide interactive opportunities for faculty and create an exchange platform. Teachers who hope to communicate with others and share with other faculty have families. Fifth, actively carry out the construction of teaching resources, make full use of modern information technology, to provide teachers with teaching support beyond the limitations of time and space, to achieve ubiquitous research.

5.3 Working Standards of Faculty Development Center

The working standards of the faculty development center are international, professional, sophisticated, and continuous. As a national demonstration center for faculty development, we must broaden our horizons, take the world-class university as the benchmark, communicate, and standardize the central work, the staff engaged in faculty development should have professional knowledge and ability to provide faculty with professional standards of teaching services; and the services provided faculty lectures, seminars, teaching consultation, etc., must be high level, with a very strong shock and impact. Therefore, helping faculty in teaching work is a long-term process, a systematic work. In order to overcome the shortcomings of point training, we should adopt snake-like training strategy. In this sense, the work of the faculty development center is to help, research, and support. The role of Faculty Development Center staff is helpers, researchers, and supporters. Faculty development center should benefit faculty at all stages of development, promote faculty to update their teaching concepts, master the necessary educational technology and teaching skills, and improve their teaching ability. We should help all kinds of faculty in all directions.

5.4 Working Content of Faculty Development Center

Faculty training
The basic vocational ability training for new faculty mainly includes how to design teaching, how to teach, how to analyze the teaching effect, etc. For experienced teachers, it is necessary to expand and study a variety of teaching methods, study their own teaching methods, and carry out teaching research with self-development significance. It should help them summarize and condense their own teaching methods and teaching theories, create a real university teacher for the school, carry out prejob training for postgraduate assistants, and carry out preservice training for postgraduate teachers to enhance their teaching ability.

Teaching consultation

Faculty as teaching individuals, in the process of teaching practice, will continue to encounter new problems, find new problems; therefore, it is urgent to have effective guidance, urgent need to discuss with the help. The Faculty Development Center provides a "point-to-point" place for faculty to explore teaching problems and provides "distribution" teaching consultation services to meet individual needs, highlighting the needs of faculty's personalized professional development. It is hoped that teachers will be able to find problems in teaching.

Teaching reform

Encourage and help teachers to carry out teaching innovation in the teaching process and carry out daily teaching and research. Try to create in the school concerned about the reform of teaching methods, concerned about the improvement of teaching effect, concerned about the positive atmosphere of student development. To help teachers actively study advanced teaching concepts, update teaching content, innovate teaching methods and models, improve teaching strategies and teaching structure, and summarize teaching experience and achievements.

Teaching research

Teaching research is the basic work of the faculty development center and it is also the vitality of the survival and development of the faculty development center. The center should focus on the working methods and strategies of the faculty development center, study how to enhance the teaching execution of university faculty, study the basic laws of faculty development in various stages of development, the ways and methods of the development of new faculty, and study the specific methods of university teaching.

Converging resources

Efforts should be made to collect and accumulate high-quality teaching resources, including famous faculty, excellent faculty, and senior faculty, for faculty to establish an effective sharing mechanism and provide faculty with high-level teaching.

5.5 Working Principle of Faculty Development Center

The working principle of the Faculty Development Centre is to focus on the key point, the characteristics, and effectiveness. Faculty who can actively participate in the activities of the Faculty Development Center is faculty who are sincerely interested in the innovation of teaching methods. They are faculty members who deserve our admiration and respect. Therefore, we must treat them kindly and try our best to think about what they think, be anxious for them, and serve them sincerely. And help these faculty members get to know each other, produce horizontal synergy, and gradually change into a long-term interactive teaching and research community. What should be emphasized here is that faculty professional development is a directional concept, not just a single improvement in teaching ability. Therefore, the work of the faculty development center not only falls on the faculty's teaching execution but also should pay attention to other aspects of faculty's professionalism. Specifically, as a university faculty, there are four major aspects of its job. One is teaching activities, disseminating knowledge, teaching and educating people, and exceeding students. The second is research activities, occupying or creating knowledge, exploring the unknown, self-cultivation and self-improvement. The third is the administrative work within the school, serving others, contributing to others, supporting the old and the young. The fourth is to serve the society, fulfill the social mission of the intellectuals, and contribute to the development of human society. In the other three aspects, the teacher development center should also play its role in helping teachers to make progress.

5.6 Faculty Development Center Assessment

Chinese faculty development center or program is positioned to serve faculty members at universities and colleges. Supporting institutions have become an international convention for faculty development program. Specifically, in contemporary Chinese higher education system, many universities' faculty development centers or programs aim at cultivating, supporting, and inspiring faculty members for teaching, researching, and serving. Therefore, Chinese faculty are often involved in various activities or projects for accelerating their academic skills and competencies. However, the attraction and pertinence of the faculty development activity are not enough. For example, it can be caused by the lack of professional consciousness and ability of project developers. There may be a lack of precise assessment of faculty's professional development needs. Therefore, how to develop faculty's professional development projects has become a religion.

Moreover, the long-term challenges and tasks faced by the faculty development centers or programs are to construct a project evaluation model for teacher professional development. By this logic, the general design of faculty professional development project is put forward currently. We can evaluate a specific project of faculty training and the evaluation should have systematic description of its objectives, as well as the benefits, values, input, output, benefits of the trained party, and so on. The assessment of faculty professional development projects is not only meaningful but also very necessary. It can be seen that both goals and needs of faculty development center play an important role in faculty development evaluation process. In other words, a variety of faculty development training or activities are organized by the faculty development center. The goal of faculty development center focuses on a concrete and actionable behavior, which is more closely related to curriculum objectives or learning objectives. For a specific institution, faculty professional development projects are actually the specific embodiment of the organizational needs of the institution. The evaluation model of faculty development is expected to meet the needs of organizations and participants at universities and colleges.

It is the main basis for judging the effectiveness of faculty's teaching development projects. Through this supply adjustment, we can improve and enhance the degree of demand to satisfy action. In the assessment model of faculty development, both the organization and the participants are the evaluation subjects. The evaluation criteria of evaluation models consist of two requirements: satisfaction and evidence.

From a political perspective, the structural reform of supply-based reform of faculty development stems from *The 19th National Congress of CPC*. The original intention is intended to be adjusted to improve the whole economic structure, which will optimize the allocation of factors and enhance Chinese economy. In other words, the structural reform of supply-based reform of faculty development more concentrates on the quality and quantity of growth. Improving the quality of supply is closely associated with promoting the structural adjustment with reform, such as distorting the allocation of corrective elements, expanding effective supply, and improving the supply structure. The adaptability and flexibility for improving faculty development at Chinese context is associated with increasing total factor production. It can better meet the needs of the broad masses of the people and promote economic society. In other words, the structural reform of supply-based reform of faculty development aims to providing sustained and healthy development for Chinese faculty member, which mainly dependent on investment and consumption within Chinese higher education system. Faculty professional development, from the perspective of supply-based structural reform, offers a specific lens to examine the essence of faculty development innovation in order to strengthen the overall quality of Chinese faculty member.

Faculty professional development is mainly based on supply-based structural perspective and this project reform creates a couple of service providers, such as the teaching development center. The faculty professional development center can be classified into cognition, skill, and emotion components. The cognitive domain can be relied on lecture-based learning, and the skill domain is dependent on learning. In the faculty development process, the cognition, skill, and emotion process is considered as a process of gradual internalization, which requires faculty members to teach and learn more than often. Reflection and communication among peers can accelerate the teaching skills and competencies in the long term. The implementation method for regular centralized lecture training can support cognition skills for faculty members. The reform of the faculty development project requires faculty's teaching development center to abandon the whole staff supply and set up the working concept of the needs of the people.

Bibliography

Al-Omari, A. A. (2012). The perceived organizational ethical climate in Hashemite University. *Asia-Pacific Education Researcher, 22*(3), 273–279. https://doi.org/10.1007/s40299-012-0033-1.
Aristotle. (1964). In E. Barber (Ed.), *The politics of Aristotle*. New York: Oxford University Press.
Aristotle. (2002). *Nicomachean ethics* (trans: Sachs, J.) Newburyport, MA: Focus Publishing.
Att Bach, P. G. (2001). *Comparative higher education: Knowledge, big learning and development [M]* (pp. 117–121). People's Education Press. Beijing: People's education Edition society.
Colby, A., Ehrlich, T., Beaumont, E., & Stephens, J. (2003). *Educating citizens, preparing America's undergraduates for lives of moral and civic responsibility*. San Francisco: Jossey-Bass.
Davis, M. (1990a). Who can teach workplace ethics. *Teaching Philosophy, 13*(1), 21–38.
Davis, M. (1990b). Who can teach workplace ethics. *Teaching Philosophy, 13*(1), 21–38.
Davis, M. (1999a). *Ethics and the university*. New York: Routledge.

Davis, M. (1999b). *Ethics and the university*. New York: Routledge.
Davis, M. (2003a). What's wrong with character education? *American Journal of Education, 110*, 32–57 (November 2003a).
Davis, M. (2003b). What can we learn by looking for the first code of professional ethics? *Theoretical Medicine and Bioethics, 24*, 433–454.
Davis, M. (2004). Five kinds of ethics across the curriculum: An introduction to four experiments with one kind. *Teaching Ethics 4*, 1–14 (Spring 2004).
Davis, M. (2009a). The usefulness of moral theory in practical ethics: A question of comparative cost. *Teaching Ethics*, 69–78 (Fall 2009a).
Davis, M. (2009b). Is engineering a profession everywhere? *Philosophia, 37*, 211–225 (June 2009b).
Davis, M. (2010). The usefulness of moral theory in teaching practical ethics: A reply to Gert and Harris. *Teaching Ethics, 11*, 51–60 (Fall 2010).
Davis, M. (2014). Professional ethics without moral theory: A practical guide for the perplexed non-philosopher. *Journal of Applied Philosophy, 6*, 1–9.
Davis, M., Laas, K., & Hildt, E. (2016). Twenty-five years of ethics across the curriculum: An assessment. *Teaching Ethics, 16*, 55–74 (Spring 2016).
Ebels-Duggan, K. (2015). Autonomy as intellectual virtue. In H. Brighouse & M. McPherson (Eds.), *The aims of higher education, problems of morality and justice* (pp. 74–90). Chicago: The University of Chicago Press.
Fan, P. J. (2016). Construction of university teacher development center: Problems and solutions [J]. *National Higher Education Research*, (10).
Han, Y. (1999). Assessment and enlightenment of foreign teachers' in-service training activities (J). In S. Rosemary, Caffarella, & F. Z. Lynn (Eds.), *National education information* (global education outlook, 2000, (06). Professional development for faculty: A conceptual framework of barriers and supports. *Innovative Higher Education, 23*(4), 241–254.
Harris, C. E. (2009a). Is moral theory useful in practical ethics? *Teaching Ethics, 10*(1), 51–68.
Harris, C. E. (2009b). Response to Michael Davis: The cost is minimal and worth it. *Teaching Ethics, 10*(1), 79–86.
Harris, C. E. (2010). A reply to Bernard Gert. *Teaching Ethics, 11*, 39–50 (Fall 2010).
Harris, C. E. (2011). A reply to Bernard Gert. *Teaching Ethics, 12*(1), 41–50.
Harris, C. E. et al. (2014). *Engineering ethics: Concepts and cases* (5th ed.). Wadsworth.
Harris, C. E., Pritchard, M. S., Rabins, M., James, R., & Englehardt, E. E. (2014). *Ethics in engineering: Concepts and cases* (5th ed.). Belmont, CA: Cengage.
Huang, J. (2003). The master of the world—On Confucius's teacher's view [J]. (1), 43.
Kagan, S. (1997). *Normative ethics. Dimensions of philosophy series*. Boulder, CO: Westview Press.
Kant, I. (1785/1998). *Groundwork for the metaphysics of morals* (trans: Gregor, M.). Cambridge, UK: Cambridge University Press.
Ke, B., et al. (2014). Construction of education and teaching standards such as teachers' professional development. The practice and application of the center in four world-class universities [J]. *Beijing University Education Review*, (04).
Keenan, J. F. (2015). *University ethics: How colleges can build and benefit from a culture of ethics*. New York: Rowman & Littlefield.
Keller, D. R. (2002). The perils of communitarianism for teaching ethics across the curriculum. *Teaching Ethics, 3*, 49–76 (Fall 2002).
Keohane, N. O. (2006). *Higher ground: Ethics and leadership in the Modern University*. Durham, NC: Duke University Press.
Li, J. (2010). *Cultivating teachers' rational quality—100 kinds of teaching that teachers should understand M*. Changchun: Northeast Normal University Press.
Matchett, N. (2008). Ethics across the curriculum. *New Directions for Higher Education*, 25–38.
Mayhew, M. J., & King, P. (2008). How curricular content and pedagogical strategies affect moral reasoning development in college students. *Journal of Moral Education, 37*(1), 17–40.
Meyers, C. (2011). Reappreciating W. D. Ross: Naturalizing prima facie duties and a proposed method. *Journal of Mass Media Ethics, 26*(4), 316–331.

Meyers, C. (2016). Universals without absolutes: A theory of media ethics. *Journal of Media Ethics, 31*(4), 198–214.
Northouse, P. G. (2013). *Leadership: Theory and practice*. Thousand Oaks, CA: Sage.
Ozar, D. T. (1977). Teaching philosophy and teaching values. *Teaching Philosophy, 2*(3–4), 237–245.
Plato. (1975). The trial and death of socrates (trans: Grube, G. M. A.). Indianapolis, IN: Hackett Publishing.
Pritchard, M. S., & Englehardt, E. E. (2015). Ethical theories and teaching engineering ethics (Chapter 8). In S. S. Sethy (Ed.), *Contemporary ethical issues in engineering* (pp. 111–120). IGI Global.
Reid, T. (2007). Practical ethics. In K. Haakonsen (Ed.), *Practical ethics*. Pennsylvania: Penn State Press.
Reid, T. (2010). Essays on the active powers man. In K. Haakonsen & J. Harris (Eds.), Edinburgh: Edinburgh University Press.
Roberts, P. (1999). A dilemma for critical educators? *Journal of Moral Education, 28*(1), 19–30.
Sia, S. (2001). Teaching ethics in a core curriculum: Some observations. *Teaching Ethics 2*, 69–76 (Fall 2001).
Taylor, C. (1989). *Sources of the self: The making of the modern identity*. Cambridge, MA: Harvard University Press.
The Hastings Center. (1980). The teaching of ethics in higher education. Hastings-on Hudson, NY: Institute of Society, Ethics and the Life Sciences.
Thoma, S. J., & Bebeau, M. J. (2013). Moral motivation and the four component model. In K. Heinrichs, F. Oser, & T. Lovat (Eds.), *Handbook of moral motivation: Theories, models, applications* (pp. 49–68). Rotterdam: The Netherlands, Sense Publishers.
Thompson, C. (2006). Unintended lessons: Plagiarism and the university. *Teachers College Record, 108*(12), 2439–2449.
Thornton, C. H., & Jaeger, A. J. (2008). The role of culture in institutional and individual approaches to civic responsibility at research institutions. *Journal of Higher Education, 79*(2), 160–182.
Tsei, L. (2002). Fostering critical thinking through effective pedagogy. *The Journal of Higher Education, 2*, 740.
Victor, B., & Cullen, J. B. (1987). A theory and measure of ethical climate in organizations. *Research in Corporate Social Performance and Policy, 9*, 51–57.
Victor, B., & Cullen, J. B. (1988). The organizational bases of ethical work climates. *Administrative Science Quarterly, 33*, 101–125.
Whitbeck, C. (1995). Teaching ethics to scientists and engineers: Moral agents and moral problems. *Science and Engineering Ethics Journal, 1*(3), 299–308.
Wolff, R. P. (1994). The myth of the neutral university. In R. L. Simon (Ed.), *Neutrality and the academic ethic* (pp. 103–109). Lanham, MD: Rowman & Littlefield.
Wu, H. (2014). Practical topic of teaching development center for university teachers. *And Other Educational Research,* (03).
Xiong, H., & Ding, Y. (2011). Currently facing the professional development of American University Teachers Dilemma [J]. *Comparative Education Research*, (03).
Yu, Z. X. (2011). *The thought of Chinese education masters [M]*. Wuhan: Huazhong Normal University Publishing Club.
Zhang, Z., & Li, J. (2011). *Educational wisdom of Chinese and foreign education masters*. Beijing: Petroleum: M Industrial Press.
Zhang, S., & Zhou, L. The vitality of ideological education—If the idea of ideological and moral education is M. Hangzhou: Zhejiang.
Zhao, Q. (1997). On confucius's view of teacher [J]. *Journal of Leshan Teachers College (Social Sciences Edition)*, (1): 57.

Part II
Practical Faculty Development at Chinese Context

Chapter 6
Interviews of Chinese Faculty Development: Narratives and Dialogues

This chapter mainly involves providing the whole landscape of Chinese faculty development from Chinese institutional perspective. A couple of experts and scholars in the field of Chinese faculty development are invited to examine the problems, difficulties, and strategies of Chinese faculty development contextually. Overall speaking, there are 40 interview transcripts, focusing on both high-frequency words and the key points.

6.1 Peking University—Liu

6.1.1 High-Frequency Words

Academic innovation ability	Academic field
University teachers	Rigid index
Cross-disciplines	Elastic system

6.1.2 Key Points of Interview

1 On the index system of innovation ability
1.1 The definition of object
  Interviewer: What's your general impression of the index system of university teachers' innovation ability?
  Liu: The indicators are not specific enough to define the concept of university teachers clearly. It is necessary to make a detailed classification of the whole university and higher education teachers.

1.2 On cross-disciplines

Interviewer: What do you think is the most important aspect of innovation ability?

Liu: To innovate, we should break the boundary of disciplines, merge different disciplines, and set up a more elastic system to fully activate teachers' creative vitality and innovative potential.

Interviewer: Do you think the classification of our index system is reasonable? Do you have any suggestions on this?

Liu: I think the comprehensive ability and cross-disciplines part should be strengthened. The learning of methodology and the cultivation of problem consciousness are most fundamental. There are different problems in different disciplines. What's your expected achievement? A questionnaire?

Interviewer: Yes.

Liu: That's really difficult. Innovation ability is very individualized. We can only make about 30–40% judgments through questionnaires. We usually use historical and qualitative research.

Interviewer: How do you think we should evaluate the creative ability of teachers?

Liu: First, pay attention to knowledge itself. Second, in different disciplines, the questions are different. Third, the process and logic of knowledge production are different from the result.

Interviewer: Compared with that of other university teachers, is there anything special about the innovation ability of teacher educators?

Liu: In the past 30 years in China, progress was made in the whole campus. However, compared with the pace of social development, the progress is too small, even too weak.

2 The influence of personnel system on the innovation ability of university teachers

2.1 On resource allocation

Interviewer: In your opinion, what are the factors that promote or hinder the academic innovation of university teachers in the current resource allocation?

Liu: The concept of resource allocation is an official one.

Interviewer: Yes.

Liu: China has been particularly keen on project system in resource allocation in recent years, which has a lot of negative effects. The government provides funds for researchers. So they have to do the given programs. Then a lot of inefficient and boring subjects arise up. If the government can provide a looser environment, researchers can do more valuable and difficult projects.

2.2 On the selection and appointment

Interviewer: How does the current mechanism of selection and appointment in universities affect the academic innovation of teachers?

Liu: Doing research and teaching must be evaluated separately. For teaching-oriented teachers, requiring them to do research would be a disadvantage. In addition, there are many levels within our universities, which I don't recommend.

Interviewer: Some rigid requirements in terms of selection and appointment will hinder the development of teachers' innovation?

Liu: No doubt about that. For everyone, his previous experience was rarely pleasant. In China, if a teacher is not a professor, he can't receive many resources, which restricts his development greatly.

Interviewer: Are there many such phenomena in China, such as one has titles, then he can get good projects?

Liu: That's right. That's a serious problem. It's necessary to give the necessary respect to academic work and guarantee the growth space of academic talents.

Interviewer: In your opinion, in such a system, can academic refreshers receive enough respect? What's the main reason for the lack of this respect?

Liu: Many researchers don't care about the tiles, positions, or the given projects. They just stick on their own domains for a long time. Finally, they produce valuable achievements.

Interviewer: In the current system, there is still some misunderstanding about whether teachers get enough respect.

Liu: They don't understand the academic field. Under the financial support, there isn't a good selection mechanism (such as an internal academic selection system) to determine how to spend the money. We had better give the money to the field or the group to let them determine how to use the money by themselves.

Interviewer: There are many rigid conditions when universities select teachers in China. However, the director of the personnel department said there would still be a few exceptions.

Liu: This is just for management.

2.3 On examination and evaluation

Interviewer: How to promote the development of teachers' innovation ability through assessment and evaluation mechanism?

Liu: Evaluate teachers once every 3 or 5 years rather 1 year. Give teachers more time and obey the rules within the academic community.

2.4 On incentive and safeguard mechanism

Interviewer: At present, how does the incentive and guarantee mechanism of university teachers affect their academic innovation ability?

Liu: I think the first is safeguard and the second is motivation. The system should be elastic and guarantee teachers' initiative and freedom. In terms of academic innovation, spending and wasting money is inevitable. So in the management of university teachers, it is necessary to ensure they can do things according to the internal logic of his academic field.

6.2 Beijing Normal University—Zhang

6.2.1 High-Frequency Words

Social ability	Academic leader
Academic innovation	Comprehensive ability
Cross-disciplines	Do some surveys

6.2.2 Key Points of Interview

1 Academic innovative social ability
1.1 Query of academic innovative social ability

Interviewer: In your opinion, is it appropriate to divide university teachers' innovative ability into three dimensions: psychological ability, knowledge ability, and social ability?

Zhang: I don't understand what is academic innovative social ability. Innovation is a matter of personal ability and tendency. One can also innovate without social support. Does the social ability of innovation mean the social support for innovation?

Interviewer: As for social ability, for example, the ability to collaborate is required in an academic team, especially in an interdisciplinary group.

Zhang: This kind of innovation is collective innovation. But the original idea was personal.

Interviewer: Now, we advocate the construction of academic teams. In the academic team, there must be an academic leader.

Zhang: That's right. After the leader has a new idea, he organizes some people to communicate and practice together. That's the leader's innovation. But he just has a group to support him.

Interviewer: Some key research bases of humanities and social sciences led by the country are innovation platforms. What do you think of this phenomenon?

Zhang: The platform is good. On the platform, researchers can sign up and apply for the funds.

1.2 The new understanding of academic innovative social ability

Interviewer: That is to say, you do not agree that academic innovation must require social skills?

Zhang: As for social ability, it's also possible to understand that innovation should be based on the needs of the country and society. If the idea is good for the country and society, we decide to do it and then form a team gradually.

2 Academic innovative psychological ability

Interviewer: Is the system of psychological ability appropriate?

Zhang: The foundation is a bit weak. Psychological ability includes insight, divergence, and associative ability and so on. Mental ability is mainly about thinking, but not limited to thinking. What's more, cognition and emotion are closely related. In addition, some indices are more important and some are less important.

Interviewer: That's right.

Zhang: Comprehensive ability is necessary. However, the requirements for the ability of knowledge crossing, knowledge integration and literature review are too low. In fact, the abilities of literature review and knowledge integration are most basally.

Interviewer: In your opinion, the ability of literature review is something that every teacher should have? This capability is not an innovation capability?

Zhang: Yes, every teacher should do that. The word "can" isn't appropriate. It should be replaced by "like" or "be good at".

Interviewer: OK. Is the system of interdisciplinary academic research ability appropriate?

Zhang: Psychologically, it is the quality of one's thinking. It is a good quality to keep an eye on the frontier in other research areas within the discipline. "I have research experience in other disciplines", "I will adopt different research methods according to my own research", and "I like to try to solve my problems in some other ways" are OK. However, "I am familiar with other disciplines" isn't appropriate.

2.1 Academic innovative knowledge ability

Interviewer: What's your opinion about academic innovative knowledge ability?

Zhang: Knowledge ability is very important. What's the ability of academic knowledge pedigree?

Interviewer: For example, the ability of sorting out knowledge history and development tendency in the future.

Zhang: That's ability of crossing disciplines.

Interviewer: The comprehensive ability of related disciplines?

Zhang: Yes. We take a combination of several subjects and take what are relevant to my research.

Interviewer: Do you have more suggestions about the indices?

Zhang: The indices are too detailed and they are arranged by expectation rather than survey.

2.2 Suggestions on future research

Interviewer: Could you give us some suggestions about the future research?

Zhang: You should do some practical surveys to understand the current situation of teachers. Use questionnaires and arrange some open-ended questions in the end.

Interviewer: What do you think of the qualitative research methods?

Zhang: We use both qualitative research approach and quantitative research methods. It's better to combine the two methods.

6.3 Northeast Normal University—Liu

6.3.1 High-Frequency Words

Innovation thinking	Innovation consciousness
Strong responsibility	Consciousness of problems
Resource allocation	Selection and appointment

6.3.2 Key Points of Interview

1 The rationality of the six indicators of innovation ability

Interviewer: Do you think the six indicators of innovation ability are reasonable?

Zhang: In my opinion, the indicators of academic innovation ability are mainly about methods. However, the key to innovation is thinking. To cultivate creative talents is to cultivate thinking talents. Creative teachers have three important abilities, the ability to enliven boring knowledge, the ability to distinguish between useful and useless knowledge, the ability to turn fragmented knowledge into systematic knowledge.

Interviewer: What's the theoretical basis of these three abilities?

Zhang: That's not important. The ability of thinking is the key. The thinking of teachers must be first.

Interviewer: What's the main type of teachers' thinking currently?

Zhang: Conformity.

Interviewer: What's the reason for conformity?

Zhang: In this society, it's difficult for everyone to innovate. Thinking is the most important. No matter what kind of thinking, the concept must be clear.

Interviewer: Can you say a bit more clearly?

Zhang: I mean the origin of thinking, the origin of coming up with a concept, the special understanding based on the existing concept. Furthermore, the logic of thinking is also important.

Interviewer: How do the categories in our indicator system reflect your views?

Zhang: You can design some indicators about teaching style, ways of getting along with different students and so on. The first task of teacher's ability cultivation is the cultivation of innovation consciousness.

Interviewer: How do we evaluate a teacher's innovation consciousness?

Zhang: How is innovative consciousness cultivated? It's cultivated in everyday life and through every little thing.

Interviewer: In your opinion, our indicator system lacks much in this aspect?

Zhang: That's right.

Interviewer: How do we evaluate university teachers' innovation ability? Is there anything special?

Zhang: It is a misunderstanding to find out something special about teacher education. Universities are just laying the foundation for students.

Interviewer: The difference in innovation ability between teachers in normal universities and teachers in other universities lies in the different objects.

Zhang: As for teacher education, there must be two attitudes. The first is strong responsibility and the second is educational reform.

Interviewer: Does our indicator system reflect the sense of innovation?

Zhang: Very little. I don't know what's knowledge innovation ability. You have to think about what is innovation ability carefully. The most important is teacher's thinking ability.

Interviewer: Only when we have determined the core of this evaluation system can we discuss the following issues?

Zhang: Yes.

Interviewer: Have NECU taken any measures to prompted teachers' creative ability?

Zhang: Yes, we have.

Interviewer: What kind of measures?

Zhang: We would like to change our scientific research concepts within 10 years. What is scientific research? Scientific research is finding a problem, finding a real problem and solving the problem. Being able to think is mainly about thinking and problem consciousness.

Interviewer: University teachers have three kinds of responsibilities, doing research, teaching, and servicing the society. Are there differences between these responsibilities and the innovation ability indicator systems.

Zhang: University teachers just have one responsibility. That is teaching students. We cultivate students with thinking ability.

Interviewer: We still have some questions about the management system.

Zhang: It's difficult to deal with the management system. In my opinion, teaching comes first.

Interviewer: In your opinion, the influence of current management system on innovation ability?

Zhang: In the understanding of management system, the elasticity is missing. Apart from teachers' creativity, I think this is the most important factor.

Interviewer: Maybe we can evaluate teachers' innovation by these dimensions?

Zhang: In my opinion, you must be around the core, thinking innovation.

2 On personnel system
2.1 On resource allocation

Interviewer: Now we think about the resource allocation…

Zhang: The more competent a university is, the less resource it should get. However, the fact is the good schools get more.

2.2 On the selection and appointment

Interviewer: In NENU, if a teacher wants to promote, is it necessary for him to have scientific …?

Zhang: That's not true. Teachers who are good at teaching and teaching for a long time can also be promoted to professors. Those who have reached 57 years old and have written teaching materials or teaching papers can get the honor of "Appointed Teacher".

Interviewer: So in NENU, there are some rigid indicators.

Zhang: Yes, it's necessary.

2.3 On examination and evaluation

Interviewer: In your opinion, how to evaluate teachers' innovation ability?

Zhang: Just through the students cultivated by the teacher.

Interviewer: Does it lack in evaluating teachers and their innovation?

Zhang: To set up an evaluation system about teachers' innovation ability, you had better do some researches about teachers and students. If a teacher's class is popular among students, then he must have innovation ability.

2.4 On incentive and safeguard mechanism

Interviewer: About the incentive and safeguard mechanism…

Zhang: Management system has also belonged to incentive and safeguard mechanism.

Interviewer: How can we set up the incentive and safeguard measures to improve their creative thinking?

Zhang: Set up a reasonable evaluation system. Doing research and teaching students are both important.

6.4 Northeast Normal University—Gao

6.4.1 *High-Frequency Words*

Innovation consciousness	Find out, propose, analyze 6.41 high-frequency words and solve problems
Personnel system	Academic innovation ability
Resource allocation	Selection and appointment

6.4.2 *Key Points of Interview*

1 The rationality of the six indicators of innovation ability

Interviewer: Do you think the six indicators of innovation ability are reasonable?

Gao: It feels like that the indicators are more suitable for teachers major in Education. I'm major in Math. I don't think cooperation is important.

Interviewer: Can you give some suggestions?

Gao: As for university teachers' innovation ability, the most basic ability is to identify, propose, analyze, and solve problems. What's more, the sense of innovation is also important.

Interviewer: How can we measure the sense of innovation?

Gao: Teachers and their students have the idea all the time that I have my own research problems and methods.

Interviewer: In this indicator system, the item of "find out, propose and solve problems" isn't very clear?

Gao: The "academic insight" doesn't mean exactly "finding problems".

Interviewer: A valuable problems?

Gao: Yes. A good problem has both application value and theoretical value. The "academic insight" may be the ability of judging research subjects. However, before this insight ability, the more important is the ability to find out and propose problems.

Interviewer: "To find out and propose problems" in our indicator system…

Gao: Maybe the most important quality is to find out the problem. Innovative person should find problems by himself.

Interviewer: In fact, "ability" is a psychological term which is difficult to measure. It can have different evaluation standards.

Gao: That's right. But it doesn't only mean the strong innovation ability. The more important is a consciousness of exploring.

Interviewer: In your opinion, teachers' innovation ability of comprehensive universities seems stronger. Can you explain it?

Gao: Maybe it's related to fields. For example, a group of excellent students are in some comprehensive universities. Sometimes they can make some direct contributions to the development of our country's economy. What's more, the faculty may be a bit better than that in normal universities. However, for teachers in normal universities, cultivating students to innovate is more important. Different universities have different missions.

Interviewer: Should the innovation be based on it?

Gao: We also need to innovate in academic research. Some researches in normal universities are also outstanding.

Interviewer: How can we innovate in Math?

Gao: In Math, the fields opened up by Chinese are little. We are big fans of learning from others. Our innovation ability isn't strong.

2 On personnel system
2.1 On resource allocation

Interviewer: In your opinion, what are the factors that promote or hinder the academic innovation of university teachers in the current resource allocation?

Gao: There may be a lack of money in the resource allocation system.

Interviewer: If a strong team get more resources, then the gap between teams will widen.

Gao: That's true. But it's hard to say whether it's bad or not.

Interviewer: A truly innovative scholar cannot stop thinking?

Gao: The most important thing is to cultivate people's ability of thinking.

Interviewer: Do you have any suggestions about how to improve the current resource allocation system?

Gao: I hope our country can give more resources to teachers to do research. The research process is more important than the results.

Interviewer: Does NENU pay close attention to resource allocation?

Gao: Yes. We give 2 million to the teacher education research institute as research funds.

Interviewer: Does it need a large amount of funds to do teacher education research?

Gao: I don't think so. Enough money would be all right.

2.2 On the selection and appointment

Interviewer: In NENU, some teacher may be accelerated promoted. Can you do something like that?

Gao: In some 985 and 211 universities, that might happen. However, in some provincial colleges and universities, it's really difficult.

Interviewer: In your opinion, does the current selection and appointment system promote or hinder the development of innovation?

Gao: This current selection and appointment system pay more attention to the results.

Interviewer: Do you have any suggestions about this problem?

Gao: We should give the innovative person some space and let him develop freely.

Interviewer: In selection and appointment of teacher educators, do we have to obey the general principles?

Gao: Yes. But they should do research about special problems.

Interviewer: Research problems?

Gao: In my opinion, the teachers major in teaching theory should do some practical research rather than theoretical research.

2.3 On examination and evaluation

Interviewer: Can you introduce the evaluation system to us?

Gao: NENU has offered 8 million to encourage teachers to do research. But a group of people want to publish papers just for the money. They can't make valuable achievements by doing this. That isn't right.

Interviewer: This problem exists all over the society.

Gao: That's right.

Interviewer: What are the evaluation indicators to promote a teacher in NENU?

Gao: I'm not very clear about that. From associate professor to professor, he has to reach two or three indicators of four, SCI papers, national projects, awards, and academic works.

Interviewer: IS this rigid evaluation system good for innovation ability?

Gao: It's right to have some requirements. Special people can be treated in a special way.

2.4 On incentive and safeguard mechanism

Interviewer: If we want teachers to innovate, we should provide teachers research funds, working conditions, and so on.

Gao: The university should create a better environment for teachers.

Interviewer: Besides research funds and better working conditions, are there some other measures, such as honor?

Gao: I don't quite agree with that much honor.

Interviewer: When we provide safeguard to teacher educators, should we consider their original situations?

Gao: I think it's right. Special care should be given to this special group.

6.5 Northeast Normal University—Jin

6.5.1 High-Frequency Words

New media	Cross-disciplines
Personnel system	Academic innovation ability
Professor committee	Selection and appointment

6.5.2 Key Points of Interview

1 The rationality of the six indicators of innovation ability

Interviewer: What do new media bring to literature?

Jin: In our faculty of literature, I find that many teachers still do research about traditional theories and frameworks.

Interviewer: In the research process about new media, is there something that begins to fall behind?

Jin: I think we have to follow the space. As for the new media theory, I think it won't fall behind within several decades.

Interviewer: We just talk about literature innovation from the notion. How about something besides notions?

Jin: Sometimes I think we should pin our hopes on new researchers. Some researchers can't keep going with new things. New media poses an unprecedented challenge to the study of literature. We are weak in research of new media.

Interviewer: How can a literary expert find the frontier theory of literature studies and make some innovation?

Jin: Through crossing disciplines. We need to cooperate and communicate. What's more, the trivial things affect teachers' innovation seriously.

Interviewer: Do you teach free normal students?

Jin: Yes.

Interviewer: Do you mainly teach courses related to Chinese teaching or just about communication or literature?

Jin: I mainly teach basic writing to undergraduates. Communication is mainly for graduate students.

Interviewer: This is crossing disciplines?

Jin: Yes.

Interviewer: Compared to other teachers, are there some special places in creativity of teachers major in teacher education?

Jin: Of course. Our students may have an important role in the future. They have to teach. So in my teaching plan, students should learn curriculum ideas, curriculum designing, and teaching methods.

Interviewer: How to evaluate teachers' innovation?

Jin: We used exams in the past. We began to use papers to evaluate about 10 years ago.

Interviewer: Is this for students or for teachers?

Jin: Teachers and students are the same. They are related closely. How can students innovate if the teacher doesn't know how to innovate?

Interviewer: As for young teachers, should we give him some space for scientific research first, or let him teach before scientific research?

Jin: They should read more at first and do scientific research before teaching.

Interviewer: Is the research ability of teaching-oriented teachers weaker than other teachers in literature faculty?

Jin: That's not the case. Students must be taught by people of high level.

2 On personnel system
2.1 On resource allocation

Interviewer: what influence does the current resource allocation have on the academic innovation of university teachers? Promoting or hindering?

Jin: There are problems within the system. It's related to national system–appointment system.

Interviewer: How does the current resource allocation system hinder the academic innovation of teachers?

Jin: In this current resource allocation system, the president has the most power. That's the disadvantages of appointment system.

Interviewer: There seems to be a committee of professors in NENU?

Jin: Yes. The professor committee should decide what the headmaster can't decide and important things about resource allocation.

Interviewer: What are the duties of professor committee?

Jin: You can search the Internet.

Interviewer: Do you perform the duties?

Jin: Actually not. The important matters are usually decided by leaders.

Interviewer: Just because of the management system?

Jin: I think so.

6.5 Northeast Normal University—Jin

Interviewer: It's also because of the wider picture.

Jin: It's problem of the high level, including the appointment limitation in our country.

Interviewer: Do you have any detailed suggestions about resource allocation system to promote teachers' innovation?

Jin: In my opinion, there should be some changes in application for research projects. More funds should be provided to support teachers.

Interviewer: How can resource allocation promote teachers' innovation effectively?

Jin: The notions of university leaders must be updated.

Interviewer: Do you mean normal teachers should update their leading concepts?

Jin: No. I mean the leaders.

Interviewer: Are there something special on resource allocation in normal universities?

Jin: I think there are some problems within this current resource allocation system. Some teachers' research can't be admitted.

Interviewer: They can't be admitted because they don't meet the requirements even though they do make some innovation?

Jin: Maybe because you don't have enough resources or you can't receive much accept ion.

Interviewer: In your opinion, what are the factors that promote or hinder the academic innovation of university teachers in the current resource allocation?

Jin: The requirements for promotion are rigid. It isn't related to innovation.

2.2 On the selection and appointment

Interviewer: Does the shortages of personnel systems mean that we failed to appoint the right teacher?

Jin: That's a complicated question. It seems that it's related to our state system sometimes.

Interviewer: Do you have the right to speak in selecting students?

Jin: Only 1%.

Interviewer: Maybe it's better in some 985 and 211 universities than that in provincial or local universities.

Jin: That's pretty much it.

Interviewer: Can the current selection and appointment system promote teachers' academic innovation?

Jin: To some extent, it can promote teachers' academic innovation. But for those who are really excellent in research, it doesn't really work. It's important to get a good peer evaluation.

Interviewer: Peer evaluation?

Jin: Peer evaluation is very important.

Interviewer: Do you have any suggestions on promoting the current selection and appointment system?

Jin: It's too flexible. It's hard to say.

Interviewer: Are there some differences in selection and appointment system between teacher educators and ordinary teachers?

Jin: Of course there are. The educational ideas of normal universities must be more advanced.

2.3 On examination and evaluation

Interviewer: It seems that there are some problems in the examination and evaluation system.

Jin: Something in Chinese culture is still working, the idleness.

Interviewer: Can you explain more about the negative effect that examination and evaluation system has on teachers' innovation?

Jin: Examination and evaluation are important. School can't solve its problems by itself.

Interviewer: There is a collegiate community.

Jin: Yes. But in our university, we all do things in our own way. It's difficult to break the boundary.

Interviewer: How does the evaluation mechanism hinder or promote the academic innovation of teachers?

Jin: The current system doesn't pay attention to innovation. There are only some rigid indicators.

Interviewer: Anything else?

Jin: The evaluation standards are the main problems.

Interviewer: Is there something in this system that can promote innovation?

Jin: Of course there is. He will admit it if we have published good papers.

Interviewer: What's your suggestion about how to promote the current system to cultivate teacher's innovation?

Jin: The ideas must change. Don't pay much attention to the forms.

Interviewer: Is there something special about teacher educators?

Jin: They should have better conational ideas.

Interviewer: Do we need to ask more about the personality of teachers and educators?

Jin: As a teacher in a normal university, the personality should be better.

2.4 On incentive and safeguard mechanism

Interviewer: Do the incentive and safeguard mechanism in universities promote or hinder teachers' academic innovation?

Jin: If the system is good enough, it can promote teachers' academic innovation.

Interviewer: Do the current incentive and safeguard mechanism in universities promote or hinder teachers' academic innovation?

Jin: A teacher may promote when he manages to achieve the standards.

Interviewer: What's your suggestion about how to promote the current system to cultivate teacher's innovation?

Jin: The key is the people who make policies.

Interviewer: Should NENU provide more on the incentive and safeguard mechanism?

Jin: We should provide more on scientific research and the promotion of innovative talents.

6.6 Northeast Normal University—Ma

6.6.1 High-Frequency Words

Accumulation of knowledge	Accumulation of methods
Cooperative consciousness	Academic innovation ability
Practical teaching experience	Assessment and evaluation

6.6.2 Key Points of Interview

1 The rationality of the six indicators of innovation ability

Interviewer: Do you think the six indicators of innovation ability are reasonable?

Ma: I think it's systematic. I agree with those indicators totally. But you should sort the system better. What's more, the calculation of knowledge and methods are important. Teachers must have academic foundation.

Interviewer: The "accusation of knowledge" isn't very clear in the system.

Ma: Yes, that's an important question. What's more, the methods are important. Having a good command of one or several research methods is important. In addition, cooperation consciousness is also important.

Interviewer: Where should we put the "cooperation" in the system?

Ma: It's an ability of getting what you want from your research team.

Interviewer: Are research capacity and academic innovation ability different?

Ma: A researcher must have enough accusation. One can come up with new things only when he combined the adulation of knowledge and methods, insight, comprehensive, and analytical abilities.

Interviewer: How about teacher education?

Ma: The field of education is actually a practical research field, while teacher education may be more practical. The real problem in education is the one that combines with education practices. However, in our research teams, a large number of researchers don't have real teaching experience. I think we should set up some policies to encourage researchers to go to primacy or secondary schools. What's more, the evaluation system of researches is bad for research and the innovation. The evaluation system is dominated by the level of papers or citation rates of papers. The achievements directly serve basic education aren't taken seriously. We should give young researchers space and time to do basic researches. A mechanism about that is needed.

6.7 Northeast Normal University—Shi

6.7.1 High-Frequency Words

Academic innovation ability	Intuition
Inductive ability	Systematic knowledge
Reflection and judgment	Assessment and evaluation

6.7.2 Key Points of Interview

1 Basic problems of the subprojects

Interviewer: In your opinion, what are the main aspects of academic innovation of university teachers?

Shi: There are three important aspects of innovation. One is the knowledge, the other is ideas and methods, and last is experience. You have mentioned innovation ability. The innovation consciousness is also important. The consciousness of innovation, the ability of innovation, and the experience of innovation are very important. What does innovation depend on? It depends on intuition. Intuition has many connotations, including association, imagination and many other things. Students get the innovation ability by understanding and comprehending rather by being taught.

Interviewer: Do you have any suggestions on our indicator system?

Shi: "The ability of sorting out discipline history" isn't necessary. But logic thinking is important. To do an excellent research, the first is to study the most critical knowledge points and improve it. The second is the assumption. A person who has systematic knowledge may not make great indentions. In my opinion, the ability of sorting out discipline history is the ability of commanding knowledge. Secondly, judgment is also important. Judgment is a step before reflection. Only quick and professional judgment produces intuition.

Interviewer: Can we get the intuition by exercising?

Shi: That's OK. We should learn this thinking method and inductive ability.

Interviewer: Are the indicators related to them?

Shi: It's not enough. Your indicator system is very difficult to carry out. There is no difference whenever we know it or not.

Interviewer: We mainly want to see whether the teacher has the ability through this system rather than promoting him to have the ability.

Shi: It has something to do with character, his knowledge structure and the objects of his teaching. There are just two standards of a good teacher. Firstly, he can inspire students to think. Secondly, he can help children form good learning habits and accumulate knowledge and experience.

Interviewer: How can we promote this system to cultivate innovative teachers?

Shi: To cultivate innovative teachers, you can leave alone the system. You can test your conclusion and then correct the conclusion. You should learn to extract theory from practice rather than guiding your ideas with theories that already exist. The intuition of teachers is the most important thing. Then you turn that intuition into a theoretical system.

Interviewer: But how can we evaluate a teacher's innovation ability?

Shi: How does he cultivate students' creativity?

Interviewer: But we want to know the teacher's innovation ability.

Shi: Analyze how he teaches students. You can ask him how he teaches students, what should be paid attention to in teaching, why he can teach like that while others can't. At last, you can generalize what they have in common.

Interviewer: We hope experts can give us some suggestions on this system.

Shi: It's not right to be comprehensive. There may only be three cores at last.

Interviewer: What's your opinion about resource allocation and teacher appointment?

Shi: Assessment is just enough. You might as well do the research like what I said.

6.8 Northeast Normal University—Department of Personnel: Zhang

6.8.1 High-Frequency Words

Innovation ability	Six indicators
Pennell system	Resource allocation
Selection and appointment	Assessment and evaluation
Incentive and safeguard mechanism	

Interviewer: What's your opinion about resource allocation?

Zhang: Resource allocation can be divided into two kinds, one is material and the other is spiritual. From the perspective of materials, including funds, living treatment, working conditions, etc. They play an important role in the innovation of teachers. From the perspective of spiritual, the first is the environment: the overall environment, the school environment, the country environment, and the local environment, as well as the small environment of your unit. The second is the academic atmosphere. The third is the interpersonal relationship.

Interviewer: Do you have any suggestions about the inceptor system of innovation ability?

Zhang: No. You did it mostly theoretically. You have to search the educational theories and other indicator systems. I just can introduce the situation to you briefly. The personnel department emphasizes the benefits of resource allocation.

Interviewer: What measures do you take to get the most benefits?

Zhang: We adopt the form of project approval when we provide investments.

Interviewer: The personnel department will consider teachers' ability comprehensively?

Zhang: Yes.

Interviewer: Do you have other opinions about resource allocation in operation?

Zhang: The allocation of resources is unreasonable at the national level. 985 universities occupy a lot of resources. However, do they achieve the corresponding positions and functions? This is the question of input and output.

Interviewer: As a normal university, does NENU have independent resource allocation for well-known teacher educators?

Zhang: Yes. Our school has set up a teacher education research center, where the university provides resources and funds separately. We will set up a teaching apartment to collect human resources and material resources to reach the most benefits.

Interviewer: In addition to the funds, project approval and other aspects, are there any other measures from the six indicators?

Zhang: Yes, there are. For example, when we design projects we would consider that. Project approval about teacher educator should be separate.

Interviewer: Are the discipline teacher educators included in the teacher education research institute?

Zhang: Yes. They belong to both teacher education research institute and their original faculty.

Interviewer: What's your opinion about the selection and appointment system?

Zhang: We now attach more importance to education degree, students, speech, achievements, and contributions in selection and appointment.

Interviewer: When assessing teacher educators, are there some differences?

Zhang: professor committee assesses them. We are still exploring the further mechanism of professor committee.

Interviewer: Do you have anything to add to our six-indicator system?

Zhang: The indicator system is definitely not perfect, because it's just from the perspective of professional teachers, from the perspective of pedagogy. You don't talk about it from the perspective of socialization. Innovation ability is a comprehensive question. You can add individual factors into the system.

Interviewer: What's your opinion about resource evaluation?

Zhang: Universities are divided into 985 universities, 211 universities and special universities. For the school development, this has a certain promotion effect. In terms of individual evaluation, assessment has an obvious promoting effect on inspiring teachers. In fact, it's a kind of unplanned assessment. What's more, this evaluation is inevitably limited to our range.

Interviewer: Does NENU have anything special on teacher's evaluation?

Zhang: Weaken the annual assessment and emphasize the developmental assessment, target assessment, and employment assessment. The venture fund proposed by us is also beneficial for teachers' innovation.

Interviewer: When do teachers can apply for the venture fund?

Zhang: They can apply for it whenever they have ideas.

Interviewer: Is there a special management organization for it?

Zhang: There is an academic committee, an organization of academic resource allocation.

Interviewer: The last question of about incentive and safeguard mechanism.

Zhang: In my opinion, high pay is an incentive measure. Our university also attaches great importance to this matter. But now universities are competing for talent, which is bad. To some extent, the vicious circle of talent competition wears away their creativity. In terms of incentives, it's more about fairness and balance. One of the more important aspects of motivation is spiritual motivation. Security or incentive refers to both material and spiritual benefits. But we're in a bit of a mess right now.

Interviewer: Are there something special incentives for teachers and educators?

Zhang: No. The pay must be the same as the ordinary teachers. The establishment of teacher education institute is also a guarantee, so they have a platform and independent space to develop.

6.9 East China Normal University—Ding

6.9.1 High-Frequency Words

Academic innovation ability	Inheritance and innovation
University teachers	Tenure system
Interdisciplinary	

6.9.2 Key Points of Interview

1 The connotation of university teachers' academic innovation ability

Interviewer: What kind of university teachers are teachers with academic innovation? What are the criteria for evaluating these teachers?

Ding: The ability to make something different from others is the basic criterion. You are not an innovative person if you just follow others' way. People with innovation ability are those who open up a road in a large field and come up with new and promising ideas. In fact, innovation is not equal to real creation.

Interviewer: How do you see the relationship between inheritance and innovation?

Ding: Inheritance is not entirely a kind of innovation, because it is a matter of historical responsibility. Just like the Four Books, we can also say that it has innovative features, because it is actually a secondary document. When it was scattered, we can only call information, but when we have sorted it out, it actually becomes a secondary document. But in the process of inheritance, it's too general to say that pure inheritance is innovation. In fact, innovation is making something new and different on the basis of old things.

Interviewer: Is innovation to the new through the old?

Ding: Yes, innovation is to forth the new through the old. For example, there is an ancient Chinese education base, and all of the ancient characters have been made into a database in the computer. This is a huge innovation by using modern technology to present old things.

Interviewer: How do you view teacher educators and who are the teacher educators in university?

Ding: From the perspective of disciplines, teacher education is the downstream of the discipline. From a broader perspective, the university teachers of all disciplines should be teacher educators and assume the responsibility of teacher education.

Interviewer: Which members do you think the teacher educator team should include?

Ding: I hope that liberal arts and science teachers should also be included. For example, although you are engaged in physics rather than physics teaching, you should bring the innovative awareness and knowledge horizon into teacher training. Teacher education should be a big undertaking, and it is necessary to get involved in more people.

Professors engaging in education should take up all upstream and downstream things and there is no intermediary. On the one hand, they should express the practical things and form new ideas, and on the other hand, they should return to the classroom by applying a new idea.

2 Factors influencing the innovation ability of university teachers

2.1 The personnel system

2.1.1 Resource allocation

Interviewer: How do you view the impact of resource allocation on the innovation of university teachers?

Ding: I implement segment management for teachers. For older generation of teachers, we have to serve them well. For middle-aged teachers, such as those who in their forties and fifties, I will not give them any preferential terms in the college, because they should prove their academic ability by making an influence in the country. For young teachers, we must give them help because they are the hope of the future.

2.1.2 Selection and appointment

Interviewer: Do you consider interdisciplinary knowledge structures as a factor in the introduction of young teachers?

Ding: Yes, I think education has to have a big field of vision. For example, if you want to engage in professional education, you'd better study labor economy such as labor economics and industrial economics. Another example is adult education, which has started to transform into human resource development. What is human resource development? Education is the first thing.

Interviewer: So, when building a teaching team, you attach great importance to the background of discipline.

Ding: Our principle Liu Fijian thought that education could not be just teaching, so he established the Institute of Educational Science. President Liu is the first to be engaged in educational science research in the country, which was called "educational science Class."

Interviewer: Educational Science Class?

Ding: In the first 3 years, the students studied the professional basic disciplines, such as history, math, physics, and in the third year, they voluntarily enrolled in the Educational Science Class to study education as an undergraduate. In 1988, I was the deputy director of the Institute of Education Science. At that time, all the teachers were interdisciplinary.

2.1.3 Examination and evaluation

Interviewer: How does the East China Normal University School of Education Science evaluate teachers? Which aspect do you value? Have you considered the academic innovation of this teacher?

Ding: Professors should publish three articles, and associate professors two articles, and lecturers one article.

2.1.4 Incentive and safeguard mechanism

Interviewer: What measures do you adopt to motivate university teachers with different titles and different academic influences?

Ding: The primary measure is to provide them more opportunities to exchange abroad and at home, and give them more financial support. In terms of bonus distribution, the weight of academic achievements should be increased and reduce the weight of teaching workload.

Interviewer: How to reward research results?

Ding: If you publish an article in SSCI journal, the college will reward you 10,000 RMB, and the school will reward you 10,000 RMB, so totally 20,000 RMB.

Interviewer: That's a great reward, especially for young and middle-aged teachers.

Ding: Yes. If you publish an article in Education Research, which is the first-level publication and has a large number of readers, you will be rewarded 10,000 RMB, 5000 RMB from the college and 5000 RMB. The article published in any CSSCI journal will be awarded.

Interviewer: If a teacher published articles in the core magazine, does it mean his academic ability is high?

Ding: Not necessarily. Academic ability depends on teachers' comprehensive ability, not on one or two articles.

Interviewer: How to provide academic development opportunities for teachers at different stages?

Ding: Just give them the chance to do scientific research. They attend academic conferences and communicate through the use of the funds provided. For example, many young teachers get involved in my project, then I finance the project team to go abroad to study. We also have all kinds of salons for young teachers.

Interviewer: Are these salons specially organized for teachers?

Ding: Yes, in these salons, many famous professors will discuss with young teachers about their interest and academic development, and lead them to make clear their research orientation.

Interviewer: Give them some guidance.

Ding: I believe I have the responsibility to help young teachers to grow up and all professors should know that the great significance of doing research project it to help the development of the team.

2.2 Other factors

2.2.1 Interdisciplinary knowledge structure

Interviewer: How do you view the impact of interdisciplinary on the academic innovation of university teachers?

Ding: As a university teacher, it's important to have a good structure of knowledge whether you study liberal arts or science. Most of the people with high innovation ability have had interdisciplinary learning experience.

Interviewer: How do you understand innovation ability?

Ding: Now liberal arts is about teamwork. For example, educational technology is interdisciplinary. I prefer those who have interdisciplinary experience when recruiting graduate students.

2.2.2 Macro research and policy research

Interviewer: How do you view the tendency of macro research and policy research?

Ding: There is much low-level repetition in the field of academic research and many details are ignored. In fact, the real policy is in the most micro, the most subtle, and the most ordinary daily life.

2.2.3 Peer review and professor classification

Interviewer: How do you view the system of peer review and professor classification in university?

Ding: I disagree with professor classification. There is no unified criterion to classify professors in different universities, so the result is meaningless.

Interviewer: So you disagree with this kind of classification?

Ding: The reason why American professors concentrate on academic without distractions is that there is no evaluation mechanism.

Interviewer: No evaluation mechanism?

Ding: No evaluation mechanism. There is only a mechanism from assistant professors to associate professors, which means tenured professors.

2.2.4 Tenure system

Interviewer: How do you view the impact of the tenure system on the academic innovation of university teachers?

Ding: Tenured professors in China are not lifelong and still have retirement ages. The treatment of tenured professors is the highest among all teachers and there is not too much evaluation on them.

Interviewer: Do you think our evaluation system play a positive role in guiding the university teachers?

Ding: In fact, this system has its own advantages and disadvantages, because the tenure system can attract some young but outstanding professors. If they become a tenured professor at young age, they concentrate more on work and achieve more. Unlike the academicians, the younger you are, the creative you are. Teachers engaging in liberal arts can never retire, because it needs a lot of accumulation.

Interviewer: Yes, learning liberal arts need accumulation.

Ding: Interdisciplinary study is required in liberal arts, the older you are, the more you accumulate, so I think tenure system is useful for liberal arts.

2.2.5 Administration of higher education

Interviewer: How do you view the relationship between degree and work?

Ding: I think the two identities should be clearly distinguished. You can get a Ph.D., even a postdoctoral degree in university, but if you go into the civil service, you're an official not an intellectual. As soon as you enter the department, you should devote yourself to the present job. But now we want to carry both identities.

Interviewer: How do you view the impact of this phenomenon on professors' academic development?

Ding: It challenges the seriousness of academic, and there should be a clear boundary between scholar and official.

Interviewer: Do you think it's a negative guide that only academicians are qualified to be principals in some universities?

Ding: Of course. Principles in foreign countries, such as the chancellor in U.K. and the president in U.S.A, whose main job is to deal with the government and get resources. But principles in our country is different, they should be responsible for everything, so the principles get administrative level and become officials.

2.2.6 Academic utilitarianism

Interviewer: Is there any other negative factors influencing the innovation of university teachers?

Ding: The orientation of reality brings a utilitarian pursuit, but most of the scientific work requires a cultural accumulation and knowledge innovation, and we need a foundation in the humanities like the natural science fund.

6.10 East China Normal University—Liu

6.10.1 *High-Frequency Words*

Academic innovation ability	Selection and recruitment mechanism
University teachers	Examination and evaluation
Rewards and incentives	

6.10.2 Key Points of Interview

1 Selection and recruitment mechanism

Interviewer: There are some selection and recruitment mechanism in university, such as one appointment for 3 years, and certain articles publishing task should be completed within the employment period, do you think such a mechanism can promote the innovation of teachers?

Liu: According to my view, most people are not pursuing academics, but seeking to survive, so it's necessary to evaluate them. I think the tenure system is not beneficial, because many people will get lazy and pursue personal enjoyment once they become tenured professors.

Interviewer: How to change this phenomenon? And what kind of appointment mechanism can be more conducive to the innovation of teachers?

Liu: I think overall assessment is more effective than individual assessment. Colleges and departments should be considered as academic communities, teachers will be examined by their own college. The college will examine these people in the college

Interviewer: Which aspect was most valued when recruiting new teachers?

Liu: Now what we are looking at most is whether you have foreign background or foreign academic experience, and the second is your achievements, but the innovation ability is not evaluated.

Interviewer: Have you ever thought about some ways to stimulate teacher's innovation?

Liu: I think the key is going back to the "academic community". Only by returning to his academic community will the real possibilities of innovation be motivated.

2 Examination and evaluation mechanism

Interviewer: Is there any special weight in terms of innovation in the evaluation of teachers?

Liu: As the head of social science department, I think the evaluation of teachers now is focused on quantity, and it's not possible to assess a teacher's innovation ability, which is due to the guiding role of the government.

Interviewer: What do you think should be reversed to effectively assess the innovation of teachers?

Liu: I think a breakthrough is to award teachers whose academic outcomes such as papers, books or research reports representing innovative ideas.

Interviewer: The articles published in academic journals of different levels have different proportion in the evaluation of teachers, do you think it can be used to judge the innovation of teachers?

Liu: The premise of this approach is wrong because the different levels of the publications do not equal to your innovation ability. When judging those who deserve awards, we should ask him which is the innovation point of his research compared with others. I don't think there should be too many awards, especially from the government, and we should emphasize the quality rather than quantity.

Interviewer: Is there classification system of teachers in your university? How do you view this phenomenon?

Liu: there are some regulations such as year of teaching, but most of them are quantified and no matter with innovation. Innovation can be evaluated by peer review, but now it's not doing well, because many people do not tell the truth for fear of offending others.

Interviewer: What do you think of the phenomenon that academic leaders take up administrative positions?

Liu: I'm against that. I think it's bad for themselves and society. Because you are an expert in one area, not necessarily in another. Some scholars will get more resource and improve their research if they engage in administrative duties, but some of them may become arrogant and suppress people who have real talents.

Interviewer: From a scholar's point of view, what factors do you think are limiting the development of innovation of young teachers, or their academic development?

Liu: I think it is the evaluation criteria hinder their development, so how to change evaluation is the problem we should consider.

3 Incentive and safeguard mechanism

Interviewer: At present, is there any incentive and guarantee mechanism to encourage academic innovation ability of university teachers?

Liu: In our university, some teachers with innovation will be promoted, but I think the promotion must be appropriate. For example, it's reasonable to promote a teacher to dean, because he can get more resource to improve his research, but if you promote him to a director, he will be negatively affected.

Interviewer: At present, schools, provinces, and cities, as well as the country provide a lot of research funds and even honorary titles for university teachers. How much of a boost do you think this would give to teachers' innovation?

Liu: It's better to have these than not to have them, but the funds for liberal arts is less than science. What's more, key laboratories of science are much more than liberal arts. I think liberal arts needs the same platforms as science.

Interviewer: However, we have seen such a phenomenon. For example, some scholars get more other resources or superimposed honors after being rated as Zijiang scholar or Yangtze River scholar, also, their research directions begin to change, and there aren't many innovative things compared to their early years.

Liu: I think the key is the system. When rating someone as a Yangtze River scholar or giving him other titles, he should be told how much responsibility he has to bear.

Interviewer: Is there any incentive system for the improvement of young teachers' innovation?

A: So the same as old teachers, such as providing them opportunities to study abroad, which will improve their innovation. In addition, give the liberal arts teachers more free time and keep them energetic.

6.11 East China Normal University—Pang

6.11.1 High-Frequency Words

Academic innovation ability	H-coefficient
University teachers	Teamwork
Lifetime professor	Academic inbreeding
The representative system of Peking University	Learning aboard

6.11.2 Key Points of Interview

1 Assessment and evaluation mechanism

Interviewer: As for the current assessment and evaluation system of university teachers, what indicators do you think are used to evaluate their innovation ability? What are the problems in the current assessment system?

Pang: There are two academically accepted definitions about innovation, one is novelty and one is adaptability. There are objective indicators in our evaluation. The first indicator is the publication of academic papers. The second indicator is the amount of papers. A new indicator called H-coefficient has been come up with now. That's the first aspect, which is from the view of research results. The second aspect is from the view of research process. In the process of research, the innovation ability depends on the question raising ability, the teamwork, and the resource utilization ability. In particular, it depends on the knowledge structures of the whole team.

Interviewer: How to evaluate an academic work or monograph in humanities and social sciences is innovative or not?

Pang: This is the same thing as I just mentioned. The h-factor, the citation rate and the quality of your publication are all valid indicators. It's a process for research findings from publication to reference.

Interviewer: Do you think the current assessment system can select innovative teachers?

Pang: It's a bit difficult. If a teacher wants to get a project, a fund or an award, academic achievements' and interpersonal relationship are both needed. However, if a teacher can stick on to a field for several years, he can get it sooner or later.

Interviewer: In the evaluation system, the lifetime professor, the Changjiang Scholar, and academician are not evaluated. Do you agree with this kind of assessment?

Pang: In my opinion, the ordinary teachers should be evaluated once a year. Those lifetime professors can be evaluated once 3 or 5 years. They also should at least give an academic lecture a year.

2 Selection and appointment mechanism

Interviewer: How can some innovative teachers be selected when selecting young teachers? Is it by the number of papers?

Pang: When we evaluate a young teacher, we may pay more attention to the quality of his papers. If he doesn't have papers of high quality, then we can see the quantity. In a word, we have no absolute quantitative limit. First, we pay attention to the quality. Second, we pay attention to the quantity.

Interviewer: What do you think is preventing the emergence of innovative or outstanding talent in the current selection mechanism for young teachers?

Pang: The indicators are too rigid. This quantitative evaluation system is a barrier.

Interviewer: What do you think is not suitable for building an outstanding teaching staff? What's your opinion of Southern University of Science and Technology 's global recruitment of outstanding teachers?

Pang: One of the worst is conferring of academic titles. It only emphasizes the first author and the independent author. To some extent, Southern University of Science and Technology 's global recruitment is like a person in fear takes special medicines. However, the body just should be taken care of for a long time. The development of a university depends mainly on the accumulation of culture.

Interviewer: What do you think of "academic inbreeding" in universities? Can you talk about what should be done to improve such a situation?

Pang: We should take a critical attitude to this issue. If his team has reached the international frontier in this field, it is OK to keep his own students because it is helpful for construction of the whole academic team. If his team isn't good enough, it's better not to keep his own students.

Interviewer: Is it good to require university teachers to study abroad especially get the doctor degree of foreign top-ranking school? What do you think about the elimination mechanism of university teachers?

Pang: Of course it's good. Talented people are hired on merit. The elimination mechanism in universities is indeed a big problem. There are good systems in the world, but we don't use them.

3 Resource allocation system

Interviewer: The most innovative period for young teachers in universities is also the period with the weakest economic foundation. What do you think of the impact of current resource allocation system on young teachers' innovation ability?

Pang: This is inevitable. Our country still doesn't have a lot of money as funds. A considerable part of the resources depends on themselves to strive for. This problem needs time to be solved.

Interviewer: But the universities may allot more resources to those lifetime professors?

Pang: If you do even the most unpopular subject, you will have a chance if you do it well. And the academic team or leading academic figures are crucial to the development of the subject.

4 Incentive and safeguard mechanism

Interviewer: In your opinion, what other incentive measures should be adopted to promote the creativity of young teachers?

Pang: Overseas exchange, including study abroad, is the most effective way. In addition to the representative system of Peking University, studying abroad and creating an achievement publication platform are also needed.

Interviewer: What do you think of the phenomenon of good scholars doing some management work?

Pang: This is very bad from an academic point of view. But the difficulties of the school are the shortage of leaders. This is a dilemma for universities.

Interviewer: What do you think of the idea that a person with strong academic organization ability can bring more resources together, makes better use of them and brings the whole team together?

Pang: I think that's really difficult.

6.12 East China Normal University—Wu

6.12.1 High-Frequency Words

Interpersonal interaction	Psychological ability
Innovation teachers	Teamwork
Originality	Insight
From the bottom to up	From top to bottom

6.12.2 Key Points of Interview

Interviewer: Do you think the indicators of university teachers' innovation ability are reasonable?

Wu: I thought of the following questions roughly. First, the index system is divided into three aspects, which may have some problems. For example, whether there is a cross between psychological ability, insight, and imagination. Second, maybe the questions in the questionnaire are a little abstract for teachers because they are only familiar in their own specific field. Third, there are several problems needed to define clearly, such as innovation teacher and innovation. It's too simple to equate innovative talents with creative directors. You have to figure out what you really want to research. What criteria are used to determine whether a person is innovative? It's a matter of originality, which is an important criterion.

About the methods: One method is doing the survey from the bottom to up. Make a list of all the reasons why these creative people have achieved what they have today. Another method is doing the survey from top to bottom. You find out the logic of innovation based on worldwide researched of innovation.

About the steps: The first thing is to capture the innovation features. The second thing is to verify the hypothesis.

At last, we're not going to describe the problem statically. The key question is to describe the situation dynamically. What is the relationship between factor one, factor two and factor three? What are the functions of factor one, factor two, and factor three? In a word, structure and process of innovation are both very important.

Interviewer: Do you think these three dimensions can cover all of the aspects?

Wu: In my opinion, the innovation talents mean the teachers of innovation students. The innovation feature of these teachers is that they can help students be familiar with the field as soon as possible. His good command of the whole situation is very important. What's more, we should pay attention to cross-discipline and teamwork. The communication and interaction with others are very important. I don't know how you think about this problem.

Interviewer: We think about this from two aspects, one is the teacher's independent innovation ability, and the other is his cooperation and communication ability in a team.

Wu: I think the three indicators that you have recognized are reasonable and it makes sense at some point. But I'm afraid you don't know the relationship between the three indicators.

Interviewer: Does the university's assessment system promote teacher innovation?

Wu: Now the system is truly a social problem, which cannot be controlled just by a university.

Interviewer: What do you think of the phenomenon of good scholars doing some management work? What's the influence on his innovation ability?

Wu: I think that should be avoided. In fact, one's time is very precious. Don't do those two things at the same time.

6.13 East China Normal University—Yan

6.13.1 High-Frequency Words

Interpersonal interaction	A quantitative system
Innovation teachers	Accumulation
Modern university system	Academic environment
Peer review	Peer acceptance

6.13.2 Key Points of Interview

Interviewer: What are your opinions on university teachers' innovation ability?

Yan: The innovation ability of university teachers mainly refers to academic innovation. The precondition of figuring out academic innovation ability is to make sure who are the most innovative in our universities. Then we find them, identify them, and find out their features of innovation. This is an empirical approach.

Interviewer: That is to say, first we should find the group of innovative person.

Yan: That's right. That's a group with the same features. Though everyone is special, we still can analyze their overall structural characteristics, which reflect the influencing factors of their innovation. Then we can do the future study on the influencing factors.

Interviewer: How to evaluate the innovation of teachers' academic achievements?

Yan: By peers.

Interviewer: Peer review?

Yan: Peer acceptance. Peer review is a narrower concept. Firstly, peer review refers to the so-called scientific literature measurement method, which has lots of problems. The first is there is a great deal of variation between disciplines. The second is s high quote rate doesn't mean that the author and the paper are good because there is an idol effect within academia. The third is the quote is sometimes a critical quote. The fourth is the following a popular topic is very common. A valuable and unpopular issue can't get enough attention. Secondly, the narrow concept of peer review refers to reviewed and evaluated by the so-called authority figures by voting or other methods. There are still problems in this progress. Although the teachers belong to the same subject, they study different fields and subjects. The reviewer may be an authority on the filed, but that does not mean he is also an authority on certain works or subjects. What's more, the social relations may have influence during peer review. There isn't an absolutely fair evaluation system at home and abroad.

Interviewer: What favorable or unfavorable influences does the current assessment system have on the development of academic innovation of university teachers?

Yan: At present, the domestic academic evaluation system is the form of quantitative indicators. The indicators are related to teachers' honors, professional titles, and allowance. This system has led to fewer and fewer people doing real research. The real academic spirit is very weak and that's related to this system. However, taking this system away will cause a serious fairness problem. There isn't a transparent oversight mechanism in the current stage of social development. We face this dilemma.

Interviewer: What do you think of lifetime professor?

Yan: The "lifetime professor" in China is different from that in western countries. Once a university teacher is employed, it's impossible to dismiss him. The "lifetime professor" in China just means a title, which is related to a teacher's income.

Interviewer: Do you mean that this title isn't good for a teacher's academic development?

Yan: I just talked about the objective fact. I didn't mention its influence.

Interviewer: What do you think of the phenomenon of academic leaders doing some management work?

Yan: I think it is key for teachers, majoring in science or engineering. But it might not be important for liberal arts. Researchers major in liberal arts need accumulation.

Interviewer: Are research funds and programs good for development of teachers' innovation?

Yan: It depends on the programs. In my opinion, some programs have a negative effect on academic innovation. In fact, many programs are applied according to government's policy needs rather than researchers' interests. That's bad for the academic development. That's why we can't get original academic achievements whether in science or engineering or literary arts.

Interviewer: How do you view the relationship between the construction of university faculty and modern university system?

Yan: First of all, I personally never mention the modern university system. The modern university system in China is just borrowed from modern enterprise system. They just borrowed the management methods from economic field or management field. We also need to reflect whether the methods of economy can work in universities. In fact, the methods in economy exactly reflect the traditional practice of universities. In some universities, they adapt the very traditional management methods, which are not modern at all. There is a "modern university system" in western countries, which means entrepreneurial university.

Interviewer: Is it helpful to build up a world-class university to employ students learning abroad?

Yan: The students can make a greater contribution if the environment is changed better. It can't help promote the entire faculty. There are serious problems in the entire academic environment and system and universities in universities.

Interviewer: Southern University of Science and Technology wants to employ the top academic team from Hong Kong University of Science and Technology. Do you think it's helpful to build up a world-class faculty?

Yan: Southern University of Science and Technology wants to follow the development model of Hong Kong University of science and technology. It may make a school look like a world-class university in the short term, but it doesn't mean it's a truly world-class university. I think environment, equipment, and conditions are very critical.

Interviewer: What factors hinder the academic innovation ability of university teachers?

Yan: The first question is the entire academic environment. A truly fair environment is most fundamental. The second question is wage and salary. A stable living condition and security is very important for young teachers. It's a complicated problem to determine whether the government should intervene and which fields should intervene. It's also important that academia should keep a fair environment for young scholars.

6.14 East China Normal University—Ye

6.14.1 High-Frequency Words

Passion	Responsibility
Innovation teachers	Accumulation
Reform of higher education	Academic environment
Peer review	Sense of self-reliance

6.14.2 Key Points of Interview

Interviewer: Do you think the indicators of university teachers' innovation ability are reasonable?

Ye: There is some crossover between the first ability (mental ability) and the second ability (intellectual ability). The first ability isn't very complete. As for the evaluation system, I think the three aspects are not enough. His passion for his work and his sensitivity to problems are also important.

Interviewer: We also divide innovation ability into intellectual factors and nonintellectual factors.

Ye: If there are other factors, they should also be considered. A teacher has a sense of responsibility and accumulation of understanding of the society, the times, and the education. He can do some in-depth studied based on these factors. That's important.

Interviewer: Compared to teachers of comprehensive universities, what are the most important characteristics of innovation ability of teacher educators?

Ye: I think that's the fundamental innovation. It's a little difficult to list the special characteristics from the perspective of teacher educators. It's a complete structure. In my opinion, first, we should analyze its current situation and find out its main problems. Second, we can carry out a research about how to change the situation. It isn't proper to put the realistic problems into a subject framework.

Interviewer: Do you agree with the idea of using an indicator system to measure a person?

Ye: I don't agree with that. First, teacher education is a complicated work needed to be involved from different facets. Second, the indicators should come from the work of teacher education.

Interviewer: Can we really evaluate teachers' creativity by using their published articles and works?

Ye: It's a problem of the university's personnel system, which isn't limited to teacher education filed. In fact, this personnel system hinders teachers' academic development to some extent. It also has an influence on university teachers' choices. Reform of higher education and reform of personnel system are very urgent now. Some of the requirements of the personnel system are even going backward. First, the requirements of the so-called 985 and 211 universities pay attention to teachers' education background and they don't care about teachers' morality, teaching, and research, which are very ridiculous. The second problem is the indicators of promotion. The indicators should be teaching first, and then the research combined with the teaching. In fact, that's the problem of system. So the promotion system should be in line with the basic law of human growth. Putting scientific research and teaching in opposite position, demanding quick success, lacking some basic guarantee are bad for young teachers' growth. The most serious problem of this personnel system is the lack of attention and care for person and for real innovation.

Interviewer: If two young teachers both published academic books, how to evaluate their academic innovation?

Ye: First, I should be familiar with the filed. Then we should see whether the author has problem awareness. Second, the book must have its topic and key problems. We can see the academic persisting and depth of the problems. Third, we should pay attention to its change of perspectives, which may be various, new or systematic. Fourth, we can see the quality of his critiques. Last, we should see the value it generates in its own field.

Interviewer: This current evaluation system pays attention to the numbers and rates of published papers. In your opinion, how to evaluate teachers' innovation ability?

Ye: I think what we did is procedural justice. My opinion is that teachers should be judged on the basis of academic standards. That's peer review. The most important is the standards of quality rather than quantity. In one field, some competition may also disturb the real academic research.

Interviewer: What do you think of the phenomenon of good scholars doing some management work?

Ye: Everyone has his own ambition. This is the policy problem if that's becomes a universal pursuit for the benefits. This reflects that the administration of colleges and universities has reached a serious degree. His own values are also questionable because he is tempted.

Interviewer: The government has provided some funds and honors for young teachers, such as the Changjiang Scholar. What do you think of that phenomenon?

Ye: The government should make accurate judgments about who should receive the funds and honors. Only those who are interested and capable in the academic field can contribute to the academic development. Now the problem is that leaders who don't know education are directing education, so the problem is getting bigger and bigger.

Interviewer: What effect does the stratification of the teacher teams have on the teacher's innovation?

Ye: Maybe it can help to cultivate several outstanding academic leaders. But it can't be the main channel. A teacher's innovation is more determined by his comprehensive ability, which can't be evaluated by several indicators. Of course, for excellent teachers, if we can give them more support, they will be better. But there are so many teachers and fields, how many problems can the limited group of scholars solve?

Interviewer: What do you think of "lifetime professor"?

Ye: First, lifetime professor is different from senior professor. Second, lifetime professor is different from Zijiang scholars. Zijiang scholars are assessed by the government while lifetime professor is assessed by the university. Third, the "lifetime professor" honor is awarded for teachers who have made real contributions to the academic field or the university. This honor shows respect for these teachers.

Interviewer: The economic pressure on young teachers is too great, resulting in their lack of interest in research, not to mention innovation. What do you think of this situation?

Ye: Academic study is never very comfortable. It's one's pursuit or interest no matter what the environment is. In fact, each generation has its own experience and suffering. The key is whether one has a sense of self-reliance. The ability to judge, to choose, and to control one's own destiny is probably the most fundamental problem.

Interviewer: Can you summarize some of the factors that currently affect the innovation of university teachers?

Ye: One is the environment conditions, such as the society, the personnel system, and the promotion system. Another one is personal responsibilities. The road of life should be taken by oneself. The real person who can make a contribution must be a strong one. The stronger one has a very clear understanding of himself, and he will ignore the external things to do what he is willing to do.

6.15 East China Normal University—Yu

6.15.1 High-Frequency Words

Passion	Responsibility
Innovation teachers	Peer review
Academic vision	Academic funds

6.15.2 Key Points of Interview

Interviewer: As the leader of a university, what do you think should be considered in evaluating teachers' academic innovation?

Yu: I think academic innovation means fundamental research. The academic innovation ability of a teacher mainly refers to his academic ability and academic development potential. In the evaluation of teacher innovation from different subjects, we repeatedly emphasize that the indicators should be different. First, other teachers from the same faculty should evaluate him. Second, the real peer should evaluate him. Last, we pay attention to his innovative potential.

Interviewer: What do you think are the main aspects of this judgment?

Yu: The first is his grasp of the frontier of the field he studies and the location of his own research works in the whole discipline. A really thoughtful and contributing teacher can speak very clearly. The second is his grasp of the discipline system and his grasp of the intersecting part between the adjacent disciplines. The third is his sensitivity to frontier issues, his logical thinking, and his passion for research.

Interviewer: Do you think peer review can promote the development of teacher innovation?

Yu: Yes, I do. The improvement of our whole teaching team has been very rapid in recent years. In a group of scholars, those who have real innovation potential and academic potential can be judged. But it's really complicated.

Interviewer: In the field of humanities and social science, can the social influence and academic influence of a scholar be used as criteria to judge whether he is outstanding or not?

Yu: It's an indicator, but it's not the complete indicator.

Interviewer: How can the university provide some good opportunities for teachers' innovation in resource allocation?

Yu: We have a concept of bundled development. First, the teacher has a flagship task and he should finish it. Then he has a team, a platform, and its projects. At last, he should have achievements. If a school wants to develop, it can only realize its great benefits if its limited resources are well concentrated on some key breakthrough points. What's more, the points are not eternal. Every year there are some new key points.

Interviewer: What do you think of the phenomenon of academic leaders taking up administrative positions?

Yu: My point is that it has both advantages and disadvantages. It has disadvantages on his academic development because he only has partial energy for academic research. The advantages are that he can organize a larger team to do research and it can help open academic horizons.

Interviewer: Do you think the current assessment mechanism in our university can promote the innovation of teachers?

Yu: We have a standard of assessment for teachers, which is a very low standard in terms of quantity, about one article a year. And we don't evaluate teachers every year. We evaluate them once about every 2 years.

Interviewer: There are some scientific research funds and honors. Do you think these research funds and honorary titles can promote the development of academic innovation of teachers?

Yu: I think the outstanding youth fund, the Zijiang scholars in Shanghai, the dawn project, etc., are actually a kind of project to promote the development of talents. Its significance is to support teachers at different stages of academic development, so that they can develop better. I think it's necessary, especially for young people, because they need some special support in their development. And that support is competitive. So I think they are beneficial. However, now it's a little bit catabolic. It is a project that supports teacher's development, but it becomes an honor or an identity.

Interviewer: As a President, in your opinion, which factors are not helpful for the development of university teachers' innovation?

Yu: I think our teachers should really demand themselves with the academic requirements and be indifferent to fame and wealth. In my opinion, working in the university, teachers should have their own moral bottom line. If one wants to strive for an opportunity and such an academic improvement, he has to work hard first.

6.16 Central China Normal University—Research on Higher Education: Liu

6.16.1 High-Frequency Words

Teaching innovation ability	Ability of grasping the direction
Environment	Teaching
Positions	Invention

6.16.2 Key Points of Interview

Interviewer: Do you think the indicators of university teachers' innovation ability are reasonable? How to evaluate teachers' innovation ability?

Liu: This indicator system basically does not reflect the teaching innovation ability, which is the biggest problem. Academics include teaching and research, which is a universal understanding. To cultivate innovative talents, teachers should have innovative ability in teaching, which is a very important point. Teaching is for students. To improve students' innovative thinking and cultivate innovative students, teachers should have the ability to guide students and transform scientific research results into teaching. The above aspects should be reflected in the indicator system. There also are three problems. The first is what the teacher was like before he went to work. The second is what the teacher is like after he went to work and what needs to be improved. The third is the environment and cultural ideas. I suggest you to do some surveys about some teachers on their experience and thinking. The first question is his ability of grasping directions. Only when he finds a direction can he goes in this direction, and only when he goes deeper and deeper can he produces achievements and make innovations. The second question is his ability of grasping subject origin. The third question is about the environment. The university leaders can change the environment and guide the teachers to change themselves by changing the environment. In our country, the first is academic freedom. Innovation, first of all, is free space, free opportunity, and free thought, which is a problem that needs to be solved. In terms of teachers' guidance, our country has some major problems, such as lack of employment system. The second is assessment, such as the quality of the assessment and awards.

Interviewer: Besides the method of peer review, is there any better suggestion on the system to make the resources allocation promote teachers' innovation ability?

Liu: The system should pay more attention to teaching. Now these assessments are mainly for scientific research, with little assessment of teaching ability and teaching achievements.

Interviewer: What do you think of the phenomenon of academic leaders taking up administrative positions? Do you think this kind of motivation is good?

Liu: I don't think so. We mainly think of this problem from the following aspects. The first depends on the number of teachers in the subject. The second is positions. The third is appointment. Positions and appointment are based primarily on schools, which have little to do with innovation. Innovation is usually at the intersection of disciplines. At present, this position setting is not conducive to interdisciplinary. The solution now is to set up some centers and some innovation teams. It's good for innovation to examine the entire innovation team rather than the individual. The current promotion system does not reflect the improvement of innovation ability. In addition, it is better for teachers to be paid annually. Honor and inspiration are special products under special historical conditions. Now these rewards have a side effect.

Interviewer: Is it because of our system?

Liu: One is the system, another one is our development process and the economic foundation.

Interviewer: Could you define innovation?

Liu: First of all, originality is innovation, but innovation is not necessarily original. There are several aspects of innovation. One is integrated creation. One is taking someone else's achievements a step further. One is new discoveries, new understandings or new approaches. And not all innovation is good.

Interviewer: There is an understanding that innovation is creation and invention, discovery, and invention. What do you think?

Liu: This is not all-sided. Discovery and invention must be innovation. Light and technology are inventions, but science is discovery.

6.17 Huazhong University of Science and Technology—Institute of Higher Education: Zhang

6.17.1 High-Frequency Words

Academic insight and imagination	Academic innovation
Science and engineering	The Matthew effect
Utilitarianism	

6.17.2 Key Point of Interview

Interviewer: Do you think the indicators of university teachers' innovation ability are reasonable? Could you give us some suggestions?

Zhang: It would be very challenging to design a very scientific indicator system of university teachers' academic innovation ability. I think the system as a whole can reflect some basic elements of innovation. For university teachers, academic insight and imagination is a very important and crucial ability, which is also very difficult to measure. The observation point designed is a kind of solution. Of course, academic insight is inseparable from the grasp of frontier knowledge. Any innovation is a breakthrough based on previous research. We should not regard innovation as too mysterious. The most typical innovation is to use new theories, methods, technologies, and practices to solve existing problems, to solve frontier problems and to use a new method to study and solve old problems. The most important innovation of liberal arts is the so-called theoretical innovation, which produces a new theory. The second is that it uses new methods or different perspectives to study the same problem. The differences between liberal arts and science are obvious in innovation. I don't quite understand the concept of "ability of knowledge pedigree". The expression seems to be aimed more at liberal arts surveys. But science and engineering are different from liberal arts. The critical ability of academic reflection is a very important issue for liberal arts and should be put in a more important position. As far as your indicator system is concerned, I think there is a high degree of correlation between the several abilities involved. For example, there is a strong correlation between academic knowledge pedigree and academic reflective critical ability. In addition, compared with other aspects of academic innovation ability of university teachers, "academic cooperation and sharing ability" has a far relationship with innovation ability. In fact, I think it is very difficult to cooperate in terms of literature, history, and philosophy. In science and engineering, collaboration is more important. I do not advocate that everything should be measured by an indicator system, including university evaluation. Some things cannot be measured and quantified. On the whole, as for your innovation indicator system, I feel the trace of liberal arts is too heavy, it may be very different from science. I think the biggest problem is that it's hard to cover all teachers' academic innovation with a single indicator system.

On personnel system

Interviewer: What promoting and hindering factors do the personnel system of colleges and universities have on the academic innovation of teachers? How to promote it?

Zhang: Our school is very typical of engineering thinking. Teachers of the liberal arts were less involved in developing the selection and appointment assessment system. I think now our overall resource allocation mechanism is called "helping the strong and not helping the weak", forming a kind of Matthew effect. In fact, the education resource allocation is basically the same across the country. This resource allocation mechanism, on the whole, hinders the development of disciplines and academic innovation.

Interviewer: What do you think of the fact that many academic leaders take on administrative positions?

Zhang: As a kind of incentive measure, it is a special phenomenon in China, but it is rare in foreign countries. Even if they take on positions, they are largely academic positions. Many academic leaders take more administrative positions and do many activities unrelated to academic work. Firstly, they will lack time and energy. Secondly, their value orientation will change. We should strongly advocate the social ethos of "just doing academic work". It is the biggest disease of Chinese academic circle to strengthen the utilitarian purpose beyond academic.

Interviewer: As a college leader, how did you overcome the contradiction between the two roles?

Zhang: Adjust your interests to meet social needs. Find a way to survive in the system.

On incentive and security mechanism

Interviewer: Would you like to talk a little bit about other incentives and how they hinder or facilitate university teachers' innovation?

Zhang: The Cheung Kong Scholars Program, National Science Fund for Distinguished Young Scholars, the million talents program, and the Thousand Talents Program are all regarded as academic awards. These rewards are not only financial, but also indicative of a person's social status. I think these incentive programs are necessary to motivate these young teachers to make more efforts in their own research. All rewards programs are not rewards for teaching. It's a bad thing not to pay attention to talent cultivation. In fact, from the perspective of stimulating the innovation of scholars, the ideal situation should be to create more favorable teaching and research conditions for teachers.

On selection and appointment

Interviewer: Can you comment on the selection and appointment system of colleges and universities?

Zhang: Focus on scientific research rather than teaching. In fact, this phenomenon is particularly serious and it will have a negative impact on teachers' academic innovation. Such appointments are guided by scientific research achievements. Why is China's overall academic creativity weak? It has something to do with our sense of utilitarian purpose.

6.18 Huazhong University of Science and Technology—Education and Economy: Fan

6.18.1 High-Frequency Words

Academic insight and imagination	Academic innovation
Science and engineering	Critical reflective ability
Professional dedication	Love students

6.18.2 Key Points of Interview

1 Basic questions of subgroups
1.1 Academic insight and imagination ability

Interviewer: What do you think of the academic insight and imagination ability in our indicator system? Do you think that's a reasonable statement?

Fan: As a university teacher, I think academic insight and imagination is a basic ability. I often tell my students to be sensitive to major changes in society, international and domestic progress and frontier in this subject. There are differences in innovation across disciplines. As a teacher educator, his academic innovation ability is more important. In a sense, it is more important to teach students the methods. As teacher educators, teachers must be able to guide students to grasp academic insight ability. In my opinion, original imagination must be built on the foundation of predecessors. If one wants to be original, he needs to grasp all aspects of national and even global economic and society.

1.2 Comprehensive crossing ability

Interviewer: How do you understand comprehensive crossing ability? Is it the basis of academic innovation?

Fan: It should be. With the development of science and technology, various disciplines are highly differentiated and highly integrated. Another advantage of this comprehension is to apply the research methods of other disciplines to this discipline.

1.3 Academic critical reflective ability

Interviewer: What do you think of the academic critical reflective ability of university teachers?

Fan: As a scholar, it is necessary to have discrimination ability and to reflect and criticize on this basis. Without academic criticism, there is no innovation.

1.4 Academic autonomy ability

Interviewer: What do you think of the academic autonomy ability of university teachers?

Fan: Personally, I think we should have our own thoughts and opinions. Some scholars still lack academic autonomy ability and their own thoughts due to the imprisonment of thoughts. Innovation requires a good atmosphere. Be innovative, be tolerant.

1.5 Academic cooperation and sharing ability

Fan: I think the academic cooperation and sharing ability proposed is very important. The collision between each other is also a kind of sharing, and the spark generated by the collision is a source of innovation.

Interviewer: Is there any special aspect to the academic innovation ability of teacher educators compared with the teachers of comprehensive universities?

Fan: First of all, teacher educators should love their work and have a professional spirit. Secondly, teacher educators should love their students. Only when he loves his students, he will try his best to cultivate them into talents.

Interviewer: How to improve the innovation ability of teachers?

Fan: In my opinion, being a manager is not conducive for an academic leader's academic innovation ability development. To improve the creativity of teachers, first, their time should be guaranteed. In the evaluation, we should not simply use such quantitative indicators, but should have a representative system. We can try the tenure system in school. The key to innovation is a good atmosphere.

Interviewer: As for our indicator system, could you give us some suggestions for improvement?

Fan: First, the reference ability should be added to the index system. Second, you should not only interview teachers from the liberal arts, but you should also consider teachers from science and engineering.

2 On personnel system
2.1 On examination and evaluation mechanism
Interviewer: Are there any specific policies for evaluating teachers' creativity?

Fan: We rely on quantitative assessment. It may solve some problems, but it certainly raises some new ones. The system led to the fickleness of teachers. Resource allocation is also involved. The whole resources allocation is unfair.

2.2 On selection and appointment system
Interviewer: What are the factors that promote and hinder the academic innovation of university teachers in the current selection and appointment mechanism?

Fan: Now the university selection and appointment mechanism have rationality and irrationality. We should see his education background, master's thesis, doctoral thesis, and mentor's recommendations.

Interviewer: How much academic innovation is involved in the selection of teachers?

Fan: For young scholars, academic innovation is reflected mainly through the representative work and what research they have participated in. They also should give a report. Good language expression ability is also an essential basic ability for university teachers. Additional, we also have image requirements.

2.3 On incentive mechanism
Interviewer: What measures does the school have to encourage teachers to be innovative?

Fan: By professional evaluation. Reward teachers each year according to the level of their published articles. The kind of reward is a double-edged sword.

6.19 Huazhong University of Science and Technology—Li

6.19.1 High-Frequency Words

University teachers	Academic innovation
Interdisciplinary abilities	Research-oriented teachers
Teaching-oriented teachers	

6.19.2 Key Points of Interview

1 Basic questions of subgroups
Interviewer: Do you think the indicators of university teachers' innovation ability are reasonable?

6.19 Huazhong University of Science and Technology—Li

Li: The "university teacher" in your system isn't very clear. At present, for colleges and universities, especially for some comprehensive universities, there are certain differences between their requirements on teachers' scientific research and our requirements on teachers' education in normal universities. In our revised document on teacher, title, and promotion this year, we set up three kinds of teachers: teachers who are research-oriented, teachers who are teaching and research-oriented and teachers who are teaching-oriented. As for the indicator system, maybe the mental ability is difficult to observe from outside. In view of the three-level indicator system, I will talk about my views. Attention ability is not academic enough. The imagination ability is too basic. It would be better to replace "interdisciplinary academic research ability" with "interdisciplinary ability". What is the relationship between historical data collection ability and previous literature review ability? Generally speaking, your indicator system gives a sense of pedant. I think this indicator system is not ideal and targeted. It is not easy to operate.

Interviewer: In what ways do you think teachers' creativity should be evaluated?

Li: By evaluating the quality of their work from the rates of articles. The system is hard to implement. As far as teacher educators, first is his moral quality, second is the teaching ability and the third is knowing elementary education.

Interviewer: Could you talk about the personnel system in the university?

Li: In China, teachers are not traditionally expected to do research. We're talking about academic innovation, and actually, a lot of people aren't really innovative. Why is the central government raising this innovation capability? Because there are serious problems in the system.

Interviewer: What is the relationship between doing research and innovation?

Li: What is innovation? If there is something new in this article, it is called innovation, we should see what kind of publication this article is published in.

Interviewer: So is the current assessment mechanism more focused on scientific research or more on teaching scientific research?

Li: We need to improve the teaching level from this year.

Interviewer: Is it unreasonable to regard scientific research as the main content of innovation evaluation?

Li: At least it's not complete.

Interviewer: If teaching is included in the content of innovation, how to evaluate it?

Li: That's really difficult.

Interviewer: Does the 3-year appointment system hinder or promote teachers' innovation?

Li: It's definitely better than having no constraints at all.

Interviewer: Some experts suggest learning the western system of tenured professors or extending the tenure to give teachers a more relaxed environment.

Li: That only solves a few problems. The Western country also has assessment.

Interviewer: Do you think the length of employment has an impact on the innovation of teachers?

Li: There is no direct impact.

6.20 Huazhong University of Science and Technology—Department of Personnel: Ren

6.20.1 High-Frequency Words

Critical reflective ability	International communication skills
The quantity and quality of papers	Research-oriented teachers
Teaching-oriented teachers	

6.20.2 Key Points of Interview

1 Basic questions of subgroups

Interviewer: Do you think the indicators of university teachers' innovation ability are reasonable? How to evaluate teachers' innovation?

Ren: In today's universities, teachers must have these basic skills. Especially in the context of internationalization, to be truly innovative, teachers must have these aspects. The index system puts forward a reflective critical ability, which I think is very important to both teachers and students. Now our educational reform also advocates critical teaching.

Interviewer: Do you have any suggestions for our innovation indicator system?

Ren: Your indicator system is relatively complete and detailed. I think international communication skills should be highlighted in your indicator system.

2 On personnel system

Interviewer: How does CCNU evaluate teachers' academic innovation?

Ren: Colleges and universities now attach great importance to evaluation. Promotion of professional title has corresponding evaluation standards. We used to pay attention to the number of papers, but now we pay more and more attention to the quality of the papers. We now classify teachers according to their different development paths: teachers who are research-oriented, teachers who are teaching and research-oriented and teachers who are teaching-oriented.

Interviewer: How do you evaluate his innovation in teaching?

Ren: We have many indicators, including teaching competition, teaching research, education and teaching reforming, teaching research papers and student evaluation.

Interviewer: What are the conditions for the selection of candidates in CCNU?

Ren: The basic condition is that he must graduate from 985 or 211 universities. I don't think there is a very scientific evaluation system. Our current talent evaluation system is problematic.

Interviewer: Does our school allocate resources according to the innovation of teachers?

Ren: We have three kinds of teachers, including teachers who are research-oriented, teachers who are teaching and research-oriented and teachers who are teaching-oriented. Each path has different requirements for teachers.

Interviewer: What do you think of the phenomenon of academic leaders taking administrative positions?

Ren: This comes from the idea of the official standard of our country. The academic leaders taking on administrative positions at the same time can definitely affect their innovation. After all, a person's energy is limited. In a strict sense, they should do their academic work and make greater use of their expertise. Administrative affairs will distract them. But it's a big appeal for teachers because of the resources. In my opinion, we should let those who are good at administration do administration, and let those who have academic innovation focus on academic development, so that we can cultivate a number of truly innovative teachers. However, on the other hand, it is also a very contradictory phenomenon to let a person without a certain academic background to be a leader to be stupid in command, which may not be conducive to innovation.

Interviewer: What kind of incentive policy does CCNU have for teachers of academic innovation?

Ren: By providing project funding, promotions, learning aboard, and improving economic benefits.

Interviewer: What do you think about giving these academic teachers some titles like "Cheung Kong scholar"?

Ren: It should be done according to the needs of national development. There are policies and plans to support talents in a special period. It has both advantages and disadvantages to attracting talent. There is no binding mechanism for the evaluation and treatment of the whole country, which is not conducive to teachers' development.

6.21 Central China Normal University—Social Sciences Department: Shi

6.21.1 High-Frequency Words

Academic innovation ability	Being original
Academic foundation	Academic vision
Academic mind	Peer recognition

6.21.2 Key Points of Interview

Interviewer: In your opinion, what is academic innovation?

Shi: Being original is an innovation, but integrating them is also an innovation. When we apply for projects, we pay special attention to innovation. We must have our own opinions. We can supplement or surpass the existing researches. In universities, innovation is mainly about scientific research. Without innovation, scientific research is meaningless and worthless. Academic innovation, I think is a kind of intelligence. As an academic innovator, first of all, he should have a solid academic foundation. Secondly, he should have a profound academic vision. Third, he should have a broad academic mind. However, as a teacher, no matter how strong his academic innovation ability is, he should never forget his job—teaching. Therefore, academic innovative ability should finally become innovative teaching ability.

Interviewer: How does the university evaluate your academic innovation ability as a section chief?

Shi: The director's appointment and removal are not based solely on academic innovation but on his work innovation ability. I think as a leader of the administrative department, the first thing to be valued is his administrative leadership and administrative innovation ability, rather than his academic innovation ability. You're looking at the more innovative teachers, and I don't want them in the management team, because people's energy and time are limited. To appoint or remove discipline leaders in universities, on the one hand, it is necessary to consider his work ability and innovation ability; on the other hand, his academic innovation ability is also necessary, in some cases, which may be necessary to be considered first. The appointment and removal of administrative leadership should emphasize its administrative innovation ability rather than academic innovation ability, which should be different.

On indicator system of university teachers

Interviewer: As far as you know, what is the evaluation of college teachers now? What are the criteria?

Shi: In liberal arts, scientific research projects, scientific research funds, scientific research achievements, scientific research awards are important. So the key is scientific research and teaching is relatively unimportant. At present, the evaluation system based on scientific research meets the needs of social development.

On selection and appointment system

Interviewer: What criteria will be used when selecting and hiring teachers? What proportion of academic innovation will take?

Shi: Strictly speaking, it has reached the stage of selecting the best among the best. Universities have their own practices, but they are strictly unscientific. What is scientific? It should be peer recognition. In the liberal arts, there is no absolute standard but only a relative standard. So most people think it's good, then that must be good. In the recruitment of college teachers, there are many considerations. First, he has to take a class, next is his educational structure, student structure, the strength of scientific research ability, and gender. Among these factors, the scientific research examines his creativity.

On incentive method

Interviewer: Are there any other incentive measures to encourage teachers besides research funds and professional promotion?

Shi: There are material rewards, professional titles, money rewards, and some honorary titles, such as New Century Talents Project and Changjiang Scholars Program. Studying abroad is no longer an incentive. I think we should be more flexible if we want to motivate the teachers.

On the rationality of indicator system

Interviewer: Do you think the indicators of university teachers' innovation ability are reasonable? Do you have any other suggestion?

Shi: On the whole, I think your six indicators of innovation ability are designed to be quite innovative and basically cover all the abilities of teachers. If your indicator system can be more perfect, it can be published as a national indicator of teacher innovation. In my opinion, first, there should be such a standard of innovation, and second, there should be differences between different disciplines. However, I am still not sure about your indicator system. Is the ability of academic cooperation and sharing a kind of academic innovation? I don't think so. This sharing ability, I think, is the most basic requirements of teachers, but it does not belong to innovation. The ability to collaborate is important, but it doesn't equal to your innovation ability.

On evaluation standards of university teachers' innovation

Interviewer: Does CCNU have special evaluation mechanism about teachers' innovation?

Shi: At present, it may be difficult for us to come up with complete evaluation criteria. How do we measure research? By its innovation, its importance and what it can provide for the society.

6.22 Central China Normal University—School of Education: Tu

6.22.1 High-Frequency Words

Academic innovation ability	The academic field of discovery
Academic foundation	Indicator system
Supportive measures	
Induction	

6.22.2 Key Points of Interview

Interviewer: What are your suggestions about this indicator system?

Tu: I don't know how you did it, but it did take a lot of work. First, what exactly does "academic" mean in academic innovation? Because now we different understanding of scholarship. The classical view of learning holds that innovation in some areas is academic. Boyer divides the academic field into four aspects, including the academic field of discovery, the academic field of synthesis, the academic field of application and the academic field of teaching. I think it's important to define it.

Interviewer: We mainly aim at research-based normal universities and universities of stronger higher education.

Tu: There are no Peking University and Tsinghua University?

Interviewer: Yes, there are. We just aim at teacher educators.

Tu: The problem is that are there normal universities can be called research universities? Maybe they are not just these six normal universities. However, these six are not necessarily research universities. What's more, University teachers and researchers are complicated groups. That reminds me of multiple intelligence theory of Gardner. Different teachers from different majors have different abilities and innovation. In that case, you should consider how to pay attention to these differences in your indicator system.

Interviewer: Do you agree with the indicator system? I'd like to hear your suggestion.

Tu: I think we can set up an indicator system, but it's not easy. The learning of teaching is not the same as the learning of discovery. The study of liberal arts is different from that of science. Therefore, it is very difficult to establish a unified and comprehensive index system in this situation. But it is true that many scholars in our country like to do indicator system now. Traditional academics may be more individualistic and modern academic innovation more team-oriented. We have different academics, different professional fields, different individuals, and different teams, so setting up such a system of indicators is quite difficult.

Interviewer: What's your opinion about the personnel system?

Tu: Everyone's opinion may not be exactly the same. In general, I think, the biggest problem is probably angering for quick success and instant benefits. On the one hand, academic innovation seems to be flourishing and everyone is doing a lot of things, but on the other hand, there is really not much real innovation. Of course, it is the problem of the whole society, and not the university itself. The problem may be difficult to alleviate in a short time, but it seems to be getting worse. Natural science may be a bit better. Now the funds are relatively abundant, which is conducive to the improvement of experimental conditions. The researchers of social sciences can't calm down now. In fact, academic innovation needs the researchers to concentrate.

Interviewer: Do leaders have some measures to promote teachers' innovation?

Tu: Young people are under a lot of pressure now, both in their lives and in their jobs and in the academic innovation. I think it's bad to just make demands for them. So we still attach importance to the cultivation of young teachers. For example, we all have corresponding support measures for going abroad for further study, research, and going out for meetings. In addition, we will provide teachers with some platforms. For example, we have key disciplines, so teachers can create it as the bases for master degree and doctoral program. Then they will become a mentor in the future. In addition, the basic working conditions are also included. We also create a more relaxed environment and atmosphere for you. These external conditions are no substitute for personal effort. Therefore, young teachers should realize that their growth is a relatively long-term process. And it's a tough process overall.

Interviewer: The most important thing is not those external conditions, the most important is the ability to calm down to read and write things. Can the research funds and honorable titles promote teachers' innovation ability?

Tu: Not much. It even has a negative influence. But now I can completely understand that phenomenon. This practice will be continued, and it will be more and more serious. Why? First, the country is now flush with funds. Second, leaders of various cities have to take political achievements. Sometimes what exists is reasonable. But we're in this whole impetuous society and in the systems of goals-oriented. Sometimes it just kills academic innovation. One of the killers of creativity is competition.

Interviewer: What are the measures of allocating resource for teachers?

Tu: The situation varies from school to school. We still took some measures, for example, improving the working conditions and scientific research conditions of teachers. Second, they are offered financial support for some academic activities.

Interviewer: How do you evaluate a candidate's academic innovation when hiring a new teacher?

Tu: First of all, the physical and mental condition of the candidate should be examined comprehensively. We first determine the indicators of admission according to actual needs, and then conduct a comprehensive survey on the education, experience, physical and mental health, ideological morality and working level of the applicant by the department, through special reports, trial lectures or symposiums. Then they form an opinion. The department's faculty committee reviewed the applicant in the department's opinion. The professor committee will focus on the applicant's academic foundation, research achievements, research ability and development potential, and then vote on the candidate.

Interviewer: How to evaluate the candidate's academic innovation?

Tu: By his academic foundation and research achievements.

Interviewer: If two people have similar conditions in other aspects, but one student has strong scientific research ability and the other student has strong teaching ability. What's the choice at this point?

Tu: There are people who are good at doing research but not good at teaching, but few. In most cases, good researchers can teach well.

Interviewer: Can we evaluate a doctoral student's innovation by his academic foundation?

Tu: That should be a comprehensive judgment.

Interviewer: So you evaluate a teacher from the rigid requirements such as published papers?

Tu: Each school has its own rules. It is certainly worth studying whether this regulation is reasonable or not. But I believe that the requirements of each school may also be connected with the actual needs of their own. The higher the level of schools is, the higher the requirements for research are, and some conditions will be higher.

Interviewer: Are you in favor of setting up an assessment system for teachers based on academic innovation?

Tu: Teachers in research universities have a variety of responsibilities, including research, teaching, and social services. In this case, it is obvious that we should have different requirements for different teachers. We're should use different criteria for different objects.

Interviewer: Do you think the overall dimension of our indicator system is reasonable?

Tu: I guess you come up with an idea first, and then listen to others' suggestions. This is one way to do it. I think you also can do it by induction like Gardner. You can select some university teachers and study what they are capable of by interviewing them and reading their books. I think it is more reliable. I do oppose the creation of a single indicator system to measure everyone. The academic innovation of different university teachers has different characteristics.

Interviewer: The best thing about a tenured professor is that he or she is free to explore and do things here.

6.23 Shaanxi Normal University—School of Education: Hao

6.23.1 High-Frequency Words

Academic innovation ability	Practical work
Basic education	Indicator system
Independent learning	Supportive measures

6.23.2 Key Points of Interview

1 Basic questions of subgroups

Interviewer: Do you think the indicator system is reasonable?

Hao: The system is divided more from the perspective of psychology, which is very detailed, but also very abstract. What we call teacher education innovation and teacher innovation, the front part is very common content. To some extent, is all the content universally applicable to scholars in the liberal arts, sciences or natural sciences? Is there a difference between measuring the creativity of ordinary people and teachers? Is there a part of it that is more appropriate for teachers than for ordinary people?

Interviewer: Is there any difference in innovation ability between teachers of comprehensive university and normal university?

Hao: From my own experience, to be innovative is to try our best to grasp the academic frontier and adapt to the development of The Times. Innovation starts with questions. How to find the problem on earth? It's too general to tell whether a person is innovative or not. We see the news every day, although the contents are not all useful, but we can feel the development of the era and there are still problems to develop. By grasping every step of the times and academic development, we can discover which problems have been solved and which have not. You should put another column in the index system to highlight the key points. At the same time, the indicator system should be more operable and easier to understand. Like what exactly is insight?

Interviewer: Is the indicator system reasonable?

Hao: First, is it possible to highlight the difference in innovation between teachers and others? Generally speaking, teachers major in education and subjects are different. Generally, scholars studying pedagogy will develop their research from a national perspective, but specific teachers will look at practical issues, such as curriculum setting and teaching methods. The system has the content of thinking, but the content of practice is less. The link between innovation and practice is very close, but it is not reflected in the indicators. There is a difference between a teacher and a scientist in theory and practice. The system should show innovation for university teachers, not for everyone. How is it defined in research, how much difference is there between scholarship and practices, and on what issues do they have differences? The present article is highly academic but has little to do with practical problems. We should solve the problem of research on practical questions isn't academic innovation and only research on macro theory is academic innovation. Whether articles of solving practical problems is innovation or not is needed further discussed. Can basic education be called academic research? If it isn't academic research, how can we develop teaching? There are also many innovations in teaching, which are to solve problems in teaching and have a great effect on practice. There are a lot of problems in education research. However, we should shift from macro and policy research to micro research on teaching practice.

Interviewer: In your opinion, how to evaluate a teachers' innovation in practical works?

Hao: Doing an experiment is a practical action. Before taken into action, the experiment should be designed well. So the researchers must be clear about the key problems and questions. Discovering other people's problems is the root of innovation, and it's important to be able to generalize about what's common in others' researches.

Interviewer: Is the dimension of academic knowledge ability in the index system reasonable?

Hao: Knowledge is needed, emphasizing reality, theory, history, and intensity. Innovation starts from reality and makes reality better by solving real problems, but you can't innovate if you don't understand what's going on in history. Knowledge is only the foundation of innovation. You can't innovative without reading books, but reading books is not necessarily useful. I put forward the view of education essence. Education is for learning. Education comes from learning. Education is a kind of instructional learning. I was inspired by the ideas of Dewey. Innovation is about discovering what you're after. We put too much emphasis on knowledge now. Broad knowledge does not necessarily lead to innovation. Three primary indicators are involved in the system. In the following study, the relationship between the three primary indicators should be clarified. Knowledge and thought promote and restrict each other.

Interviewer: The last dimension is the social ability of academic innovation, which mainly includes academic autonomy ability and academic sharing ability. Is it appropriate?

Hao: Some people are stubborn. Maybe that's not good in other people's eyes, but perhaps it's good for academic research, because he's autonomous and independent, and he can say the reasons. I usually write for myself. When I write, I am free from other distractions and have my own framework and ideas. Then I fill my own frame with other people's researches. In fact, to prove your academic ability, you should choose what others have done and then present your own ideas. From a philosophical point of view, innovation is about being able to change, and above all is about changing basic concepts. Teacher–student dialogue is emphasized in the teaching theory. What is the meaning of conversation? I usually emphasize conversations that don't need to talk. Dialogue is first and foremost a spiritual communication. We should pay attention to this in our cooperation. Cooperation takes many forms. Explicit cooperation is important, but implicit cooperation is also important. Sometimes autonomy and cooperation are at odds. Too much autonomy means no cooperation. You should be able to express your own views in cooperation.

2 On personnel system
2.1 On resource allocation

Interviewer: In your opinion, what resources should be provided for teachers in the allocation resources of university teachers to better promote their innovation?

Hao: The issue of housing is very important. It is the security of life. There should also be some guarantee of income.

Interviewer: Besides the basic resources you just mentioned, how to improve the allocation of resources so as to improve the innovation of teachers?

Hao: In teaching, the basic conditions are important. Not only housing and living problems should be solved, but also research facilities and conditions. Another problem is the computer facilities. A teacher should have a computer. Books and materials are also important.

2.2 On selection and appointment

Interviewer: As for teacher educators, is there something special about the selection and appointment mechanism to ensure the improvement of their innovation?

Hao: There are rigid conditions for selection and appointment. Some people think you can't evaluate too often, which is the hope of real academics. To the average person, if you don't judge him, he is lazy. The standard isn't very high. We rely on the internal motivation for our articles.

Interviewer: How to improve the selection and appointment system?

Hao: There should be some requirements. In a certain extent, no requirement is harmful to the teachers. For young teachers, language expression ability is a basic requirement. The level of publishing houses and magazines does not necessarily represent the innovation of teachers. It's impossible to expect everyone to innovate. It's also impossible to select the innovators. We can only choose people who meet the general conditions and then give them more cultivation.

Interviewer: How to pay attention to the evaluation of ideas and promote the creativity of university teachers?

Hao: It's mostly a moral aspect. Ideological evaluation mainly advocates the three aspects, which is embodied in telling the truth, doing practical things and being an honest person.

Interviewer: How to evaluate teachers' innovation ability? How to promote teachers' innovation ability?

Hao: By their published works and papers. Universities have their own evaluation system. The social scale is generally balanced. The assessment is only for a few people. However, to avoid the phenomenon of academic immorality and promote teachers' innovation mainly depends on their individual morality and the initiative to abide by academic norms, rather than external evaluation.

2.3 Incentive and security

Interviewer: As for teacher educators, what is special about the incentive and guarantee mechanism to improve their innovation?

Hao: What is more important for young people is a life guarantee. Incentives should be graded, but not too obviously. Financial security, exchange abroad, domestic exchanges are all important.

6.24 Shaanxi Normal University—School of Education: Chen

6.24.1 High-Frequency Words

Academic insight and imagination ability	Prototype inspiration
Academic autonomy	Scholarship of teaching
Research achievements	

6.24.2 Key Points of Interview

1 Basic question of subgroups

Interviewer: Do you think the indicator system is reasonable? Do you have any suggestions? How to evaluate teachers' innovation ability?

Chen: There are several indicators below the first level. The first is academic insight and imagination ability. I think this one is ok. As college and university teachers, they should have an insight and be sensitive to academic research. This insight may include insights into forefront issues in international research as well as practical ones. Any creation has a kind of prototype inspiration, so academic imagination ability is still very important. The point is that can you find this prototype and what you can get from this prototype. I don't think there is a complete and absolute originality. Any invention or creation has a prototype. But how closely this prototype is related to the creation is different. As for insight ability, I think academic researchers should be sensitive to academic development. I take your intellectual insight as a kind of sensitivity. We should quickly notice and even interested in new issues. When I teach my students, I will read foreign papers and attend academic conferences, and then tell them problems that are worth studying. I am not sure whether the academic comprehensive ability and the interdisciplinary ability can be placed under the academic psychological ability. In my opinion, literature review ability is not a kind of discipline and professional ability, which seems better in the academic knowledge ability. The design of knowledge pedigree ability is relatively targeted. The reflective ability of academic innovation knowledge ability is also very important. Academic critical ability and critical thinking are also ok. Abiding by academic ethics in academic autonomy ability is very good. I am very concerned about academic standardization. While advocating academic innovation, it is wise to stick to academic standards.

Interviewer: Is there a necessary link between academic autonomy ability and academic innovation?

Chen: We think about autonomy from two aspects. One is to think autonomously. The other is independent intellectual property rights. We can form our own ideas through such activities.

Interviewer: Is academic autonomy ability?

Chen: Academic autonomy is sometimes a kind of consciousness. Innovation requires awareness, but it also requires capacity. I think two things can be added together, such as changing academic autonomy ability to academic autonomy consciousness and ability.

Interviewer: Are there necessarily differences in creativity between teachers who do their own research and those who are directed?

Chen: This varies from person to person. Some people can be equally innovative in project-based researches and interest-based researches. Some people will be limited by the projects. The classic research results that I've seen in the past, they're irrelevant to the project. But now everyone has projects. The subject has both advantages and disadvantages. On the one hand, it is not conducive to the free study of intellectuals; on the other hand, it supports them to conduct large-scale research and academic exchanges. The liberal arts are less obvious, the sciences are more obvious. You can't do research without some instruments in sciences. In this case, the awareness and ability of innovation must be integrated with the projects. Therefore, we cannot treat different situations as the same. Academic cooperation ability belongs to academic society ability. As a broad sense of social competence, that's ok. As a member of the academic community, scholars should have exchanges, cooperation, and communication ability.

Interviewer: Can these six points evaluate teachers' innovation perfectly?

Chen: In addition to the question of whether the academic comprehensive ability and the interdisciplinary ability can be placed under the academic psychological ability, it is questionable to discuss. Moreover, the academic research in academic innovation of university teachers mentioned here refers to scientific research. But we still have teaching research. The university has three tasks: teaching, scientific research, and social service. The comprehensive university emphasizes teaching and scientific research. In my opinion, universities should put teaching first. I mention scholarship of teaching. In addition to scientific research, we have teaching research. Teachers of normal universities should pay special attention to scholarship of teaching.

Interviewer: What is the difference in innovation between teachers of normal universities and those of comprehensive universities?

Chen: The two types of teachers have different job contents. In addition, teachers of comprehensive universities have wider platforms for academic exchanges, more opportunities, and better support. In addition, many teachers in comprehensive universities have a foreign background and international vision. They have more prototypes of academic imagination and stronger interdisciplinary comprehensive ability.

2 On personnel system
2.1 On resource allocation
2.2 On selection and appointment

Interviewer: How to evaluate academic innovation when selecting and employing teachers?

Chen: There is no indicator of innovation when hiring teachers. But we're looking at the academic potential of a teacher. The basic teaching ability, existing research achievements, research interests, and future research directions are generally investigated.

Interviewer: How to tell if a teacher is innovative?

Chen: In terms of personal experience, the first is to look at his subject background, the second is to look at the research achievements, the third is the degree of internationalization, such as English level, the degree and ability to dabble in foreign literature, and the fourth is to look at whether he has academic sensitivity through communication.

Interviewer: How to improve the personnel system to improve the innovation of teachers?

Chen: At present, the personnel system of colleges and universities is favorable for innovation. Some honors can encourage teachers to constantly research and innovate. I personally think it is too complicated to evaluate the creativity of new teachers individually. Generally, the evaluation based on the standard system is rather time-consuming and laborious. In addition, such assessments of imported academic leaders show that they are not fully accepted. But from a normative perspective, this kind of evaluation system can be tried in the future.

Interviewer: How does the university evaluate teachers' innovation?

Chen: By evaluating the innovation of the project and teachers' awards experience.

Interviewer: How to improve the assessment mechanism based on the six indicators?

Chen: One is the innovation of scientific research achievements and the other is the innovation of teaching. As for the research results, we should not only pay attention to the number of published articles, but also the innovation of the papers. We should try to evaluate innovation separately. For example, 100 articles published in leading journals are reviewed by experts, and 80 articles that are truly innovative can be rewarded. There will be weighting issues between the indicators in the future.

2.3 Incentive and security

Interviewer: How to encourage innovation of teachers by incentive and security system?

Chen: Two ways: research grants and funds reward. The former is a reward for scientific research and can be used for life. The latter can only be used for deep research, not for anything else.

6.25 Shaanxi Normal University–School of Education: Fang

6.25.1 High-Frequency Words

Academic insight and imagination ability	Interdisciplinary
Academic autonomy	Extensive and in-depth
Research achievements	Critical reflective ability

6.25.2 Key Points of Interview

1 On reasonability of the indicator system

Interviewer: Do you think the indicator system is reasonable?

Fang: I don't know how to divide insight and imagination in practice. Academic insight ability should be measured. It's also called intuition. Academic insight and imagination ability are different for different teachers. This ability is based on long-term research and the accumulation of experience. A teacher must first be an observant and conscientious person. Then he must learn new things. This ability is available only to experienced teachers. I think the comprehensive interdisciplinary ability is actually the ability to control knowledge. A really good research must be interdisciplinary. This ability is impossible for young teachers. It requires considerable experience and practice. I don't know what the knowledge pedigree ability is. I personally think there are two trends within the discipline. One trend is that the subject content is becoming more and more specialized and more and more refined. On the other hand, research must be interdisciplinary. Two trends should exist simultaneously. Extensive and in-depth should be combined with each other. From the perspective of research and the perspective of social science, extensive and in-depth are very necessary. Creative teachers and workers must be proficient in one area and have a wide range of knowledge. Academic autonomy ability is important. Some domestic scholars are more fickleness and profitable. However, some scholars are more considerable and aren't influenced by environment. We cannot say that the former teacher has no autonomy. The first type of teacher also has autonomy because he can choose to do which project. Some people do research for pleasure and some others just for a living. But a real scholar should have the academic spirit of doing what he likes. Autonomy and autonomy are not directly related to innovation ability. People are malleable and their abilities can be cultivated. Critical reflective ability is important. Good researchers must be critical. But the critical spirit is not reflected by expressing, but reflected in the process of thinking. The importance of collaborative sharing depends on different researches. There's nothing wrong with emphasizing teamwork. Engineering projects require teams. But some basic research doesn't require teams. Not all-innovative research needs to be done as a team. It depends on the projects.

Interviewer: What is unique about teachers and educators?

Fang: Teachers in normal universities obey the rules more, but those in comprehensive universities and engineering colleges are livelier. From the perspective of cultivating people, normal colleges are very good. But there are drawbacks to cultivating innovative talented students. Comprehensive universities give children a lot of space for their nature and activity. I really appreciate what's done abroad. You can't judge people easily. The evaluation of a person is diversified. We should pay more attention to guidance rather than a qualitative judgment.

2 On personnel system

Interviewer: When you hire teachers, will you specifically evaluate their academic innovation ability?

Fang: There are no specific measures of innovation. We will consider their academic potential, which will include academic innovation. We will reform this year. First of all, there is a basic threshold, after the basic conditions are met, the materials of the candidates will be sent to at least 10 comparable universities or higher universities for peer review. The evaluation of innovation must be deep. The judgment of innovation is hard and may hurt the candidates. From the psychological point of view, people who can make big achievements are of a stable personality and able to stick to research.

Interviewer: How to evaluate teachers' academic innovation?

Fang: There is no single way to evaluate academic innovation. Usually, a teacher is evaluated from the school to the department and then to the school's academic review committee. But the problem with this approach is that Chinese society has human relations. There is too much humanity involved in the selection process. After reaching the evaluation at school level, it is not just about academic evaluation. It is related to the control of quota and the comprehensive ability, which is irrelevant to the innovation ability.

Interviewer: How to improve the existing incentive and guarantee mechanism to enhance the innovation of teachers?

Fang: At present, there is no mechanism for teachers' innovation. In terms of personnel system, the past learning experience, research achievements, the thinking ability, and the understanding of researches are highly valued. A person who is engaged in research is constantly experiencing the pleasure of doing research. But it's hard to tell from scientific achievements. We can tell whether he is innovative through face-to-face communication and investigation. We think more about this person's developmental potential, which is also associated with innovation. We are also trying to adjust the evaluation and assessment methods of teachers in the system.

6.26 Shaanxi Normal University–School of Education: Huo

6.26.1 High-Frequency Words

Teacher quality	Academic spirit
Innovation spirit	Teacher education
Inheritance and innovation	

6.26.2 Key Points of Interview

1 On reasonability of the indicator system

Interviewer: Do you think the indicator system is reasonable? Do you have any suggestions?

Huo: The structural model of teacher quality of Latos in American is instructive. From the outside to the inside, it has environment, behavior, ability, faith, professional identity, and mission. I think their model is more reasonable. We focus on the competence. But competence is just an accessory. The core of teachers' quality is their mission, faith, and professional spirit. Besides academic ability, it would be better if academic spirit could be integrated into it. In terms of psychological quality, there should be a spirit of innovation. Ability is not the core of a teacher. The spirit should be more prominent. Although your indicator system also focuses on teachers' spirit, it is too scattered. Our evaluation mechanism has a very short cycle. We assess teachers one a year and hire them once every 3 years. In one respect, there are some advantages to avoid the phenomenon of some people muddling along. But for those who really want to do scholarship, the institutional approach is a short-term system. I have a question now, how do we achieve these ideas when we turn them into scales? Academic personality ability or academic personality should be added to academic mental ability. Academic communication ability, or international communication ability, that is, international perspective should be added to knowledge pedigree ability.

Interviewer: Is international communication ability a kind of knowledge ability or social ability?

Huo: Both, actually. The hardest part of doing this work is front and back testing. You should do a big sample test, take more samples, and do a matrix analysis.

Interviewer: What is the difference in innovation between teachers in normal schools and teachers in comprehensive universities?

Huo: Normal universities have more restrictions, while comprehensive universities have more academic freedom. The development focus of teachers' innovation ability is relatively low, because they focus on teaching students well. Teachers in comprehensive universities have more personality in terms of innovation ability. The most central characteristic of normal university teachers should be on teacher education. There's got to be more first-rate achievements on teacher education. Chinese teachers are very dedicated and should have their own characteristics in the world. In addition, I think teachers of normal university are less confident than those of science and engineering.

2 On personnel system
2.1 On resource allocation

Interviewer: What are the factors that promote and hinder the academic innovation ability of the university teachers in resource allocation mechanism?

Huo: The macro aspect is right. But the micro-mechanism needs to be strengthened. For example, discipline construction mainly focuses on discipline leaders, doctoral programs, master programs, laboratories, bases, and research teams. In fact, there are schools, journals, and academic research bases for discipline construction. These micro-mechanisms have a great influence on students. China's relative weakness is that we have no world-renowned academic leaders. But more importantly, foreign researchers focus on school teams, and school ideas can be passed down from generation to generation. However, once our academic leader dies, we can't inherit it. No inheritance, no innovation.

Interviewer: What are the causes of promotion or hindrance?

Huo: There are many deficiencies in micro-mechanism and academic environment.

Interviewer: Based on the six innovation index systems proposed by us, how to improve the existing resource allocation mechanism to improve teacher's innovation?

Huo: The most fundamental way is depending on our own teachers and students. Education is a long-term career.

2.2 On selection and appointment

Interviewer: What are the factors that promote and hinder the academic innovation ability of the current universities teachers in selection and appointment mechanism?

Huo: Now we mainly evaluation comprehensively by achievements, which is decided by leaders.

Interviewer: How to improve the selection and employment mechanism based on the innovation index system?

Huo: Necessary investigation is required. But the key is to have a long-term mechanism and a long-term plan for the cultivation of teachers' creativity.

2.3 On evaluation and assessment

Interviewer: Putting the indicator system aside, what aspects do you think innovation should be evaluated from?

Huo: Now we mainly focus on the efficiency and outcomes. Now we don't care about the spirit of innovation, we can only see the results first. So efficiency is a more operational indicator.

Interviewer: In the case of the same articles, what aspects should be assessed on teacher innovation?

Huo: In my opinion, as a scholar, innovation is not the most important thing. The most important thing is a national spirit, such as the attitude toward academics and the relationship with colleagues. I really appreciate that teachers give in-depth guidance in some good universities. Only when teachers and students make progress together can they have persisting power. To be a teacher, the most important thing is not academic, but his character and style.

2.4 On incentive and security

Interviewer: What are the promoting and hindering factors for the academic innovation of teachers in the current universities in incentive and guarantee mechanism? What are the causes of promotion or hindrance?

Huo: Now the reward is not enough, we should increase the reward. In addition, other mechanisms should be gradually improved. We should give more awards to young and middle-aged people and less to academic leaders.

Interviewer: What is the difference in the incentive mechanism between young and middle-aged teachers and older teachers?

Huo: We should not only pay attention to published papers. If a teacher has papers or books or teaches well, he should be awarded. Young teachers should be encouraged to keep their research directions stable and produce more achievements and good achievements. There should be differences between academic leaders.

6.27 Shaanxi Normal University—School of Literature: Li

6.27.1 High-Frequency Words

Innovation sense	Academic interests
Undergraduates	System reforming
Tenured faculty	

6.27.2 Key Points of Interview

1 On reasonability of the indicator system

Interviewer: Do you think the indicator system is reasonable? Do you have any suggestions?

Li: It feels that there is a big gap in the concept of innovation at home and abroad. Innovation country needs innovation talent. Innovation talent needs innovation education. Innovation education needs innovation teacher. Innovation ultimately requires an innovative class. The current curriculum stifles students' sense of innovation. The teacher talked on and the students are not allowed to talk. The teacher teaches according to the teaching plan and textbook, and the student learns according to what the teacher says. Foreign students study in advance. They go into class with questions and go out with questions. Domestic students come into the classroom with problems, but go out without problems. We should start from kindergarten to create innovative country. Domestic teaching values time over efficiency. Chinese people attach great importance to innovation, but teachers have no ability to innovate. The cultivation of innovation should start from the baby, and start from the cultivation of interest. When students are eager to learn, they will have many ideas. And then there will be a debate among the students, and there's innovation. Many people who don't read much are better able to adapt to society and innovate. Innovation needs direction. Domestic orientation is quantity, not quality. This index system is a self-test. It takes me a long time to think about it. The index system is for scientific research, but the teaching ability of university teachers is more important. More attention should be paid to undergraduate teaching in talent cultivation.

Interviewer: What is the difference in innovation between teachers in normal schools and teachers in comprehensive universities?

Li: The normal universities cultivate teachers and indirectly promote innovation through training innovative students. The innovations of comprehensive universities are immediately effective.

2 On personnel system
2.1 On resource allocation

Interviewer: What are the factors that promote and hinder the academic innovation ability of the university teachers in resource allocation mechanism? What are the causes of promotion or hindrance?

Li: The universities' facilities are not designed for innovation, but for discipline construction and school development. The measure of innovation is still published articles.

2.2 On selection and appointment

Interviewer: What are the factors that promote and hinder the academic innovation ability of the current universities teachers in selection and appointment mechanism? What are the causes of promotion or hindrance?

Li: Nowadays, it is difficult to confer academic titles for university teachers, only doctors can be evaluated. Recently only overseas doctors can be evaluated. Some teachers with several academic achievements can't teach students. But they can be promoted to professors quickly.

Interviewer: How to improve the selection and employment mechanism based on the innovation index system?

Li: As for the teachers from foreign contrives, they should participate in the defense meeting in the assessment of teaching and make a report in the assessment of research.

2.3 On evaluation and assessment

Interviewer: What are the promoting and hindering factors for the academic innovation of teachers in the evaluation mechanism of university teachers at present? What are the causes of promotion or hindrance? Based on the six innovation index systems proposed by us, how to improve the existing assessment and evaluation mechanism to improve teacher innovation?

Li: We should reform the evaluation system. Administrative agency evaluation, expert evaluation, and student evaluation can be added into the system.

2.4 On incentive and security

Interviewer: Based on the six innovation index systems proposed by us, how to improve the existing incentive and guarantee mechanism to improve teacher innovation?

Li: As long as the university wants to inspire teachers, there are many ways. They should gather the teacher to discuss. But the most immediate incentives are job titles. If teachers are not active in class reforming, they should be encouraged to carry out class reforming and be provided with financial support. If teachers are highly motivated, we can set it as a basic requirement. SNNU is studying the tenured faculty. We try to stop evaluating teachers who have an academic interest and just provide them with security and spiritual rewards. The young professors should teach well first and then get research funds. As for teachers in sports, music, and art, we can see whether they are national athletes or not. In addition to the above, I have some other suggestions. You should first understand the current state of innovation and then study the institutional norms and incentives. Then use students' initiative to create an innovative atmosphere. The third is letting students enjoy your class. If they are interested, they will have a sense of innovation.

6.28 Shaanxi Normal University—Social Sciences Administration Department: Ma

6.28.1 High-Frequency Words

Teaching innovation	
Research innovation	Resource allocation
Management innovation	

6.28.2 Key Points of Interview

1 On reasonability of the indicator system

Interviewer: Do you think the indicator system is reasonable? Do you have any suggestions?

Ma: The way of development in each era is different, so is the way of human development. Different development times determine the different human development modes. We should talk about the innovative ability of teachers according to the characteristics, pattern, and people of the times. The innovation of teacher's ability must be based on the pattern and characteristics of the times. As to whether the indicator system is reasonable or not, I am not sure whether the proposal is reasonable since I have not studied it. The index system is set according to intension. Do we have other indicators? What drives innovation? On the other hand, my personal feeling is that the indicator system refers more to scientific research. In fact, there are problems in academic innovation of talent cultivation. The innovation of talent cultivation is reflected in teaching and scientific research. If it is sorted by the first-level dimension of the indicator system, it should be knowledge, psychology, and society, because knowledge is the foundation of innovation. The order embodies the inherent logic of the indicators. I think the index system can be more abundant and more perfect. More dimensions might be involved, but I'm not sure what they are. In terms of specific and detailed indicators, I think literature review and knowledge integration ability should belong to knowledge ability, not psychological ability. The ability of academic criticism and reflection belongs not only to knowledge but also to academic insight. As to whether you should put critical and reflective ability into psychological ability, I have not made clear.

Interviewer: Are there other elements of innovation besides these six indicators? What is unique about teacher educators?

Ma: Normal university teachers are educating people. They should not only impart knowledge but also educate people, involving the formation of the next generation's world outlook and values. Teachers of normal university have higher requirements and more responsibilities. Teachers of normal university must have comprehensive ability to ensure that students are trained to be excellent talents. For teachers in normal schools, doing is more important than speaking.

Interviewer: What is the difference in innovation between teachers in normal schools and teachers in comprehensive universities?

Ma: Teachers should have a unique way to cultivate talents. They should have a choice on ways of educating, teaching methods, and teaching contents. They need to talk more about excellent culture and talk less about negative aspects. Children who grow up in a healthy environment are more likely to be healthy and have a better chance of development. Teachers should hold a positive attitude toward students. Teacher's innovation should include teaching innovation. A teacher's education style can affect students' life. Ideological innovation is the biggest innovation. This is probably the biggest difference between teachers of normal universities and those of comprehensive universities. The innovation of normal university in education is always based on the innovation of scientific research. Many scientists are also educators. Therefore, it is wrong to separate teaching innovation from scientific research innovation. Scientific research innovation is the basis of education innovation. Since teacher innovation is proposed, we should combine teaching innovation and scientific research innovation.

2 On personnel system
2.1 On resource allocation

Interviewer: What are the factors that promote and hinder the academic innovation ability of the university teachers in resource allocation mechanism?

Ma: Different universities have different historical traditions, resources, and management methods, so it is difficult to have a unified standard. The standard of resource allocation is closely related to the universities' historical tradition, resource quantity, and category. It is not possible to generalize which resource allocation methods are promoting or hindering to universities. In China, administrative department plays a controlling role in resource allocation. Such a system can be a hindrance to solving urgent problems, but it can be a boost to other problems.

Interviewer: Which resource allocation of SNNU has promoted the innovation of teachers?

Ma: We do not have a truly good mechanism for allocating resources. The most important principles of resource allocation are fairness and openness. The problem is how to integrate and allocate the resources of each department. The key is the structure of resource allocation.

Interviewer: Based on the six indicators, how to improve the resource allocation and personnel system?

Ma: The principle should be centered on scientific research and teaching. One thing to pay attention to resource allocation is to improve management level. To realize the innovation of teachers, it is important to realize the management innovation.

2.2 On evaluation and assessment system

Interviewer: What are the factors that promote and hinder the academic innovation ability of the current universities teachers in evaluation and assessment system? What are the causes of promotion or hindrance?

Ma: At present in China, on the whole, the number of papers, the evaluation of publishing houses and so on can promote the academic development. This is necessary. A certain amount of fundamental and repetitive research is also necessary. On academic research, it is necessary to assess 90% of people in terms of articles, but 5% should be assessed in other forms. Some assessments are too frequent, which is unnecessary. Assessment period should be adjusted, 3–5 years is the most appropriate.

Interviewer: How do you judge the creativity of teachers who have the same number of achievements?

Ma: Part of the evaluation of innovation is by journals, presses, and some other ways. There are peer reviews in journal reviews. We should set some requirements for 95% of people, manage their goals, and promote their innovation.

Interviewer: Based on the index system, how to improve the assessment system?

Ma: This index system is only a theoretical study. The real system is more of a management problem. On the one hand, teachers should cultivate the spirit of innovation; on the other hand, they should take innovation as a pursuit. At the same time, we use the policies to encourage the teachers.

Interviewer: How to see whether a teacher has academic pursuit or not?

Ma: Some people may just take classes and do nothing else. We need to create an incentive atmosphere through policies.

2.3 On incentive and security

Interviewer: What are the promoting and hindering factors for the academic innovation of teachers in the incentive and security mechanism of university teachers at present? What are the causes of promotion or hindrance?

Ma: First, there should be good policies; second, there should be a relatively basic material guarantee; third, there should be policy orientation and promotion. On the one hand, it provides working conditions; on the other hand, it provides living security. Compensation is also an important mechanism. Teachers now treat this job more as a means of making a living. We can only promote teachers through policies to do researches. The incentive mechanism is nothing more than fame and profit, spiritual, and material rewards. The safeguard mechanism is to provide conditions for them. The administrative department must elect a good president. The real educator should be elected as president. The principal's style and ideas determine the mechanism and top-level design of a university. But real problems are more complex than theoretical assumptions. It is very prudent for any department to come up with a policy. The policy is the result of the investigation and compromises. But policies are unlikely to take care of everyone's needs.

6.29 Shaanxi Normal University—Wang

6.29.1 High-Frequency Words

A narrow range of knowledge	Basic skills
Ability of capturing and digesting knowledge	Basic knowledge
Teaching ability	

6.29.2 Key Points of Interview

1 Basic question of subgroups

Interviewer: Do you think the indicator system is reasonable? Do you have any suggestions? How to evaluate teachers' innovation?

Wang: Teachers nowadays have a narrow range of knowledge. Innovation requires basic skills first. I think we should study the training mechanism in addition to the personnel system. My own practice is to organize discussion classes and presentations, and encourage students and young teachers to attend academic conferences. It is very important to consolidate the foundation. As a college teacher, we are never too old to learn. We should gain new insights through reviewing old material. All six aspects of the indicator system are good. There are some personal experiences that are already mentioned in the indicators. I think learning is about respect and transcendence. To learn, we should respect others first. Respect is the ability to seriously read others' books and achieved results. To transcend means we can't be limited by them. This is the reconsidering and critique ability. It is the information society now. The natural science development is simply changing with each passing day. Should the ability of being sensitive to information, capturing information and digesting information be come up with? If you can't detect the information and the latest research related to your research, you will lose the opportunity for innovation. We must be able to keep pace with the times. How to keep up with the times? First is to have solid foundation, second is to be sensitive to new information, which is interdisciplinary ability. I mean we should be sensitive to information, be able to capture it and digest it and let it be a part of ourselves. Then we can make innovation combined with our major. I find that many young teachers have great ambitions and plan to learn a lot. But they don't want to do the most solid work. My experience is that more haste and less speed. We also should accumulate. The knowledge pedigree ability is very good. We should be clear about which problems needed to be solved.

Interviewer: What abilities do basic researches need?

Wang: I'm not familiar with these abilities. But the most important ability is being clear with basic knowledge.

Interviewer: Does the basic knowledge mean knowledge within the discipline?

Wang: Yes. One can innovate if he has a firm knowledge foundation.

Interviewer: What is the difference in innovation between teachers of normal universities and teachers of comprehensive universities?

Wang: Teachers in normal colleges should pay more attention to teaching methods, which may be the difference.

2 On personnel system
2.1 On resource allocation

Interviewer: What are the factors that promote and hinder the academic innovation ability of the university teachers in resource allocation mechanism? What are the causes of promotion or hindrance? Based on the six innovation index systems proposed by us, how to improve the existing resource allocation mechanism to improve teacher innovation?

Wang: In my opinion, the most important resource allocation is books and materials, as well as experimental means and facilities.

2.2 On selection and appointment

Interviewer: How to assess their innovation when hiring new teachers?

Wang: Our school is doing better now. In addition to the number of published papers, we also see the teacher's teaching effect. And now the teaching load is added into the assessment system. If the teaching workload is not up to the standard, the teacher is not qualified to apply for the professional title. There was a time when we only looked at the number of articles published by teachers. Now we also look at teaching levels and teachers' morality.

2.3 On evaluation and assessment system

Interviewer: What are the factors that promote and hinder the academic innovation ability of the current universities teachers in evaluation and assessment system? What are the causes of promotion or hindrance? Based on the six indicators of innovation proposed by us, how to improve the existing assessment and evaluation mechanism to improve teachers' innovation ability?

Wang: Logical construction ability should be considered in the evaluation mechanism. Reflective ability is also very important. The ability of being sensitive to information, being able to capture it and digest it is necessary.

Interviewer: What is special about the evaluation mechanism of teachers' innovation ability from normal universities?

Wang: We should set up an assessment system that does not rely solely on the number of articles published. One way to do that is to train teachers and then have them write about it and use this as a factor for teachers' promotion. In fact, these problems are hard to solve. The current leadership lacks stability. Teaching philosophy should be consistent.

2.4 On incentive and security

Interviewer: What are the promoting and hindering factors for the academic innovation of teachers in the incentive and security mechanism of university teachers at present? What are the causes of promotion or hindrance?

Wang: In terms of incentive and security mechanism, each school has different degrees of rewards. In SSNU, teachers will get 300 Yuan a month for 3 years as rewards once they published an SCI paper. It's good for the rise in school rankings. The bad thing is that many people become desperate for quick results in writing. But the rewards are necessary. It's hard to keep balance.

Interviewer: Can the six capability indicators correspond to the four types of mechanisms to improve teacher innovation?

Wang: The resource allocation of books and materials is closely related to the comprehensive academic ability. Resource allocation is also closely related to the ability to collect knowledge and historical materials.

6.30 Shaanxi Normal University—School of Psychology: You

6.30.1 High-Frequency Words

Information literacy	De-administration
Research innovation	Resource allocation
Teaching innovation	

6.30.2 Key Points of Interview

1 On reasonability of the indicator system

Interviewer: Do you think the indicator system is reasonable? Do you have any suggestions? How to evaluate teachers' innovation ability?

You: As a kind of ability, literature review ability is not called literature review ability, but information literacy. It refers to the ability and awareness to obtain information, and the analysis and summary of information. In fact, it refers to how to find information. Literature review and comprehensive intercross ability can be integrated into information literacy ability. What does interdisciplinary intersecting mean? You should change the word into communication between fields. What is the difference between academic critical ability and academic evaluation ability? What is the difference in evaluate ability between academic critical ability and academic cooperative ability? The academic ability, communication ability, and coordinate ability are for people while the academic evaluation ability is for a task and efficiency. So the questions should be clearer.

Interviewer: What is the difference in innovation between teachers of normal universities and teachers of comprehensive universities?

You: Science and engineering majors pay more attention to innovative solutions to problems. The humanities may attach more importance to the acquisition, combing, and analysis of literature.

2 On personnel system
2.1 On resource allocation

Interviewer: What are the factors that promote and hinder the academic innovation ability of the university teachers in resource allocation mechanism? What are the causes of promotion or hindrance?

You: Our university administration is not scientific enough. The allocation of scientific resources in universities is not scientific. Realizing scientific allocation is important. The tasks and functions of departments are related to resource allocation. The problem of unreasonable resource allocation is a problem that should be studied scientifically, not solved administratively.

2.2 On selection and appointment

Interviewer: What are the factors that promote and hinder the academic innovation ability of the current university teachers in selection and appointment mechanism? What are the causes of promotion or hindrance?

You: It's still the problem of human resource allocation. We should bring in the best talent, that's the principle. How to evaluate their future development is a key issue. It is problematic to define proportions from an artificial perspective.

Interviewer: What do you think of innovation when bringing in talent?

You: University teachers should not only focus on academic innovation, but also on teaching innovation. Teaching innovation is an important indicator. It's a pity that the index system only reflects academic innovation.

Interviewer: How to improve the selection and appointment system based on the index system?

You: The index system should not be used to evaluate a teacher. It should be used to evaluate a work. The core is literature synthesis ability and critical reflection ability.

2.3 On evaluation and assessment system

Interviewer: What are the factors that promote and hinder the academic innovation ability of the current universities teachers in evaluation and assessment system? What are the causes of promotion or hindrance? How to improve it?

You: The academic evaluation mechanism is too crude. The assessment and evaluation mechanism should be more detailed. If the humanities were simply reviewed every 3 years, it might not promote innovation, but eliminate it. In engineering and science, you can't just look at the influencing factors, and you have to divide the disciplines. Subdisciplines within the same discipline should also be distinguished, not only by influencing factors but also by their relative positions within the discipline. There should be a period of assessment for each subject. The humanities have a relatively long period.

2.4 On incentive and security

Interviewer: What do you think of the current incentive and guarantee mechanism for university teachers' academic innovation?

You: The teacher's motivation is both material and spiritual. The core problem is that teachers' innovation ability is different, and the incentive system should be very different.

Interviewer: Do other people need incentives?

You: We need to motivate others. Eighty percent of people maintain the university and 20% lead the university. These few people are very important to the development of the university.

6.31 Shanghai Jiaotong University (SJTU)—Institute of Higher Education: Liu

6.31.1 High-Frequency Words

Academic innovation ability	Academic accumulation
Academic foundation	Academic evaluation
Academic leaders	Academic awards
Self-fulfillment	

6.31.2 Key Points of Interview

1 On selection and appointment system

Interviewer: When selecting and recruiting young teachers, will you take innovation into account?

Liu: It is certainly considered, and its weight is very high in the selection indicator system. Innovation is closely related to academic accumulation, without which there is no innovation. We evaluate their creativity mainly in terms of academic accumulation. For all candidates, the first interview is to do an academic report, by which we can evaluate his responsiveness and communication ability. We will consider the university where he graduated from, but the report is more important.

Interviewer: Do you have any special requirements in terms of education background and achievements?

Liu: No, we don't. In fact, sometimes his early achievements don't matter, which we don't pay special attention to. What we actually care is his academic accumulation and responsiveness. We still will set some standards about educational background and so on. But personally, I'm not inclined to list some indicators. I think everyone can express themselves. In general, we offer candidates an opportunity for an interview.

Interviewer: What are the indicators that your school focuses on when recruiting teachers?

Liu: The index of our school is very simple. The candidate should get his or her doctor's degree from the overseas university or world famous university. What's more, the graduates of this school cannot stay.

2 On evaluation and examination

Interviewer: From the perspective of your research, what are the factors that affect the academic innovation of the university faculty?

Liu: The evaluation or evaluation system is not conducive to academic development. Any evaluation will boost what you want, as long as the indicator system is designed to meet your starting point. The most important is we have to be clear about what kind of teachers do we really need.

Interviewer: At present, most universities take scientific research output as the most important criterion to evaluate teachers. Do you think this can promote the development of teacher innovation?

Liu: Of course it can. But I do have an idea of what kind of effect your evaluation is going to have, and that's the key thing. But now the evaluation falls into a circle. There seem to be no evaluation criteria without quantification standards. I think it's just a tool, not the whole thing. But at the moment it seems to be the only standard because it is the most convenient.

3 On incentive and security mechanism

Interviewer: Academic leaders may take up administrative positions. What effect do you think this may have on his innovation?

Liu: Academic leaders and proxies should be held by people with strong academic ability. At least they should have stronger academic insight ability. However, I think few academic leaders will hold the positions of administrative service departments. If one takes a long time to do administrative work, it's basically hard to get back to academic work. But in social science, this may be different. Sometimes it's good for his academic development. The key is to classify.

Interviewer: The school will promote the development of teachers' innovation through scientific research funds or national research funds and honor systems, such as the Changjiang Scholar and Zijiang Scholar. Do you think these really work?

Liu: I haven't done any research on that. In fact, I think the talent awards are definitely needed, especially in such a competitive era. You may give up a lot of good people by not rewarding them. I think there is a lot of overlap in the current talent incentive policy, or the directionality is very unclear. From the perspective of cultivation, it should be divided into stages, and the cultivation goal should be very clear. But to a large extent, the Changjiang scholars and outstanding young teachers have actually become a kind of honor. If it's an honor, it's actually a reward for your early work, not a promotion for your later work.

Interviewer: Is there any difference in the incentive and safeguard measures for young teachers and young backbone teachers in SJTU?

Liu: Actually, our school is not representative. One is that our school is very small; the other is that we have only run for more than 2 years, which is also very short. According to my research, such hierarchical management and hierarchical reward mechanism are not particularly good. Not just our schools, but across the whole country, people pay more attention to lagging evaluation. For example, there are many academicians who are supposed to retire after the review. But because of the academician, he will not retire. If he doesn't retire, his achievements aren't particularly impressive. And he may care more about the researchers who came after him. His creativity may have declined, but it may have helped in other ways. So it's hard to say. Maybe it makes a big difference, maybe there are problems like this or that. In general, I think the country's attention to young teachers is still too weak. Today's pay system often makes life especially tough for young teachers. Our basic security now cannot meet their basic living needs, which is problematic. In fact, the reform of the salary system should be a guaranteed system in the future. It's not an efficient way to get paid through competition. When such a guaranteed salary system is established, the living environment of our teachers may be much better. Teachers should not rely on projects to improve their treatment. A project should be something of honor, not something of substance.

Interviewer: What aspects do you think should be done to improve the teacher motivation and guarantee mechanism?

Liu: By salaries. Every university should have lots of money as scientific research funds. The universities guarantee the basic salary. They cannot let the teachers earn their salary through scientific researches. Another phenomenon is that schools now often use average salaries to represent teachers' pay. In fact, this is extremely unscientific because subjects are different. The country still should do more work on this kind of safeguard system.

4 On university teachers and innovation

Interviewer: What do you think is the relationship between university teachers' creativity and teachers themselves?

Liu: In such a situation, I think, it is relatively early for teachers to be innovative. Maslow's hierarchy of needs tells us that the self-actualization needs can be met only after a number of low-level needs have been met. Self-actualization is the highest requirement. In China, probably many people do not reach such a level. Especially for young teachers, they are still in the stage of unmet needs for survival. Without changing other factors, it is impossible to think about self-fulfillment now. The reason for the unsatisfactory may be that the conditions and the environment are not good enough; the other may be that there are problems in the big direction, may be unrealistic requirements. We all have a desire for self-fulfillment and living a decent life. People will have the need for self-fulfillment when they are living a decent life.

6.32 Southwest University—Chen

6.32.1 High-Frequency Words

Academic innovation ability	Teaching and doing research
Academic autonomy	Academic quality
Academic cooperation ability	

6.32.2 Key Points of Interview

1 On the rationality of the index system

Interviewer: Do you think our six indicators of innovation are reasonable? Do you have any suggestions? How to evaluate the innovation of teachers?

Chen: On one hand, the indicator system is too detailed to do the research. On the other hand, the indicator system is too professional. "The ability to collect historical material" is a little broad. "Academic intuition" is more abstract. If there are too many indicators, it is too troublesome to operate.

Interviewer: The questions are too many and board?

Chen: Be more popular and don't be too professional.

Interviewer: Are these indicators related to the dimensions of teachers' innovation?

Chen: This is okay.

Interviewer: What is unique about the teacher educators? What are the differences in innovation between teachers from normal universities and those from comprehensive universities?

Chen: Fundamentally, they are no different in terms of academic innovation. They just focus on different areas. Normal education pays more attention to education dynamics, basic education and the whole world education dynamics. The comprehensive universities will pay more attention to their own field problems.

2 On personnel system

2.1 On resource allocation

Interviewer: What are the factors that promote and hinder the academic innovation ability of the university teachers in resource allocation mechanism? What are the causes of the promotion or hindrance? Based on the six innovation index systems proposed by us, how to improve the existing resource allocation mechanism to improve teachers' innovation?

Chen: Academic leaders control academic resources, but they are not necessarily creative. Research funding should be divided into two parts, one for individuals or teams, the other for research teams and universities. The universities know who can do the researches. This gives teachers who have been willing to do this research for a long time the opportunity to participate in the research. Research funds should be divided into two parts. Some can be got by declaring and some are designed from the bottom to up by research universities. Top-down and bottom-up should be combined.

Interviewer: Which ability in the indicator system do you think can get help in providing academic resources to teachers?

Chen: Academic autonomy ability needs to be strengthened. Changing the system of resource allocation can mobilize teachers' autonomy.

2.2 On selection and appointment

Interviewer: What are the factors that promote and hinder the academic innovation ability of the university teachers in selection and appointment mechanism? What are the causes of the promotion or hindrance? Based on the six innovation index systems proposed by us, how to improve the existing selection and appointment to improve teachers' innovation?

Chen: Teachers are still judged on their achievements. Some teachers were more productive when they were students, but they don't have a strong innovative ability. The administrative department is responsible for the assessment, without examining the potential. In foreign countries, professors would talk to candidates and then evaluate them while the HR department has no right to evaluate them. The role of experts should be played in selection and appointment. Experts can see clearly the breadth and depth of academic knowledge and the understanding of the problem. Some of the papers were issued along with the subject, which did not indicate his academic potential.

Interviewer: When you are interviewing a teacher, what do you mainly look at?

Chen: The first is teaching ability and the second is academic quality by talking. We not only look at the paper but also the background of the paper and the author's views on the issue.

2.3 On assessment and evaluation

Interviewer: What are the factors that promote and hinder the academic innovation ability of the university teachers in assessment and evaluation mechanism? What are the causes of the promotion or hindrance? Based on the six innovation index systems proposed by us, how to improve the existing assessment and evaluation system to improve teachers' innovation?

Chen: It is very difficult to assess academic innovation in academic system.

Interviewer: Whether the evaluation mechanism of achievements assessment can promote the development of innovation?

Chen: It does promote. But psychologically, the system is too professional to carry out. Assessments of teachers are conducted by the personnel department, the department of science technology or assessment center rather than by professional people.

Interviewer: Does the system hinder the development of innovation?

Chen: The standards are too uniform. It is impossible to judge innovation ability by valuing quantity, hierarchy and influencing factors of papers. It is a question whether the ability of academic innovation of teachers can be assessed through articles. But now we don't have any other method. Young teachers can't be innovative in a short time. They need to cultivate innovation in the course of academic research.

Interviewer: What do you think of innovation?

Chen: The system of higher education has to change. For universities, the teacher's task should be combined with the basic duties. This kind of innovation is permanent. To maintain the innovative ability of university teachers, it should be related to the responsibilities. The creativity of teachers is related to interest and professional belief.

Interviewer: You mentioned changing the teachers' fickleness?

Chen: We should respect the rules of academic growth of teachers. However, the current national evaluation method has influenced the teachers' long-term attention to problems and led to short-term innovation. A large number of achievements don't represent the ability to innovate. Now we evaluate whether a person is innovative or not based on his achievements. But none of the evaluation mechanisms have long drawn the attention of teachers to research. Now the evaluation time is too short to let teachers calm down to do more creative researches.

Interviewer: Where is the root of this irrational method?

Chen: The fundamental value orientation at the national level is important.

Interviewer: What abilities in the indicator system do you think can be examined?

Chen: The cooperative spirit of university teachers is not good. Academic cooperative ability is very important. There is very little assessment of participation right now. The truly innovative people in science were the ones who participated. This evaluation mechanism is not conducive to the development of innovation. Without the ability to collaborate and share, it's hard to innovate.

Interviewer: How can the personnel system be revised to assess the innovative ability of participants?

Chen: Now the evaluation is mainly about the results. You can evaluate a team. But now the assessment is all about the individuals. Individuals are assessed by the team, while the teams are assessed by the university.

2.4 On incentive and security mechanism

Interviewer: Is there any advanced experience abroad?

Chen: The assessment of teachers in the United States and Canada is mainly on teaching. Teachers don't have too many scientific achievements. There is no such importance attached to scientific achievements.

Interviewer: What do foreign countries mainly concern about?

Chen: They stress the teacher's job. After the teachers have finished teaching, they will do scientific research. Motivation can lead to the improvement of teachers' innovation ability, but it will hinder the development of teachers' innovation ability at last.

Interviewer: How to motivate and protect these teachers who are willing to pursue academic careers?

Chen: Emphasize the job and combine teaching and research. You can't follow the hot spots. If you follow the hot spots, there will be a lot of achievements, but the academic quality will be greatly affected. Teaching and research are unified. Teaching is an important way of scientific research and teaching is not the burden of scientific research.

6.33 Southwest University—Huang

6.33.1 High-Frequency Words

Academic innovation ability	Motivation factors
Academic accumulation	Resource allocation
Teaching ability and research ability	Academic community

6.33.2 Key Points of Interview

1 Basic questions of subprojects

Interviewer: Do you think our six indicators of innovation are reasonable? Do you have any suggestions? How to evaluate the innovation of teachers?

Huang: The indicators are reasonable. However, there are many factors that affect academic innovation. Ability is a factor, but motivation is another factor. Motivation is about personality. You need to think about which dimensions of motivation should be in and which are the most important. The motivation to satisfy academic interest and curiosity is different from the motivation to seek fame and fortune. Innovation isn't all about money. A lot of innovation happens in tough conditions. Teachers can innovation with curiosity rather than with pressure. The motivation is a kind of value. There is another problem: knowledge accumulation is necessary for learning. Where should be academic experience and energy placed in? Academic accumulation affects the depth and breadth of the problem. The same question can be looked at from different angles. The key is what you focus on. Your indicator system is more focused on ability. There are some deep factors. In the academic research of the arts and sciences, interdisciplinary comprehensive ability is very important.

Interviewer: What is unique about the innovation of teacher educators? What are the differences in innovation between teachers in normal universities from those in comprehensive universities?

Huang: There is no essential difference. Teachers of normal university have a higher level of teaching, and the scientific research ability of comprehensive university is relatively strong. Teaching is an art which should bring beauty to students. Teaching is also a kind of scientific research. Only by taking scientific research very seriously and taking teaching as a process of cultivating people will you know what to do and what not to do. Teachers of normal universities should combine teaching with scientific research, which requires higher ability of them.

2 On personnel system
2.1 On resource allocation

Interviewer: What are the factors that promote and hinder the academic innovation ability of the university teachers in resource allocation mechanism? What are the causes of the promotion or hindrance? Based on the six innovation index systems proposed by us, how to improve the existing resource allocation mechanism to improve teachers' innovation?

Huang: The biggest problem of resource allocation is too many wasted resources, insufficient support for young teachers, and unfair resource allocation. The strong should have more resources, the weak should have less. Each department does its own job, and there will be no competition for resources. Administrative departments do well in service, teaching departments do well in teaching, and scientific research departments do well in scientific research.

2.2 On selection and appointment

Interviewer: How to evaluate the innovation of teachers when employing them?

Huang: It mainly focuses on scientific research and teaching. If he does not have one teaching materials, his teaching ability is not good. If he doesn't have a high-quality article, his research ability is not good. When we evaluate published articles, we should not only look at the level of the journal in which the article was published, but also see how valuable the article itself, which should be evaluated by experts. The assessment of ability should still be reflected by achievements. For example, his published textbooks, lecture notes in class, and even exam questions can reflect his innovative teaching ability.

Interviewer: How to evaluate the two teachers' level of innovation if they publish the same number of articles and the same level of journals?

Huang: They will be evaluated by the academic community.

2.3 On assessment and evaluation

Interviewer: What are the factors that promote and hinder the academic innovation ability of the university teachers in assessment and evaluation mechanism? What are the causes of the promotion or hindrance? Based on the six innovation index systems proposed by us, how to improve the existing assessment and evaluation system to improve teachers' innovation?

Huang: Current assessment is linked to bonus and professional titles. In addition, the exit mechanism within the university is insufficient. The rationality of assessment standards needs to be considered. If the university takes published papers of SCI as standards, teachers have to follow the directions and interests of foreigners. We will lose our academic autonomy. When can we have our special research? Engaging with international trend is different from keeping academic autonomy. In addition, academic evaluation should have multiple indicators. The Chinese characteristics in the study and the actual effects of the study on China's social development and even on local social development should be taken as indicators of academic evaluation system. This indicator system is a self-evaluation scale, which is certainly not enough. Everyone has a sense of self-affirmation. This evaluation system can be used to evaluate teachers' innovation ability, and it can be further improved after the first attempt. No questionnaire is perfect.

Interviewer: Who can also evaluate teachers?

Huang: They can be assessed by the teaching and research section and students. The weights should be different and they should have different questionnaires.

2.4 On incentive and security

Interviewer: What are the factors that promote and hinder the academic innovation ability of the university teachers in incentive and security mechanism? What are the causes of the promotion or hindrance? Based on the six innovation index systems proposed by us, how to improve the existing incentive and security mechanism to improve teachers' innovation?

Huang: Our school not only provides financial awards but also uses the points system. There is a problem in this kind of incentive system. It will form an incentive orientation focusing on quantity but not quality. The incentive mechanism should focus on quantity as well as quality and quantity.

Interviewer: How to evaluate the quality of academic achievements?

Huang: There are several methods. One is evaluated by the academic community, and another is evaluated by users of academic achievements, such as the government. The quality of academic achievements should be evaluated from a variety of perspectives. However, in practice, academic evaluation is influenced by interpersonal relationship and other factors.

6.34 Southwest University—Jin

6.34.1 High-Frequency Words

Academic innovation ability	New methods
Spiritual quotient	Values
Flowing	Academic community
Utilitarianism	

6.34.2 Key Points of Interview

1 Basic question of subprojects

Interviewer: Do you think our six indicators of innovation are reasonable? Do you have any suggestions? How to evaluate the innovation of teachers?

Jin: The current indicator system focuses on the personality quality of teachers, which is relatively static, such as psychology and knowledge. However, the ability of innovation should be realistic and involve the possibility and premise of innovation. The ability to innovate should be viewed dynamically. No matter how good the personal qualities are, there is no way to be creative without new methods and ideas. The academic innovation of universities teachers is not only to build basic ability. The whole process of research should be evaluated.

Interviewer: As for the basic abilities, do you think the indicator system is reasonable?

Jin: Li Kaifu once said that talents in the twenty-first century should have intelligence quotient, emotional quotient, and spiritual quotient. Social competence mainly involves emotional intelligence. But the lack of spiritual quotient is a problem of values. Scientific competence should include scientific spirit, scientific attitude, and scientific ethics.

Interviewer: Do you think there is anything else to add?

Jin: Add indicators about ethics and values.

Interviewer: What is unique about the innovation of teacher educators? What are the differences in innovation between teachers in normal universities from those in comprehensive universities?

Huang: There is no essential difference. Their cultivation subjects are different. They also have differences in the teaching process. Comprehensive university teaches focus on academic ability training while normal university teachers pay attention to the teaching of students.

2 On personnel system
2.1 On resource allocation

Interviewer: What are the factors that promote and hinder the academic innovation ability of the university teachers in resource allocation mechanism? What are the causes of the promotion or hindrance? Based on the six innovation index systems proposed by us, how to improve the existing resource allocation mechanism to improve teachers' innovation?

Jin: Teacher resource allocation mainly includes teacher allocation and training. Resource allocation has an impact on the social capability in the indicator system. Overall, resource allocation mechanisms are mandatory. There is little mobility of teachers. The lack of reasonable mobility is detrimental to the development of teachers' innovative social abilities. Many abilities are formed in the flow process.

Interviewer: How does it flow?

Jin: In a university system, teachers should be able to move freely. I can go to Peking University today and Tsinghua University tomorrow. Internal flows between universities are important. Today's universities are less mobile.

Interviewer: What are the causes of the less flowing?

Jin: On the one hand, the planning and enforcement of the system are too strong. On the other hand, it's not competitive enough.

2.2 On selection and appointment

Interviewer: How to judge the innovative ability of new teachers whose academic achievements are not abundant?

Jin: It depends on the interviewers of universities. We should look at his achievements, but not the number of articles. We should look at his way of thinking, his thoughts, his expressions, and other aspects through the articles. If a Ph.D. doesn't have a paper published, then we will look at his doctoral dissertation or the topic. Specific problems should be analyzed in detail. It is difficult to choose people according to the same standards. One's potential can be judged by the discussion in the academic committee. The article is not the most important while the potential is the most important. Potential can be judged by experience, doctoral thesis, human qualities, etc.

Interviewer: What abilities do you value most personally?

Jin: Personally, I think the experience is very important. At the same time, we should also look at the achievements, including the topic selection and writing, especially the topic selection of the doctoral dissertation. The judgment of academic innovation should be made by committees and peers.

Interviewer: What items are needed in selecting candidates?

Jin: Perception, attention, and recognition ability are not needed. However, literature review ability, interdisciplinary ability, and logic construction ability are needed.

2.3 On assessment and evaluation

Interviewer: What are the factors that promote and hinder the academic innovation ability of the university teachers in assessment and evaluation mechanism? What are the causes of the promotion or hindrance? Based on the six innovation index systems proposed by us, how to improve the existing assessment and evaluation system to improve teachers' innovation?

Jin: The assessment mechanism is result-oriented, and scientific research results are quantitatively oriented. There is a lack of effective evaluation system. We're too utilitarian.

Interviewer: How to evaluate teachers' academic achievements and abilities?

Jin: Evaluation should be based on integrity mechanism. Peer evaluation of the good achievements is very good. For example, I choose my good results this year, and then I ask five teachers to evaluate them. Two professors are from other universities and two are from my university.

Interviewer: How to evaluate innovation ability?

Jin: It's difficult to assess the basic ability of innovation, such as perception ability, attention ability, literature review ability, etc. The ability to innovate must be judged by something. Knowledge integration capability is an internal processing mechanism, which cannot be evaluated. This indicator system can be used as a reference in the training of university teachers, but it is difficult to be used as a standard for assessment.

2.4 On incentive and security

Interviewer: What are the factors that promote and hinder the academic innovation ability of the university teachers in incentive and security mechanism? What are the causes of the promotion or hindrance? Based on the six innovation index systems proposed by us, how to improve the existing incentive and security mechanism to improve teachers' innovation?

Jin: University incentive systems are materially oriented. This orientation is the root of utilitarianism. But what matters are dignity and the value of culture. It is important to create an atmosphere of free development for teachers.

Interviewer: How is cultural motivation reflected in measures?

Jin: The shaping of this culture is a long process. Substance-based reward systems are not acceptable.

Interviewer: Based on the index system, what can improve the mechanism?

Jin: Social innovation is valuable. Autonomy must be culturally guaranteed. Poor atmosphere building has an impact on ability. How to create an atmosphere of academic autonomy and academic cooperation ability according to the indicators should be considered.

6.35 Southwest University—Human Resource Office: Liu

6.35.1 *High-Frequency Words*

Academic innovation ability	Autonomy ability
Social ability	Mental ability
Resource allocation system	Research funds

6.35.2 Key Points of Interview

1 On the innovation indicators

Interviewer: Do you think our six indicators of innovation are reasonable? Do you have any suggestions? How to evaluate the innovation of teachers?

Liu: Some items in the system are too detailed and there is a crossover. For example, free press ability involves many external factors and it's not a personal ability. You can change it to the best effort I have paid in the publishing process. Social ability and academic sharing ability are more connected. Is autonomy ability a kind of social capacity? Autonomy ability and society ability are the relations of opposition and unity. Self-control ability should be mental ability.

Interviewer: Are psychology, knowledge, and social ability appropriate in terms of dimensions?

Liu: As for innovation knowledge ability, knowledge and innovation are two levels in nature. Knowledge is the study of predecessors. Innovation is the process of reprocessing knowledge and finding new theories, technologies or other aspects based on the understanding of nature and society. I agree with both psychological and intellectual abilities, but can social abilities be lumped together? Social skills are important, but not absolute. Cooperation is right, but not absolute. It is technically correct, but not rigorous. Scientific innovation depends on individuals. During the development of informatization, knowledge is valued more. Mental ability is very important. Mental ability refers to whether people are stable and whether it can provide strong psychological support for people to deal with problems when the academic environment is unfavorable. The dimensions are good, but they don't fit very well. Academic comprehensive ability, literature review ability, and knowledge integration ability do not belong to psychological ability. Literature review ability involves thinking and writing. There is no specific index for the dimension of mental ability. Mental ability refers to a person's state, which should refer to the academic psychological ability.

Interviewer: What does psychological ability include?

Liu: Psychological abilities include the ability to master oneself, resist temptations from the outside world and the ability of bearing the pressure of work tasks from the society and the work units. To make academic innovation, first is the interests, the second is the ability to eliminate the interference, the third is finding one's own way of combination and the last is the methods. All of these capabilities are required.

Interviewer: Is academic innovative knowledge capability reasonable?

Liu: As for knowledge, I think there are two aspects: one is ability to master knowledge, and the other is ability to reflect on others' knowledge.

Interviewer: What is unique about the innovation of teacher educators? What are the differences in innovation between teachers in normal universities from those in comprehensive universities?

Liu: There is no essential difference. Teachers of normal university and comprehensive university are similar in structure and humanity. Comprehensive universities have a complete set of subjects. The impact of these two universities on students is basically the same.

2 On personnel system
2.1 On resource allocation

Interviewer: What are the factors that promote and hinder the academic innovation ability of the university teachers in resource allocation mechanism? What are the causes of the promotion or hindrance?

Liu: There are many kinds of resource allocation mechanism in domestic universities. In this university, the promotion effect of academic innovation on teachers is that if they do well, more funds will be given, and it is more secure in the enrollment of students. It depends on how hard they work. There are differences in our evaluation. Humanity, science, and technology are not very understanding of each other. Different composition of leadership or evaluation groups leads to different understandings of different disciplines. We could not to recruit students and allocate resources. The most important thing is that the knowledge and understanding of the subject are too simple.

Interviewer: How to improve resource allocation?

Liu: If the allocation of resources is administered by the state, then a good evaluation mechanism, the results and the contribution to the university and to the society are important. Now there's a concept called performance. We allocate resources based on performance.

2.2 On selection and appointment

Interviewer: How to judge the innovative ability when hiring new teachers?

Liu: By judging the representative outcomes. We used to focus on quantity, and then on quantity and quality, but now we focus on representative outcomes. There are differences between theory and practice. In theory, teachers' innovative thinking is very important, but in practice, it is very difficult to evaluate. Opportunities should be given to teachers to innovate.

Interviewer: What should be provided for young teachers?

Liu: Provide various opportunities for them, such as the opportunity to promote education background, the opportunity to conduct academic exchanges and the opportunity to cooperate in scientific researches, etc.

2.3 On assessment and evaluation

Interviewer: Whether there is a mechanism to evaluate teachers' academic innovation?

Liu: There is no clear index to evaluate academic innovation. Assessment is the hardest thing, but also the most basic thing.

Interviewer: Based on the six innovation index systems proposed by us, how to improve the existing assessment and evaluation system to improve teachers' innovation?

Liu: First of all, we should learn from foreign countries, and then we should do it according to the actual situation of our university and country. People's ideas are hard to reverse. We should properly handle the distribution of interests.

Interviewer: How to promote the evaluation system?

Liu: You should solve the problem of who will make the indicator system and conduct the evaluation. The system should be operative and objective. The observation point has to be specific.

Interviewer: What are the factors that promote and hinder the academic innovation ability of the university teachers in incentive and security mechanism? What are the causes of the promotion or hindrance?

Liu: In addition to the normal funding for teaching and research results, our university has additional financial incentives, which is up to 100,000. There are different rewards at the school level and at the student level. For the old teachers, they can have the reward only when they have papers in good journal. To young and middle-aged teachers, they can get the rewards once they have achievements. Rewards vary depending on the objects. There is also special money for research projects.

Interviewer: How to motivate teachers who are good at academic work?

Liu: By evaluating. If they don't perform well during an employment period, they will be downgraded.

6.36 Southwest University Faculty of Arts–Liu

6.36.1 High-Frequency Words

Academic innovation ability	Academic achievements
Resource allocation system	Academic background
Teaching ability	

6.36.2 Key Points of Interview

1 On the innovation indicators

Interviewer: Do you think our six indicators of innovation are reasonable?

Liu: This system based on the frontier of psychology is good in theory, but there is no way to operate them in practice. On the one hand, hiring teachers is the task of the human resources department. On the other hand, it's impossible for personnel and management departments to hire people with indicator systems. Recruitment generally depends first on teaching ability and then on scientific research ability. Are systematic observation points, such as academic insight, evaluated by the individual or by other departments? Are they selective or not? This isn't conducive for academic innovation.

Interviewer: By the five-point scale.

Liu: The items are too detailed that it can be difficult to give the points by both oneself and managers. It's ok as a psychological self-test. Many indicators are subjective and difficult to judge. It is a very vague question for us to judge a teacher. As the teacher and the dean, we judge a teacher according to the terminal things, such as whether his research direction is stable, whether there is a connection between the results, and whether finally the article published in the high-level journals. Personally, I do not agree with judging the teacher's level by journals, but now there is no way. The level of a teacher depends on the results. Self-assessment is unreliable and troublesome. It is also not reasonable for the leaders or the teaching and research offices to make judgments.

Interviewer: So how do you design the evaluation mechanism for a certain part, such as literature review ability?

Liu: The ability of literature review can be reflected in the doctoral dissertation. It is not easy to design a mechanism without relying on specific topics and projects.

Interviewer: Assessments on partial abilities also should be made according to achievements?

Liu: How to evaluate a teacher's ability systematically? The cadre's meeting will carry on very detailed evaluation of the cadre, includes whether he drinks the wine, whether he accepts the ceremony and whether he likes to read books, etc.

Interviewer: Evaluation of facts?

Liu: They can also be assessed as a whole, based on ordinary performance. But the items were not designed clearly enough.

2 On personnel system
2.1 On resource allocation

Interviewer: What are the factors that promote and hinder the academic innovation ability of the university teachers in resource allocation mechanism? What are the causes of the promotion or hindrance?

Liu: China's resource allocation is unfair. There are differences in the allocation of resources between universities, for example, 985 universities have more resources. The allocation of resources in universities is also problematic. Science has more resources than liberal arts.

Interviewer: How to allocate resources based on innovation?

Liu: Resources will be allocated according to the discipline level, such as the first-level discipline will have more enrollment and research resources.

Interviewer: What is the impact on innovation?

Liu: It's motivating innovation. If there are less research, projects, and results, then there will be fewer enrollments. Away from projects, awards, and immediate interests, researches out of academic interests are really valuable.

Interviewer: How to take care of those who really do researches in system?

Liu: It can't be changed. Without papers, the university won't accept them.

2.2 On selection and appointment

Interviewer: What are the factors that promote and hinder the academic innovation ability of the university teachers in selection and appointment mechanism? What are the causes of the promotion or hindrance?

Liu: Neither Beijing normal university nor southwest university has a real hiring mechanism. Colleges have no exit mechanism. Personnel departments and colleges are afraid to weed out teachers. The fundamental problem is to change the university system. The evaluation cycle is too short now, and it's too utilitarian.

Interviewer: How to evaluate innovation when hiring new teachers?

Liu: It's time to think about their achievements, not their motivation. There is a group interview for a new teacher. It can be seen from the materials, such as the topic of the doctoral thesis, whether a teacher has the basic quality of engaging in research. Now we will also consider the study background, such as undergraduate and master's research background. Under the same conditions, we will choose the one with a better background rather than relationships and the tutor.

Interviewer: How to evaluate his research ability?

Liu: By seeing if his topic has academic value and whether it has the value that continues to study. Being able to teach is also ok. It mainly depends on the achievements, academic background, academic experience and the influence of published articles.

2.3 On evaluation and assessment

Interviewer: What are the factors that promote and hinder the academic innovation ability of the university teachers in evaluation and assessment mechanism? What are the causes of the promotion or hindrance?

Liu: You can't promote innovation through assessment. Whether a person can be a teacher or innovative is innate. Although there are teachers through efforts to achieve a certain level, but as a talent, he is very general. When hiring new teachers in the future, they have to give lessons for 3 months to see their state of mind, expression ability, etc.

Interviewer: Who will evaluate the teaching ability during the employment process?

Liu: Ten or twenty people, including academic leaders, personnel, and academic staff.

Interviewer: How does the conclusion that the teacher cannot teach well come out?

Liu: The first is student evaluation. But sometimes there are problems. Some teachers are not really bad, but have no teaching experience. Whether a teacher can give a lecture is a comprehensive judgment, including factors such as fluency, sense of humor, and appearance. In general, students' evaluation of their teachers is 80% accurate. It's hard to evaluate innovation. It depends on whether your academic achievements are recognized by the academic community. Being able to raise and solve problems in the field is innovation. Make innovation within the discipline, push the discipline progress a little bit and the thesis has value in the discipline domain are innovation.

Interviewer: What really demonstrates the innovation of teachers?

Liu: Work hard and make influential achievements in the discipline. High-level universities do not require high numbers of teachers' academic achievements because they trust academic committees. Academic authority is more destructive if it fails to exert its power properly. The reason why some people advocate a systematic evaluation system is that the objective system is free from human interference.

2.4 On incentive and security

Interviewer: What are the factors that promote and hinder the academic innovation ability of the university teachers in incentive and security mechanism? What are the causes of the promotion or hindrance?

Liu: First, there are basic guarantees. On the basis of basic guarantee, the reward is given according to the contribution without the top limitation. There is also the research points system. After each project and article, teachers will be given a different score. Points are accumulated and a reward is given when a certain amount is reached.

Interviewer: Incentives for academic innovation are material?

Liu: There are also honorary and title incentives.

6.37 Southwest University—Song

6.37.1 High-Frequency Words

Academic innovation ability	The ability to ask questions
the ability to solve problems	The operability of the system
Appointment system	

6.37.2 Key Points of Interview

1 On the innovation indicators

Interviewer: Do you think our six indicators of innovation are reasonable? Do you have any suggestions?

Song: As a whole, it is important to define the innovation ability. In innovation, one kind of ability is the ability to ask questions, and the second kind is the ability to solve problems. Sometimes, the ability to ask questions is more difficult than the ability to solve problems. The ability to ask questions is the foundation of innovation. The division of the system is basically ok, but there are two problems. Question 1: Does the index system have different weight? All indicators should be weighted. Question 2: is the academic knowledge pedigree appropriate? Are all indicators are named by "ability"? The system involves dimensions, first, second, and third indexes and observation points. There are three points need to be considered. First, the consistency of indicators and their connotation should be considered. Second, whether the observation point reflects the corresponding indicator should be considered. Third, the operability of the system should be considered. The indicator system is very difficult, which needed to be considered carefully. The index system is decomposed into three-level index system. Some of them can be quantitatively analyzed, while others cannot.

Interviewer: How to operate it?

Song: The first thing is to discuss carefully, the second is to try a little, and then is to organize multidisciplinary experts form statistics, evaluation, psychology, and logic to discuss.

Interviewer: What is unique about the innovation of teacher educators? What are the differences in innovation between teachers in normal universities from those in comprehensive universities?

Song: Normal university teachers' innovation includes academic innovation, teaching method innovation, and talent cultivation mode innovation. The innovation of normal universities should focus on the talent training mode and education method.

Interviewer: What's the difference in ability?

Song: To make students innovative, our teachers should be innovative in terms of teacher education.

2.1 On resource allocation

Interviewer: What are the factors that promote and hinder the academic innovation ability of the university teachers in resource allocation mechanism? What are the causes of the promotion or hindrance?

Song: Should we consider the differences between different types of universities and different subjects in the allocation of resources?

2.2 On evaluation and assessment

Interviewer: What are the factors that promote and hinder the academic innovation ability of the university teachers in evaluation and assessment mechanism? What are the causes of the promotion or hindrance?

Song: Can we adopt innovations in the employment system? Some universities use appointment system, some use personnel agency, some hire teachers for a year, some hire teaches all the time. Can we use different ways on selection appointment system?

Interviewer: What is the downside of the current selection system?

Song: Change lifetime system and use appointment system besides a few people.

2.3 On evaluation and assessment

Interviewer: What are the factors that promote and hinder the academic innovation ability of the university teachers in evaluation and assessment mechanism? What are the causes of the promotion or hindrance?

Song: At present, as for the assessment of teachers, many schools are engaged in the form, not really promoting the development of teachers through the process of teachers' evaluation. Academic papers are now highly valued. In terms of evaluation orientation, besides theoretical orientation, it should also be related to social value. Many universities have a very low application of scientific research achievements. The development of society should be considered.

2.4 On incentive and security

Interviewer: What are the factors that promote and hinder the academic innovation ability of the university teachers in incentive and security mechanism? What are the causes of the promotion or hindrance?

Song: There should be incentives and constraints.

6.38 Southwest University—Institute of Psychology: Zhang

6.38.1 High-Frequency Words

Academic innovation ability	Value orientation
the ability to find problems and analyze problems	Published papers
Professional dedication	De-administration

6.38.2 Key Points of Interview

1 On the innovation indicators

Interviewer: Do you think our six indicators of innovation are reasonable? Do you have any suggestions?

Zhang: The indicators are relatively comprehensive and operable. The third level indicators are more specific, and the later indicators are easier to quantify. So it's good in terms of structure and quantization. In my opinion, academic innovation ability depends on value orientation. Some people prefer to follow the rules, with no risk. Some people are willing to risk failure to innovate. This personality trait could affect innovation. Value orientation refers to whether teachers think innovation is important to them and whether they are willing to innovate. Teachers can be innovative, but they may not be willing to do it. There are many reasons, such as the possibility that innovation could affect the interests of vested interests. In addition to emphasizing knowledge and ability, it is also necessary to emphasize the transformation of potential possibilities into actions, the intrinsic motivation of innovation and the intrinsic value orientation of innovation.

Interviewer: Do you think the psychological ability of academic innovation is reasonable?

Zhang: I looked around and it was very comprehensive. Do you mention the ability to learn from foreign literatures in literature review ability? In the process of innovation, it is important to learn something from others. To reform, we should find and analyze problems. According to the present teaching situation, the ability to find problems and analyze problems does not seem to be clearly put forward.

Interviewer: What is unique about the innovation of teacher educators? What are the differences in innovation between teachers in normal universities from those in comprehensive universities?

Zhang: Comprehensive universities pay more attention to whether the students they cultivate can go to the forefront of scientific development and attach more importance to the source and foundation of academic innovation. Teachers in normal universities do not directly create science and technology, but train teachers in primary and secondary schools. The innovation ability of normal university cannot catch up with that of comprehensive university, but more attention is paid to human development and growth. Teachers should be more innovative in the development of pedagogy and psychology.

2 On the impact of personnel system on teachers' innovation
2.1 On resource allocation

Interviewer: What are the factors that promote and hinder the academic innovation ability of the university teachers in resource allocation mechanism? What are the causes of the promotion or hindrance? Based on the six innovation index systems proposed by us, how to improve the existing resource allocation mechanism to improve teachers' innovation?

Zhang: I think people are creative, just different. In resource allocation, different resources should be given to different people. We should give consideration to all aspects and give prominence to key points.

Interviewer: How to distinguish the grades?

Zhang: Although I oppose the results theory, at present, we have no other methods and we can only allocate resources based on the achievements.

2.2 On evaluation and assessment

Interviewer: What are the factors that promote and hinder the academic innovation ability of the university teachers in evaluation and assessment mechanism? What are the causes of the promotion or hindrance?

Zhang: First we will see his resume and published results. If the published results are generally up to our standards, then we will interview him. During the interview, an academic report should be made, during which his oral expression ability and teaching skills, as well as the depth of academic thoughts and the prospect of future development, are assessed. However, it is not very successful at present, so the effect of talent introduction is not good enough. On the contrary, the students we have cultivated have strong ability of innovation.

Interviewer: What other capabilities should you pay attention to?

Zhang: It's necessary to see his basic conditions and achievements. When selecting now teachers, we should pay more attention to research interests and professional dedication. Value orientation is very important.

2.3 On evaluation and assessment

Interviewer: Can the index system provide reference for the assessment and evaluation mechanism?

Zhang: Different evaluations are for different things. For example, the liberal arts should be judged by the standards of the liberal arts; the science should be judged by the standards of science. These are academic reviews, which are not the same as academic innovation.

Interviewer: What does an academic review cover?

Zhang: Such as awards, research projects, honorary titles, key laboratories or bases. These extensive reviews should be conducted according to certain procedures. The innovation system is a survey of the current situation and can even be used as a basis for teachers' self-improvement, but it can't be used as a means of administrative management.

2.4 On incentive and security

Interviewer: What are the factors that promote and hinder the academic innovation ability of the university teachers in incentive and security mechanism? What are the causes of the promotion or hindrance? Based on the six innovation index systems proposed by us, how to improve the existing incentive and security mechanism to improve teachers' innovation?

Zhang: At present, China's higher education problem is very big, which seriously hinders the development of teachers' ability. A lot of people think it should be de-administrated, but I don't think so. It's really all about evaluation and incentive systems, which pay more attention to results. Titles, honors, and projects are coming along with published papers. As a result, teachers are eager for quick success and instant benefits, but have no time to care about their own work and innovation in their own work. The invisible, slow, down-to-earth innovations are often suppressed. In terms of the evaluation of projects and awards, it is often judged by academic experts and academic authorities. The evaluation results are given in the name of the evaluation team, and the results are decided collectively. First, it is not an individual act, so no one can be consulted; second, it's a decision of authority; third, it has administrative relevance. This has many drawbacks in the actual operation. Instead of experts voting to decide whether or not to win, experts should set quantitative standards and publish them on the Internet. Applicants should grade themselves according to the standards, and then publish them on the Internet. It is then up to the administration to decide whether to award the prize. If the administrative decision is wrong, the administrative person should be responsible for it. If there is a problem with the standards, the experts should be held accountable. If the filer cheats, the filer is disqualified for the awards. There is now an academic field of a bunch of authoritative people who can help each other win prizes. It's also frustrating for innovation. People in their 70s and 80s have lost their ability of academic innovation, but they still reject new ideas and opinions from young people and suppress their development. This, on the one hand, suppressing the enthusiasm of young people, and on the other hand, making young teachers lose confidence and lose their academic aspirations.

Interviewer: How to encourage teachers to release innovation through incentive mechanism?

Zhang: The innovation of normal universities is ultimately for the development of students. Teachers are judged by their students' development in turn. The teacher is evaluated by the student's evaluation and the student's achievements.

Interviewer: What is the key to China's academic environment reform?

Zhang: Great reforms lead to emancipation of the mind, but great reforms are a long process. The first is the need that comes from the base; the second step is that some elites recognize this thing, summarize it and conduct propaganda, mobilization, and struggle. The third step involves political change. Although I am not in favor of de-administration, there should be accountability. The rules are not transparent or public. China is now moving to the second step.

6.39 Southwest University Office of Academic Affairs—Zhou

6.39.1 High-Frequency Words

Academic innovation ability	Five-point scale
Evaluation indicators	Interests
Meta-innovation	Spiritual stimulus

6.39.2 Key Points of Interview

1 On the innovation indicators

Interviewer: Do you think our six indicators of innovation are reasonable? Do you have any suggestions?

Zhou: The critical reflection ability as knowledge ability is a little far-fetched. It should belong to the psychological ability. And the comprehensive crossover ability belongs to the knowledge ability. Only with a solid foundation of knowledge can we achieve integration and crossing.

Interviewer: Is the indicator system sound?

Zhou: There is a cross within the index system. It is difficult to draw a clear line between each other. This indicator system is used for self-test. How to define its contents?

Interviewer: By the five-point scale.

Zhou: Chinese people fill out forms according to other people's needs, so it's not objective enough. If the indicator is self-testing, the teacher will have a subconscious sense of self-protection. The problem is how to solve the objective problem of teachers' self-test. The effectiveness and authenticity of the investigation remain to be considered. In addition, the concept of the index system is a little fuzzy. If the concept is not clear, or the boundaries are not clear, it is difficult for the teacher to figure out what you are trying to say. The most difficult problem in domestic evaluation is that many concepts are only understood in a macro sense, but they are often different in the real evaluation. Students may judge teachers poorly because of their own prejudices or unmet personal needs, or they may judge teachers well because they want to cater to them. The innovation of a domestic teacher is evaluated by journals and influence factors, but in fact, the people who win the Nobel Prize abroad are not the ones who have published many articles on SSCI. How to explain this phenomenon? For university faculty, it's hard to have one indicator of innovation. We usually evaluate a university by the degree level of teachers, major projects, the number of scholars of Yangtze River, the number of doctoral guides, the number of papers and scientific research achievements, but the actual situation is hard to tell.

Interviewer: What is unique about the innovation of teacher educators? What are the differences in innovation between teachers in normal universities from those in comprehensive universities?

Zhou: These don't exist. Innovation has nothing to do with the type of schools. There is no fundamental difference in the innovation of teachers in different schools.

2 On the impact of personnel system on teachers' innovation
2.1 On resource allocation

Interviewer: What are the factors that promote and hinder the academic innovation ability of the university teachers in resource allocation mechanism? What are the causes of the promotion or hindrance?

Zhou: At present, there is a great waste of human and material resources in universities. There are tens of millions of devices out there, which are wasteful. Some laboratory staff at the bottom is not valued, and these are the real people who do things.

Interviewer: Based on the six innovation index systems proposed by us, how to improve the existing resource allocation mechanism to improve teachers' innovation?

Zhou: Leaders should use their superior wisdom to allocate human and material resources. To allocate manpower and materials effectively, they should focus on making people use what they have and what they use. They should let people with different abilities do what is right for them. They should reasonably arrange people's work, fully respect their personality and value of work, and give full play to their abilities.

2.2 On evaluation and assessment

Interviewer: How to evaluate the potential of teachers when recruiting new teachers?

Zhou: Now we usually look at the current results, which show that he has the ability in the early stage. But that is wrong.

Interviewer: What abilities do you pay attention to?

Zhou: Traditionally we pay attention to the ability of expressing, logic, grasping knowledge, and summarizing. Interviews are important.

Interviewer: What else to look at besides the current results?

Zhou: The key is his ambition. The first is to see if he has enough energy and good health, mainly the spirit. But the general evaluation index tends not to see those. I usually look at people's potential comprehensively. Publishing many articles doesn't mean he has a strong ability to innovate.

2.3 On evaluation and assessment

Interviewer: How do you think teachers' creativity should be evaluated?

Zhou: I think no comment is the best comment. The innovation that we usually say includes meta-creativity, technology innovation, and digest-integrated type innovation. Different innovations have different values for society. The knowledge we have is abundant enough. We human beings do not lack original innovation, but what we lack is technological innovation and integrated innovation. Our country has led us to the path of meta-innovation, which has led to a lot of academic fraud. We allow some people to do meta-innovation, but it's a disaster for the whole country to do it. It would be better than original innovation if we could digest and absorb the technologies that can best protect human society from catastrophic upheaval. Our university scientists and professors need to do more than just meta-innovation.

2.4 On incentive and security

Interviewer: What are the factors that promote and hinder the academic innovation ability of the university teachers in incentive and security mechanism? What are the causes of the promotion or hindrance?

Zhou: External motivation is not the most important, while the most important is the inner motivation. The most effective stimulus is the career and drawing a very meaningful blueprint on the management level.

Interviewer: Many examples of spiritual leaders such as Gaddafi and MAO Zedong have shown that sometimes spiritual forces are more powerful than physical ones. There are usually material incentives like job titles, which are needed, but they don't do much. The real motivation is to understand what the other person is really willing to do and to create the conditions to meet the teacher's interest. Interest is the best teacher.

Interviewer: How to implement spiritual management?

Zhou: Real innovation depends not on institutions but on interest. They should stimulate people to face the world with a positive attitude. Institutional work does not inspire innovation.

6.40 Southwest University—Zhu

6.40.1 High-Frequency Words

Academic innovation ability	Cultivate talents
Evaluation indicators	Normal students
Differences in disciplines	

6.40.2 Key Points of Interview

1 On the innovation indicators

Interviewer: Do you think our six indicators of innovation are reasonable? Do you have any suggestions?

Zhu: The system is too formalized. Some indicators may be more while some may be less. The basis of indicators and internal logic should be studied. Statistical software should be used to deal with the observability and controllability of indicators.

Interviewer: Do you think it is appropriate to be divided into three dimensions: psychology, knowledge, and society? Are there any supplements?

Zhu: To study the innovative ability of university teachers, we need to make the differences clear. How does the innovative ability of university teachers differ from that of other organizations? What are the differences? The most basic function and responsibility of a university is knowledge innovation, talent cultivation, and serving the society, while the center is talent cultivation. Academic innovation does not exist in isolation, but is related to the personnel training mode. So you have to think about the relationship between them.

Interviewer: What do you think is the difference between a teacher in a normal university and a teacher in a comprehensive university in terms of the elements of innovation?

Zhu: Teachers' academic innovation should be more in line with the national education medium- and long-term development and planning. The directivity of teacher training is very strong, especially in the universities that recruit free normal students. We should train excellent teachers according to the outline of the state.

Interviewer: You mentioned the culture object is different. What do you think is different in terms of capabilities?

Zhu: Our teachers' academic innovation should be integrated with our students and their future work as well as the national requirements for normal students. If we do not have a large number of excellent teachers engaged in high-level research and our teachers' understanding of the whole education, the subject, the teaching contents, and teaching methods and the ability of innovation are not enough, we cannot require the students to have a certain quality and ability. It is necessary to have an international perspective and understand the latest development trend of global basis education and have local consciousness to master domestic circumstance. The free normal university students are a carrier to realize the vision of the future. If they are not nurtured well, then the gap between wishes and reality will be very big. If we look at the fundamental education problem from multiple perspectives, a lot of the problems in the economic transition are related to one another. If we have a reasonable distribution mechanism, the most basic and strategic problem is education fairness. The academic innovation of normal colleges should take education as the starting point to deepen things.

2 On the impact of personnel system on teachers' innovation

2.1 On resource allocation

Interviewer: How to improve the allocation of resources to promote the innovation of university teachers?

Zhu: Universities need to provide adequate basic support and security. The key facilities of the university should cover all departments and the resources should be shared. Each department should handle the allocation of resources. Of course, schools should also focus on the specific sectors to support. This involves dealing with the collaborative relationship between academic leaders and the team.

2.2 On evaluation and assessment

Interviewer: What are the factors that promote and hinder the academic innovation ability of the university teachers in evaluation and assessment mechanism? What are the causes of the promotion or hindrance?

2.3 On evaluation and assessment

Interviewer: What are the factors that promote and hinder the academic innovation ability of the university teachers in evaluation and assessment mechanism?

Zhu: The first is disrespecting disciplinary research and managing it too digitally. The rankings of universities are based on quantitative criteria such as how many books are published and how many programs are in charge. This has a lot to do with our higher education management system. This is mainly due to the increase in quantity rather than ability, and there will also be academic misconduct, which will cause harm to the society.

Interviewer: Based on the six innovation index systems proposed by us, how to improve the existing assessment and evaluation mechanism to improve teachers' innovation?

Zhu: Academic innovation should have a relatively independent evaluation system, rather than a unified evaluation system. There are great differences between normal colleges and universities. For normal colleges and universities in general, it is more of fundamental and theoretical discussions. In general, our country has invested less in the scientific research of teachers' colleges at least in the past. Basic theoretical research depends on long-term accumulation. We should pay attention to the differences in subjects.

Interviewer: How do you evaluate teachers if you really want to improve creativity?

Zhu: We should go back to the organizational trend of colleges and universities. Now the management of colleges and universities has copied the administrative management mode, which has caused problems.

Interviewer: De-administration?

Zhu: If the frame problem of higher education is not solved, it's useless to solve the problem of details. How to enhance the autonomy of colleges and universities is very important. We need to explore effective patterns. The reform of university management system and internal reform should be involved.

Interviewer: How to evaluate teachers' innovation?

Zhu: The problem of who to evaluate, how to evaluate and the evaluation cycle should be solved first. On the one hand, the humanities and social science department should take 3 years as an assessment cycle. On the other hand, we should consider how to ensure that university teachers do research in peace. To ensure individual and team innovation, the team organization ability must be included in the capacities.

Interviewer: Based on the six innovation index systems proposed by us, how to improve the existing incentive and guarantee mechanism to improve teachers' innovation?

Zhu: In addition to dedication, people have to face real life. So when use incentives, we need to balance relationships, careers, money, and academic interests. They should be respected and responded positively. In addition, the internal management of universities should be converted to service-oriented.

Chapter 7
Analysis of Interviews of Chinese Faculty Development

This chapter concentrates on analyzing the previous interviews of Chinese faculty development from a qualitative approach. NVivo 12 is to be used for analyzing 40 interviews and to obtain a series of analytical results. Along with the analytical results, we can observe that the high-frequency words are generally identical, and they occurred in different interviews with different proportions, which we can get the corresponding key points of the interview. It also indicates that with different positions, it is possible that the ideas and opinions can be different toward the same question.

7.1 Introduction and Summary

Qualitative analysis is a set of analysis that took the researcher as the research instrument, carry on a deep and comprehensive research toward the research object via multiple data collection methods so that a conclusion can be drawn, and a theory can be formed from the original data, which is different from and more difficult than quantitative analysis since we need to clean the raw data so that it can be meaningful and well managed. The key step of the qualitative analysis is collecting and analyzing the data and construct the feasible theory. In this report, we use NVivo 12 to analyze 40 reports and obtain a series of results.

7.2 Comprehensive Analysis

7.2.1 Basic Information

In this case, there are totally 40 interviews included in the report. The interviewees are from nine different universities in China. Here, we summarize the basic informa-

Fig. 7.1 The High-frequency-word cloud based on interviews

tion of the interview, including interviewee's name, university, interview key words, length of the interview, and question amounts in Table 7.1.

Here, we need to notice that the qualitative analysis is based on the existed text, that is to say, we will only obtain the description result but not inference result. This indicates that it is possible that the result will be different though the text is in the same meaning but with different contents. This is the reason why the qualitative analysis has an unavoidable error. Coding is the key step for our analysis. Here, we use NVivo 12 to set each question as a code before our analysis.

7.2.2 High-Frequency Word Analysis

First, we take all 40 interviews as a whole and do the high-frequency word analysis. This can help us to refine the interviews. Suppose if a word occurs more than 80 times in all interviews, i.e., it occurs in each interview twice on average, it is called high-frequency word. Note that the corresponding derivative words, such as noun, verb, adjective, adverb, plural, -ing, -ed, etc. are included. We always use the noun to represent the set of words. For example, for the word "innovative", we use word "innovation" to represent, and the set of words include "innovate", "innovating", "innovation", "innovations", "innovative", "innovator", "innovators" (Table 7.2).

Straightforwardly, we can see the high-frequency-word cloud as shown in the picture below (Fig. 7.1).

7.2 Comprehensive Analysis

Table 7.1 Basic information of interviews

No.	Interviewee name	University	Key words	Length of interview (words)	The amount of questions
1	Liu	Peking University	Academic innovation ability; Academic field; University teachers; rigid index; cross-disciplines; elastic system	848	12
2	Zhang	Beijing Normal University	Social ability; academic leader; academic innovation; comprehensive ability; cross-disciplines; do some surveys	675	14
3	Liu	Northeast Normal University	Innovation thinking; innovation consciousness; strong responsibility; consciousness of problems; resource allocation; selection and appointment	858	25
4	Gao	Northeast Normal University	Innovation consciousness; find out, propose, analyses and solve problems; personnel system; academic innovation ability; resource allocation; selection and appointment	944	28
5	Jin	Northeast Normal University	New media; cross-disciplines; personnel system; academic innovation ability; professor committee; selection and appointment	1244	44
6	Ma	Northeast Normal University	Accumulation of knowledge; accumulation of methods; cooperative consciousness; academic innovation ability; practical teaching experience; assessment and evaluation	303	5
7	Shi	Northeast Normal University	Academic innovation ability; intuition; inductive ability; systematic knowledge; reflection and judgment; assessment and evaluation	523	10
8	Zhang	Northeast Normal University	Innovation ability; six indicators; pennell system; resource allocation; selection and appointment; assessment and evaluation; incentive and safeguard mechanism	745	17

(continued)

Table 7.1 (continued)

No.	Interviewee name	University	Key words	Length of interview (words)	The amount of questions
9	Ding	East China Normal University	Academic innovation ability; inheritance and innovation; university teachers; tenure system, Interdisciplinary	1731	30
10	Liu	East China Normal University	Academic innovation ability; selection and recruitment mechanism; university teachers; examination and evaluation; rewards and incentives	900	14
11	Pang	East China Normal University	Academic innovation ability; H-coefficient; university teachers; teamwork; lifetime professor; academic inbreeding; the representative system of Peking University; learning aboard	943	14
12	Wu	East China Normal University	Interpersonal interaction; psychological ability; innovation teachers; teamwork; originality; Insight; from the bottom to up; from top to bottom	493	5
13	Yan	East China Normal University	Interpersonal interaction; a quantitative system; innovation teachers; accumulation; modern university system; academic environment; peer review; peer acceptance	949	13
14	Ye	East China Normal University	Passion; responsibility; innovation teachers; accumulation; reform of higher education; academic environment; peer review; sense of self-reliance	1084	13
15	Yu	East China Normal University	Passion; responsibility; innovation teachers; peer review; academic Vision; academic funds	687	9

(continued)

7.2 Comprehensive Analysis

Table 7.1 (continued)

No.	Interviewee name	University	Key words	Length of interview (words)	The amount of questions
16	Liu	Huazhong University of Science and Technology	Teaching innovation ability; ability to grasp direction; environment; teaching; positions; invention	624	6
17	Zhang	Huazhong University of Science and Technology	Academic insight and imagination; academic innovation; science and engineering; The Matthew effect; utilitarianism	858	6
18	Fan	Central China Normal University	Academic insight and imagination; academic innovation; science and engineering; critical reflective ability; professional dedication; love students	750	11
19	Li	Central China Normal University	University teachers; academic innovation; interdisciplinary abilities; research-oriented teachers; teaching-oriented teachers	488	10
20	Ren	Central China Normal University	Critical reflective ability; international communication skills; the quantity and quality of papers; research-oriented teachers; teaching-oriented teachers	572	8
21	Shi	Central China Normal University	Academic innovation ability; being original; academic foundation; academic vision; academic mind; peer recognition	755	7
22	Tu	Central China Normal University	Academic innovation ability; the academic field of discovery; academic foundation; indicator system; eager for quick success and instant benefits; supportive measures; induction	1252	15

(continued)

Table 7.1 (continued)

No.	Interviewee name	University	Key words	Length of interview (words)	The amount of questions
23	Hao	Shaanxi Normal University	Academic innovation ability; practical work; basic education; indicator system; independent learning; supportive measures	1390	13
24	Chen	Shaanxi Normal University	Academic insight and imagination ability; prototype inspiration; academic autonomy; scholarship of teaching; research achievements	1156	12
25	Fang	Shaanxi Normal University	Academic insight and imagination ability; interdisciplinary; academic autonomy; extensive and in-depth; research achievements; critical reflective ability	804	5
26	Huo	Shaanxi Normal University	Teacher quality; academic spirit; Innovation spirit; teacher education; inheritance and innovation	954	12
27	Li	Shaanxi Normal University	Innovation sense; academic interests; undergraduates; system reforming; tenured faculty	785	7
28	Ma	Shaanxi Normal University	Characteristics of the times; teaching innovation; research innovation; resource allocation; management innovation	1249	11
29	Wang	Shaanxi Normal University	A narrow range of knowledge; basic skills; ability to capture and digesting knowledge; basic knowledge; teaching ability	942	10
30	You	Shaanxi Normal University	Information literacy; de-administration; research innovation; resource allocation; teaching innovation	679	9

(continued)

7.2 Comprehensive Analysis

Table 7.1 (continued)

No.	Interviewee name	University	Key words	Length of interview (words)	The amount of questions
31	Liu	Shanghai Jiao Tong University	Academic innovation ability; academic accumulation; academic foundation; academic evaluation; academic leaders; academic awards; self-fulfillment	1176	10
32	Chen	Southwest University	Academic innovation ability; teaching and doing research; academic autonomy; academic quality; academic cooperation ability	1259	19
33	Huang	Southwest University	Academic innovation ability; motivation factors; academic accumulation; resource allocation; teaching ability and research ability; academic community	1018	9
34	Jin	Southwest University	Academic innovation ability; new methods; spiritual quotient; values; flowing; academic community; utilitarianism	1062	16
35	Liu, G	Southwest University	Academic innovation ability; autonomy ability; social ability; mental ability; resource allocation system; research funds	1084	14
36	Liu, M	Southwest University	Academic innovation ability; academic achievements; resource allocation system; academic background; teaching ability	1197	18
37	Song	Southwest University	Academic innovation ability; the ability to ask questions; the ability to solve problems; the operability of the system; appointment system	638	9
38	Zhang	Southwest University	Academic innovation ability; value orientation; the ability to find problems and analyze problems; published papers; professional dedication; de-administration	1337	12

(continued)

Table 7.1 (continued)

No.	Interviewee name	University	Key words	Length of interview (words)	The amount of questions
39	Zhou	Southwest University	Academic innovation ability; five-point scale; evaluation indicators; interests; meta-innovation; spiritual stimulus	1034	13
40	Zhu	Southwest University	Academic innovation ability; cultivate talents; evaluation indicators; normal students; differences of disciplines	1026	12

Table 7.2 The summary of high-frequency words

Word	Length	Amount of occurrence	Weighted (%)
Innovation	10	809	4.84
Teacher	7	787	4.71
Ability	7	538	3.22
Academic	8	524	3.14
University	10	383	2.29
System	6	377	2.26
Research	8	311	1.86
Evaluation	10	302	1.81
Indices	7	191	1.14
Teaching	8	166	0.99
Resource	8	165	0.99
Promotion	9	161	0.96
Difference	10	155	0.93
Mechanism	9	153	0.92
Problem	7	145	0.87
Educator	8	137	0.82
Allocation	10	130	0.78
Assessment	10	120	0.72
Student	7	97	0.58
Development	11	95	0.57
Knowledge	9	91	0.54
Incentive	9	90	0.54
Improvement	11	87	0.52
Factor	6	85	0.51
Scientific	10	83	0.50
Selection	9	80	0.48

7.2 Comprehensive Analysis

According to the analysis result above, we can observe that "innovation" is the most frequent word (4.84%) and the words whose the amount of occurrence exceed 500 are "teacher" (4.71%), "ability" (3.22%), and "academic" (3.14%). These words are highly related to the innovation and reform of teachers in higher education, which is the topic of interviews'.

Then, based on the high-frequency words we obtained above, we endeavor to get the coverage percentage of these words in each interview. The coverage percentage for each high-frequency word is summarized in Tables 7.3, 7.4, 7.5, and 7.6.

According to the tables above, for the analysis of high-frequency word coverage percentage, for each interview, we can summarize the information of each high-frequency word in Table 7.7.

Now, take each interviewee as our analysis object. Despite the word "innovation" which is the common and determined topic for all interviews, i.e., remove the word "innovation" as the key word, we independently analyze each interview and take the most frequent three to five words as the labels of each interview. Notice that these words may not be one of the twenty-six high-frequency words what we obtained before. The result are summarized in Table 7.8.

7.3 Correlation Analysis for High-Frequency Words

In this case, we use spherical graph to observe the correlation between the high-frequency words. Since there are too many words, we only select 30 notional words, shown in Figs. 7.2, 7.3, 7.4, and 7.5.

According to the figures above, we can observe that in whole, the high-frequency words can be divided into two groups. Since all the interviews are long, so not every word has a connection with all the words. However, based on the terminal of the tree, we can obtain some basic ideas about these interviews. For example, we can observe that "resource" and "allocation" are together, which indicates that there is probably an issue about how to allocate the resource fairly; "promote" and "mechanism" are together, which indicates that there is probably an issue about how to promote the mechanism in higher education; "teachers" and "innovative" are together, which indicates that the teachers in higher education should be innovative; and "evaluation" is highly related to "university", "systems", "teachers", and "innovative" which implies that evaluation is quite important in universities for both system and teachers.

(3) Cluster analysis based on interviewees

Further research is to explore the similarity among interviews. Based on the word's similarity, we use cluster analysis toward all interviews. The figure is shown in Fig. 7.6.

According to the figure above, we can observe that it is reasonable to classify all the interviewees into four clusters. The result of cluster analysis based on the interview similarity is summarized in Table 7.9.

Table 7.3 The coverage percentage of high-frequency words in each interview (Word 1–7)

	Innovation (%)	Teacher (%)	Ability (%)	Academic (%)	University (%)	System (%)	Research (%)
PKU-Liu	2.61	2.36	1.36	1.94	2.22	1.16	1.01
BNU-Zhang	4.36	0.48	4.97	2.82	0.22	0.26	2.35
NENU-Liu	3.87	2.29	2.68	0.14	1.29	1.34	0.85
NENU-Gao	3.26	1.97	1.58	0.77	2.03	0.97	2.10
NENU-Jin	3.17	2.28	0.25	0.95	1.45	1.66	1.31
NENU-Ma	2.43	1.07	2.14	1.17	0.00	1.46	5.40
NENU-Shi	4.11	1.97	2.67	0.47	0.29	1.23	0.47
NENU-Zhang	0.97	2.15	0.54	0.46	1.97	0.83	0.46
ECNU-Ding	2.21	2.73	0.68	1.34	1.62	0.48	0.78
ECNU-Liu	3.84	2.88	0.61	1.55	1.05	0.42	0.84
ECNU-Pang	1.68	1.97	0.82	1.95	2.52	1.03	0.54
ECNU-Wu	5.17	1.71	1.36	0.00	0.97	0.58	0.58
ECNU-Yan	2.40	1.22	0.45	2.05	4.20	1.35	0.43
ECNU-Ye	1.73	2.18	1.11	1.38	1.51	1.04	0.69
ECNU-Yu	2.79	2.65	0.33	3.16	1.16	0.14	1.30
HUST-Liu	5.92	1.52	2.06	0.61	0.71	1.18	0.59
HUST-Zhang	3.37	0.85	1.28	3.27	1.49	1.17	0.71
CCNU-Fan	3.16	3.04	3.04	3.48	1.42	0.95	0.32
CCNU-Li	3.60	3.03	2.16	0.96	2.28	1.80	2.40
CCNU-Ren	3.06	3.87	0.54	1.83	1.17	1.07	1.43

(continued)

7.3 Correlation Analysis for High-Frequency Words

Table 7.3 (continued)

	Innovation (%)	Teacher (%)	Ability (%)	Academic (%)	University (%)	System (%)	Research (%)
CCNU-Shi	6.73	1.71	2.96	3.18	1.51	0.71	2.10
CCNU-Tu	2.11	1.55	0.63	2.61	1.79	0.98	1.94
SNNU-Hao	3.75	1.79	0.78	1.52	0.81	0.87	1.32
SNNU-Chen	3.04	1.61	2.68	3.88	1.71	0.54	2.85
SNNU-Fang	2.80	1.86	2.39	1.94	1.12	0.56	2.37
SNNU-Huo	2.67	3.11	1.65	2.40	1.79	0.77	0.55
SNNU-Li	6.66	3.55	0.54	1.08	1.88	1.31	0.46
SNNU-Ma	4.15	2.56	0.94	0.88	1.73	1.17	1.10
SNNU-Wang	2.64	2.46	2.29	0.67	1.14	0.92	0.43
SNNU-You	3.42	1.33	3.29	2.22	2.74	1.28	0.17
SJTU-Liu	1.36	1.93	0.38	2.06	1.28	0.83	1.04
SWU-Chen	4.20	2.46	1.71	2.32	1.74	1.19	1.69
SWU-Huang	3.25	1.52	1.66	2.49	1.57	1.02	1.42
SWU-Jin	3.43	1.86	2.68	1.45	2.71	1.33	0.22
SWU-Liu, G	3.04	1.43	3.69	1.56	1.95	0.68	0.47
SWU-Liu, M	2.57	2.32	1.37	2.16	1.64	0.71	1.18
SWU-Song	4.67	2.18	2.60	1.49	2.83	2.09	0.19
SWU-Zhang	4.10	1.54	1.29	1.65	1.26	0.45	0.18
SWU-Zhou	4.37	1.72	1.57	0.48	1.30	0.56	0.12
SWU-Zhu	3.39	1.37	0.93	1.30	3.36	0.74	0.59

Table 7.4 The coverage percentage of high-frequency words in each interview (Word 8–13)

	Evaluation (%)	Indices (%)	Teaching (%)	Resource (%)	Promotion (%)	Difference (%)
PKU-Liu	0.79	0.18	0.28	0.72	0.25	0.95
BNU-Zhang	0.00	0.46	0.00	0.00	0.00	0.20
NENU-Liu	1.39	1.46	1.22	0.54	0.25	0.66
NENU-Gao	0.81	1.10	0.13	1.06	0.47	0.44
NENU-Jin	1.26	0.24	0.77	1.06	1.51	0.13
NENU-Ma	1.46	1.46	0.78	0.00	0.00	0.44
NENU-Shi	0.53	0.82	1.03	0.23	0.47	0.29
NENU-Zhang	0.97	1.08	0.15	2.11	0.35	0.21
ECNU-Ding	0.69	0.00	0.28	0.36	0.00	0.56
ECNU-Liu	1.68	0.00	0.14	0.44	0.66	0.47
ECNU-Pang	1.70	1.13	0.13	0.86	0.12	0.00
ECNU-Wu	0.00	0.97	0.00	0.00	0.23	0.00
ECNU-Yan	0.59	0.32	0.00	0.00	0.11	0.43
ECNU-Ye	0.76	0.85	0.46	0.00	0.39	0.39
ECNU-Yu	1.26	0.65	0.19	0.40	0.65	0.63
HUST-Liu	0.20	0.69	1.96	0.22	0.39	0.00
HUST-Zhang	0.18	1.15	0.43	0.43	0.28	0.67
CCNU-Fan	0.79	0.55	0.10	0.34	0.14	0.22
CCNU-Li	1.11	1.38	1.68	0.00	0.48	0.33
CCNU-Ren	2.14	1.20	2.24	0.46	0.48	0.46
CCNU-Shi	1.15	1.29	0.48	0.00	0.18	0.58
CCNU-Tu	0.49	1.14	0.56	0.10	0.17	1.82
SNNU-Hao	0.82	0.73	0.62	0.49	0.39	0.78
SNNU-Chen	1.12	0.61	1.09	0.10	0.00	0.61
SNNU-Fang	1.55	0.34	0.00	0.00	0.00	0.50
SNNU-Huo	0.61	0.71	0.24	0.38	0.64	0.49
SNNU-Li	1.88	0.35	1.09	0.31	1.25	0.19

(continued)

7.3 Correlation Analysis for High-Frequency Words

Table 7.4 (continued)

	Evaluation (%)	Indices (%)	Teaching (%)	Resource (%)	Promotion (%)	Difference (%)
SNNU-Ma	0.49	1.16	0.78	1.50	1.07	0.79
SNNU-Wang	0.97	0.80	0.94	0.80	0.99	0.49
SNNU-You	2.14	0.58	0.51	1.22	1.18	1.03
SJTU-Liu	1.55	0.52	0.00	0.00	0.31	0.52
SWU-Chen	1.57	0.89	0.77	0.60	0.75	0.35
SWU-Huang	2.68	0.86	1.54	1.11	0.71	0.98
SWU-Jin	1.53	0.92	0.32	0.67	0.67	0.57
SWU-Liu, G	1.56	0.40	0.11	0.93	0.77	1.10
SWU-Liu, M	1.78	0.50	0.64	1.34	0.91	0.26
SWU-Song	1.63	1.58	0.35	0.58	1.70	1.58
SWU-Zhang	1.26	0.57	0.18	0.57	0.55	0.64
SWU-Zhou	1.42	1.00	0.00	0.64	0.48	1.00
SWU-Zhu	1.80	0.88	0.24	0.52	0.44	1.31

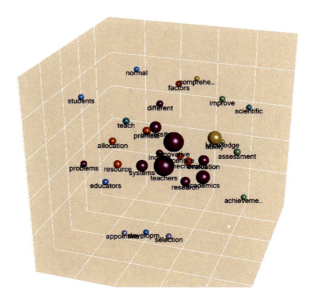

Fig. 7.2 3D clustering graph for correlation analysis of high-frequency words

Table 7.5 The coverage percentage of high-frequency words in each interview (Word 14–20)

	Mechanism (%)	Problem (%)	Educator (%)	Allocation (%)	Assessment (%)	Student (%)	Development (%)
PKU-Liu	0.79	0.39	0.32	0.71	0.18	0.00	0.78
BNU-Zhang	0.00	0.18	0.00	0.00	0.00	0.00	0.24
NENU-Liu	0.46	0.61	0.49	0.51	0.00	1.09	0.00
NENU-Gao	0.15	1.87	0.73	0.97	0.00	0.39	0.47
NENU-Jin	0.54	0.56	0.56	1.19	0.00	0.86	0.00
NENU-Ma	0.44	0.34	2.63	0.00	0.49	0.00	0.00
NENU-Shi	0.00	0.23	0.00	0.29	0.59	0.94	0.00
NENU-Zhang	0.52	0.00	1.94	1.55	1.68	0.15	0.35
ECNU-Ding	0.40	0.00	2.08	0.18	0.00	0.14	0.58
ECNU-Liu	1.26	0.12	0.00	0.00	0.56	0.00	0.58
ECNU-Pang	0.91	0.37	0.00	0.34	0.84	0.27	0.37
ECNU-Wu	0.00	1.20	0.00	0.00	0.32	0.52	0.00
ECNU-Yan	0.14	0.63	0.00	0.00	0.16	0.26	1.06
ECNU-Ye	0.00	1.60	1.43	0.00	0.23	0.00	0.32
ECNU-Yu	0.21	0.00	0.00	0.23	0.46	0.00	2.88
HUST-Liu	0.00	0.91	0.00	0.25	1.01	0.59	0.27
HUST-Zhang	0.48	0.67	0.16	0.53	0.18	0.00	0.37
CCNU-Fan	0.71	0.16	1.05	0.40	0.20	0.95	0.43
CCNU-Li	0.27	0.48	0.81	0.00	0.60	0.00	0.00
CCNU-Ren	0.23	0.00	0.51	0.20	0.00	0.38	1.12
CCNU-Shi	0.18	0.00	0.22	0.00	0.00	0.14	0.22

(continued)

7.3 Correlation Analysis for High-Frequency Words

Table 7.5 (continued)

	Mechanism (%)	Problem (%)	Educator (%)	Allocation (%)	Assessment (%)	Student (%)	Development (%)
CCNU-Tu	0.00	0.35	0.34	0.12	0.12	0.26	0.14
SNNU-Hao	0.20	1.12	1.10	0.33	0.11	0.08	0.60
SNNU-Chen	0.12	0.10	0.00	0.13	0.27	0.10	0.14
SNNU-Fang	0.34	0.13	0.17	0.00	0.19	0.15	0.00
SNNU-Huo	1.73	0.00	0.57	0.47	0.38	0.50	0.17
SNNU-Li	1.04	0.31	0.35	0.38	0.77	1.50	0.21
SNNU-Ma	0.77	0.56	0.95	1.56	0.79	0.20	0.80
SNNU-Wang	1.37	0.27	0.00	1.00	0.94	0.13	0.18
SNNU-You	0.96	0.77	0.00	1.71	0.85	0.00	0.47
SJTU-Liu	0.37	0.22	0.24	0.00	0.00	0.00	0.60
SWU-Chen	0.88	0.28	0.65	0.48	1.65	0.10	0.53
SWU-Huang	0.93	0.41	0.13	0.89	1.01	0.24	0.33
SWU-Jin	1.27	0.21	0.13	0.98	0.78	0.11	0.31
SWU-Liu, G	0.63	0.21	0.25	1.06	0.42	0.43	0.15
SWU-Liu, M	0.92	0.30	0.00	0.99	0.76	0.09	0.00
SWU-Song	0.84	0.74	0.63	0.70	1.16	0.19	0.51
SWU-Zhang	0.72	0.62	0.21	0.55	0.55	0.44	1.01
SWU-Zhou	0.41	0.32	0.14	0.70	0.30	0.12	0.00
SWU-Zhu	0.66	0.75	1.06	0.44	0.88	0.71	0.32

Table 7.6 The coverage percentage of high-frequency words in each interview (Word 21–26)

	Knowledge (%)	Incentive (%)	Improvement (%)	Factor (%)	Scientific (%)	Selection (%)
PKU-Liu	0.32	0.32	0.00	0.12	0.00	0.90
BNU-Zhang	1.78	0.00	0.00	0.00	0.00	0.00
NENU-Liu	0.76	0.61	0.12	0.10	0.51	0.31
NENU-Gao	0.00	0.15	0.11	0.11	0.00	0.73
NENU-Jin	0.00	0.43	0.00	0.08	0.48	0.64
NENU-Ma	1.75	0.00	0.00	0.00	0.00	0.00
NENU-Shi	1.85	0.00	0.21	0.00	0.00	0.00
NENU-Zhang	0.00	1.08	0.00	0.14	0.00	0.52
ECNU-Ding	0.40	0.08	0.00	0.24	0.18	0.08
ECNU-Liu	0.00	0.65	0.56	0.12	0.00	0.47
ECNU-Pang	0.15	0.30	0.12	0.10	0.00	0.69
ECNU-Wu	0.00	0.00	0.00	1.16	0.00	0.00
ECNU-Yan	0.00	0.00	0.00	0.34	0.16	0.00
ECNU-Ye	0.00	0.00	0.00	0.50	0.14	0.00
ECNU-Yu	0.00	0.00	0.51	0.16	0.23	0.00
HUST-Liu	0.00	0.00	0.64	0.00	0.49	0.00
HUST-Zhang	0.48	0.66	0.00	0.12	0.53	0.48
CCNU-Fan	0.00	0.18	0.49	0.14	0.00	0.71
CCNU-Li	0.00	0.00	0.21	0.00	1.20	0.00
CCNU-Ren	0.00	0.23	0.23	0.00	0.25	0.23
CCNU-Shi	0.00	0.54	0.00	0.14	2.18	0.54
CCNU-Tu	0.00	0.00	0.25	0.00	0.25	0.07
SNNU-Hao	0.60	0.31	0.43	0.00	0.00	0.47
SNNU-Chen	0.35	0.23	0.27	0.00	0.77	0.23
SNNU-Fang	0.50	0.17	0.13	0.00	0.19	0.17

(continued)

7.3 Correlation Analysis for High-Frequency Words

Table 7.6 (continued)

	Knowledge (%)	Incentive (%)	Improvement (%)	Factor (%)	Scientific (%)	Selection (%)
SNNU-Huo	0.28	0.42	0.46	0.33	0.00	0.42
SNNU-Li	0.00	0.73	0.67	0.40	0.19	0.52
SNNU-Ma	0.66	0.44	0.26	0.26	0.85	0.00
SNNU-Wang	1.51	0.45	0.59	0.45	0.00	0.15
SNNU-You	0.00	0.79	0.30	0.75	1.15	0.58
SJTU-Liu	0.00	0.37	0.19	0.19	0.54	0.37
SWU-Chen	0.11	0.11	0.64	0.34	0.60	0.43
SWU-Huang	0.13	0.80	0.74	0.90	1.04	0.13
SWU-Jin	0.25	0.50	0.68	0.29	0.70	0.50
SWU-Liu, G	1.50	0.26	0.29	0.29	0.28	0.13
SWU-Liu, M	0.00	0.49	0.00	0.45	0.13	0.35
SWU-Song	0.21	0.65	0.00	0.65	0.23	0.42
SWU-Zhang	0.10	0.52	0.45	0.24	0.11	0.10
SWU-Zhou	0.68	0.42	0.21	0.32	0.15	0.00
SWU-Zhu	0.27	0.28	0.62	0.21	0.15	0.00

We can also obtain some information from the Pearson correlation coefficient matrix. (It contains 1600 numbers, which is too large to show it here). Based on the Pearson correlation coefficient matrix, we can concentrate the information in the following statements. Generally speaking, the interview between SWU-Huang and SWU-Chen's is most similar (0.846) and the interview between NENU-Zhang and BNU-Zhang's is least similar (0.210).

7.4 Analysis by Universities

If we want to know more characteristics about different universities, we'd better take the university and a group, then separately analyze the interviews. In this case, based on the sample size in each university, we only consider five universities, i.e., Central China Normal University (CCNU), East China Normal University (ECNU),

Table 7.7 The highest and lowest coverage percentage of each high-frequency words in each interview

Key word	Interviewee	Highest coverage percentage (%)	Interviewee	Lowest coverage percentage (%)
Innovation	CCNU-Shi	6.73	NENU-Zhang	0.97
Teacher	CCNU-Ren	3.87	BNU-Zhang	0.48
Ability	BNU-Zhang	4.97	NENU-Jin	0.25
Academic	SSNU-Chen	3.88	ECNU-Wu	0.00
University	ECNU-Yan	4.20	SNNU-Ma	0.00
System	SWU-Song	2.09	NENU-Shi	0.14
Research	SNNU-Ma	5.40	SWU-Zhou	0.12
Evaluation	SWU-Huang	2.68	BNU-Zhang; ECNU-Wu	0.00
Indices	SWU-Song	1.58	ECNU-Ding; ECNU-Liu	0.00
Teaching	CCNU-Ren	2.24	BNU-Zhang; ECNU-Wu; ECNU-Yan; SSNU-Fang; SJTU-Liu; SWU-Zhou	0.00
Resource	NENU-Zhang	2.11	PKU-Liu; SNNU-Ma; ECNU-Wu; ECNU-Yan; NENU-Ye; CCNU-Li; CCNU-Shi; SSNU-Fang; SJTU-Liu	0.00
Promotion	SWU-Song	1.70	BNU-Zhang; SNNU-Ma; ECNU-Ding; SSNU-Chen; SSNU-Fang	0.00
Difference	CCNU-Tu	1.82	ECNU-Pang; ECNU-Wu; HUST-Liu	0.00
Mechanism	SNNU-Huo	1.73	BNU-Zhang; NENU-Shi; ECNU-Wu; NENU-Ye; HUST-Liu; CCNU-Tu	0.00

(continued)

7.4 Analysis by Universities

Table 7.7 (continued)

Key word	Interviewee	Highest coverage percentage (%)	Interviewee	Lowest coverage percentage (%)
Problem	NENU-Gao	1.87	NENU-Zhang; ECNU-Ding; ECNU-Yu; CCNU-Ren; CCNU-Shi; SNNU-Huo	0.00
Educator	SNNU-Ma	2.63	BNU-Zhang; NENU-Shi; ECNU-Liu; ECNU-Pang; ECNU-Wu; ECNU-Yan; ECNU-Yu; HUST-Liu; SSNU-Chen; SNNU-Wang; SNNU-You; SWU-Liu, M	0.00
Allocation	SNNU-You	1.71	BNU-Zhang; SNNU-Ma; ECNU-Liu; ECNU-Wu; ECNU-Yan; NENU-Ye; CCNU-Li; CCNU-Shi; SSNU-Fang; SJTU-Liu	0.00
Assessment	NENU-Zhang	1.68	BNU-Zhang; NENU-Liu; NENU-Gao; NENU-Jin; ECNU-Ding; CCNU-Ren; CCNU-Shi; SJTU-Liu	0.00
Student	SNNU-Li	1.50	PKU-Liu; BNU-Zhang; SNNU-Ma; ECNU-Liu; NENU-Ye; ECNU-Yu; HUST-Zhang; CCNU-Li; SNNU-You; SJTU-Liu	0.00

(continued)

Table 7.7 (continued)

Key word	Interviewee	Highest coverage percentage (%)	Interviewee	Lowest coverage percentage (%)
Development	ECNU-Yu	2.88	NENU-Liu; NENU-Jin; SNNU-Ma; ECNU-Shi; ECNU-Wu; CCNU-Li; SSNU-Fang; SWU-Liu, M; SWU-Zhou	0.00
Knowledge	NENU-Shi	1.85	NENU-Gao; NENU-Jin; NENU-Zhang; ECNU-Liu; ECNU-Wu; ECNU-Yan; NENU-Ye; ECNU-Yu; HUST-Liu; CCNU-Fan; CCNU-Li; CCNU-Ren; CCNU-Shi; CCNU-Tu; SNNU-Li; SNNU-You; SJTU-Liu; SWU-Liu, M	0.00
Incentive	NENU-Zhang	1.08	BNU-Zhang; SNNU-Ma; NENU-Shi; ECNU-Wu; ECNU-Yan; NENU-Ye; ECNU-Yu; HUST-Liu; CCNU-Li; CCNU-Tu	0.00
Improvement	SWU-Huang	0.74	PKU-Liu; BNU-Zhang; NENU-Jin; SNNU-Ma; NENU-Zhang; ECNU-Ding; ECNU-Wu; ECNU-Yan; NENU-Ye; HUST-Zhang; CCNU-Shi; SWU-Liu, M; SWU-Song	0.00

(continued)

7.4 Analysis by Universities

Table 7.7 (continued)

Key word	Interviewee	Highest coverage percentage (%)	Interviewee	Lowest coverage percentage (%)
Factor	ECNU-Wu	1.16	BNU-Zhang; SNNU-Ma; NENU-Shi; HUST-Liu; CCNU-Li; CCNU-Ren; CCNU-Tu; SNNU-Hao; SSNU-Chen; SSNU-Fang	0.00
Scientific	CCNU-Shi	2.18	PKU-Liu; BNU-Zhang; NENU-Gao; SNNU-Ma; NENU-Shi; NENU-Zhang; ECNU-Liu; ECNU-Pang; ECNU-Wu; CCNU-Fan; SNNU-Hao; SNNU-Huo; SNNU-Wang	0.00
Selection	PKU-Liu	0.90	BNU-Zhang; SNNU-Ma; NENU-Shi; ECNU-Wu; ECNU-Yan; NENU-Ye; ECNU-Yu; HUST-Liu; CCNU-Li; SNNU-Ma; SWU-Zhou; SWU-Zhu	0.00

Northeast Normal University (NENU), Shaanxi Normal University (SSNU), and Southwest University (SWU), whose sample size is 5, 7, 6, 8, and 9, respectively. In the following steps, we will repeat what we do in a comprehensive analysis and make the comparison with the result in whole. Still, we define the high-frequency word in group analysis as same as in comprehensive analysis. That is, if a word occurs more than 80 times, it is called high-frequency word.

Table 7.8 The labels of each interview based on high-frequency words

Interviewee	High-frequency words
PKU-Liu	Teacher (5.61%), Academic (3.32%), University (3.06%)
BNU-Zhang	Ability (10.09%), Academic (5.05%), Research (4.10%), Social (4.10%)
NENU-Liu	Teacher (6.56%), Ability (5.77%), Thinking (3.94%)
NENU-Gao	Teacher (4.53%), Research (4.03%), Problem (3.78%)
NENU-Jin	Teacher (6.68%), System (4.27%), Promotion (3.15%)
NENU-Ma	Research (8.39%), Ability (4.20%), Accumulation (4.20%), Education (4.20%)
NENU-Shi	Ability (5.91%), Teacher (4.09%), Intuition (3.18%), Knowledge (3.18%), System (3.18%)
NENU-Zhang	Teacher (4.94%), Resource (3.78%), Education (3.20%)
ECNU-Ding	Teacher (5.13%), Education (3.05%), Academic (2.32%)
ECNU-Liu	Teacher (6.32%), Academic (3.02%), Evaluation (2.758%)
ECNU-Pang	Teacher (4.07%), Academic (3.56%), University (3.56%)
ECNU-Wu	Teacher (4.195%), Ability (3.14%), Factory (3.14%)
ECNU-Yan	University (5.42%), Academic (3.47%), System (3.04%), Teacher (3.04%)
ECNU-Ye	Teacher (5.89%), Problem (3.16%), Academic (2.53%), System (2.53%)
ECNU-Yu	Teacher (6.08%), Academic (5.74%), Development (4.05%)
HUST-Liu	Ability (4.41%), Teacher (4.41%), Teaching (3.68%)
HUST-Zhang	Academic (5.52%), System (2.64%), Teacher (2.64%)
CCNU-Fan	Ability (5.91%), Academic (5.91%), Teacher (5.65%)
CCNU-Li	Teacher (7.47%), Ability (4.15%), Research (4.15%), System (4.15%)
CCNU-Ren	Teacher (8.33%), Teaching (3.99%), Academic (3.26%), Evaluation (3.26%)
CCNU-Shi	Ability (5.92%), Academic (5.63%), Teacher (3.94%)
CCNU-Tu	Academic (4.63%), Research (3.21%), Teacher (3.21%)
SNNU-Hao	Teacher (3.99%), Academic (2.71%), Practice (2.23%), Research (2.23%)
SNNU-Chen	Academic (6.74%), Ability (5.32%), Research (4.79%)
SNNU-Fang	Ability (4.88%), Research (4.07%), Teacher (4.07%)
SNNU-Huo	Teacher (6.64%), Academic (4.20%), Ability (3.32%)
SNNU-Li	Teacher (6.02%), Student (3.01%), System (2.76%)
SNNU-Ma	Teacher (4.48%), System (2.65%), Resource (2.49%)
SNNU-Wang	Teacher (5.61%), Ability (4.44%), Knowledge (2.34%)
SNNU-You	Ability (6.63%), Academic (3.92%), University (3.61%)
SJTU-Liu	Teacher (4.35%), Academic (3.93%), Evaluation (2.48%)
SWU-Chen	Teacher (6.11%), Academic (4.19%), Ability (3.49%)

(continued)

7.4 Analysis by Universities

Table 7.8 (continued)

Interviewee	High-frequency words
SWU-Huang	Academic (4.30%), Evaluation (4.10%), Teacher (3.69%)
SWU-Jin	Ability (4.96%), Teacher (4.20%), University (3.44%)
SWU-Liu, G	Ability (7.40%), Teacher (3.20%), Academic (2.80%)
SWU-Liu, M	Teacher (4.50%), Academic (3.78%), Ability (2.70%), Evaluation (2.70%)
SWU-Song	Ability (5.28%), System (4.95%), Teacher (4.29%)
SWU-Zhang	Teacher (3.59%), Academic (2.94%), Ability (2.61%)
SWU-Zhou	Teacher (4.09%), Ability (3.02%), Evaluation (2.160%)
SWU-Zhu	University (4.40%), Teacher (4.19%), Evaluation (2.73%)

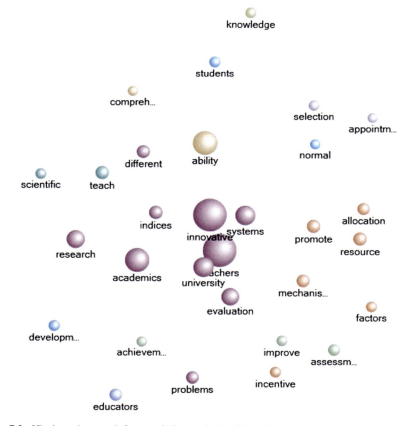

Fig. 7.3 2D clustering graph for correlation analysis of high-frequency words

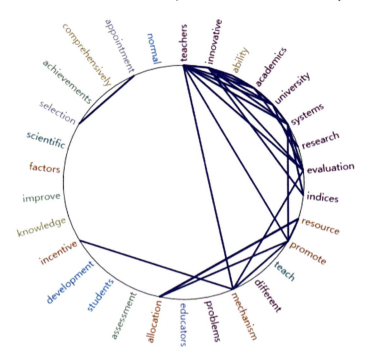

Fig. 7.4 Circle graph for correlation analysis of high-frequency words

Table 7.9 The result of cluster analysis based on the interview similarity

Clusters	Labels
ECNU-Wu; HUST-Liu; NENU-Liu; NENU-Shi	Ability; Teacher
NENU-Ma; SNNU-Chen; SNNU-Fang; BNU-Zhang; SWU- Liu, G	Ability; Research
ECNU-Yan; ECNU-Ye; ECNU-Yu; CCNU-Tu; CCNU-Shi; HUST-Zhang; ECNU-Ding; ECNU-Liu; ECNU-Pang; SJTU-Liu	Academic; Teacher
NENU-Zhang; CCNU-Li; CCNU-Ren; NENU-Gao; NENU-Jin; SWU-Zhou; SWU-Zhang; SNNU-Li; SNNU-Ma; SNNU-Hao; SWU-Zhu; SNNU-Wang; SWU-Jin; SNNU-You; SWU-Song; PKU-Liu; SWU-Liu, M; SWU-Chen; SWU-Huang; CCNU-Fan; SNNU-Huo	Ability; Academic; Teacher; System

7.4 Analysis by Universities

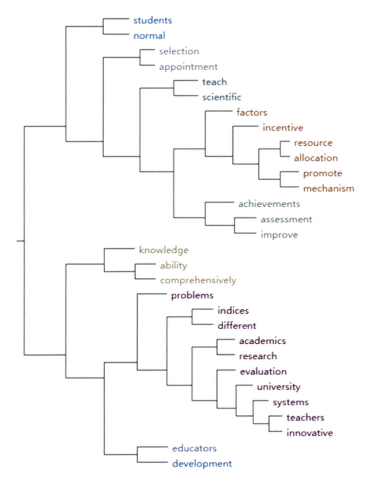

Fig. 7.5 Tree graph for correlation analysis of high-frequency words

7.4.1 For Central China Normal University (CCNU)

First, we take all five interviews from CCNU as a whole and do the high-frequency word analysis. The result is as shown in Table 7.10.

Straightforwardly, we can see the high-frequency-word cloud as shown in the picture below (Fig. 7.7).

According to the analysis result above, we can observe that "Teacher" is the most frequent word (5.25%), which is slightly different from the result of comprehensive analysis. Moreover, the words whose amount of occurrence exceed 150 are "innovation" (5.11%) and "academic" (4.33%). Still, these words are highly related to

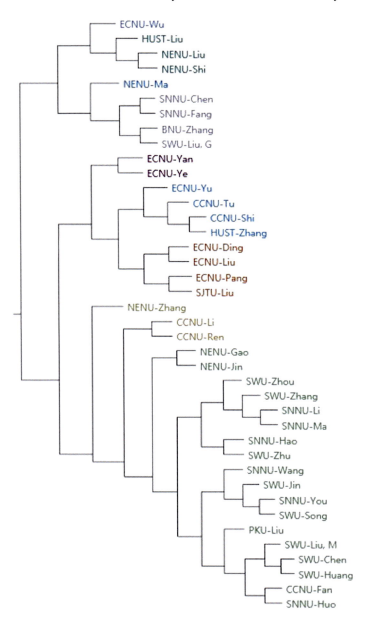

Fig. 7.6 Cluster analysis for interviews

7.4 Analysis by Universities

Table 7.10 The summary of high-frequency words in CCNU interviews

Word	Length	Amount of occurrence	Weighted percentage (%)
Teacher	7	183	5.25
Innovation	10	178	5.11
Academic	8	151	4.33
Ability	7	120	3.44
Research	8	98	2.81
System	6	87	2.50

Fig. 7.7 The high-frequency-word cloud based on interviews of CCNU

the innovation and reform of teachers in higher education, which is the topic of interviews'.

Then, based on the high-frequency words we obtained above, we endeavor to get the coverage percentage of these words in each interview. Note that for the group analysis, we take the university as the whole population. So, the result will be slightly different from the result of comprehensive analysis. The coverage percentage for each high-frequency word is summarized in Table 7.11.

According to the tables above, for the analysis of high-frequency word coverage percentage, for each interview, we can summarize the information of each high-frequency word in Table 7.12.

Second, we apply correlation analysis for high-frequency words in the following statement. Similarly, in this case, we use spherical graph to observe the correlation between the high-frequency words. Since there are too many words, we only select 30 notional words, as shown in Figs. 7.8, 7.9, 7.10, and 7.11.

Table 7.11 The coverage percentage of high-frequency words in each interview of CCNU

	Teacher (%)	Innovation (%)	Academic (%)	Ability (%)	Research (%)	System (%)
CCNU-Fan	3.04	3.16	3.48	3.04	0.32	0.95
CCNU-Li	3.03	3.60	0.96	2.16	2.40	1.80
CCNU-Ren	3.87	3.06	1.83	0.54	1.43	1.07
CCNU-Shi	1.71	6.73	3.18	2.96	2.10	0.71
CCNU-Tu	1.55	2.11	2.61	0.63	1.94	0.98

Table 7.12 The highest and lowest coverage percentage of each high-frequency words in each interview of CCNU

Key word	Interviewee	Highest coverage percentage (%)	Interviewee	Lowest coverage percentage (%)
Teacher	CCNU-Ren	3.87	CCNU-Tu	1.55
Innovation	CCNU-Shi	6.73	CCNU-Tu	2.11
Academic	CCNU-Fan	3.48	CCNU-Li	0.96
Ability	CCNU-Fan	3.04	CCNU-Ren	0.54
Research	CCNU-Li	2.40	CCNU-Fan	0.32
System	CCNU-Li	1.80	CCNU-Shi	0.71

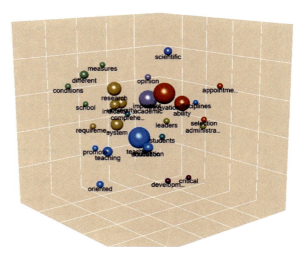

Fig. 7.8 3D clustering graph for correlation analysis of high-frequency words of CCNU interviews

7.4 Analysis by Universities

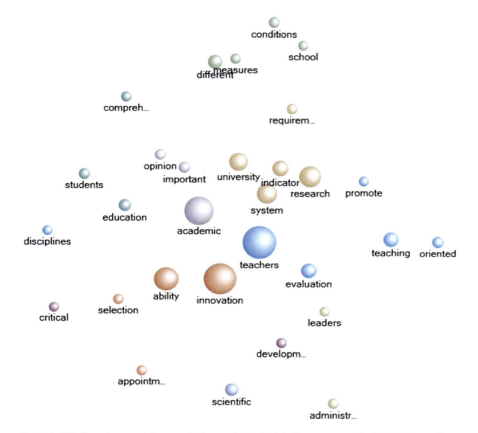

Fig. 7.9 2D clustering graph for correlation analysis of high-frequency words of CCNU interviews

According to the figures above, similarly, we can observe that in whole, the high-frequency words can be divided into two groups and almost every word has a connection with another word. However, based on the terminal of the tree, we can obtain some basic ideas about these interviews, which embodies the situation of CCNU. For example, we can observe that "innovation" and "ability" are together, which indicates that the innovation is based on teacher or researcher's ability; "administrative" and "leader" are together, which indicates that it is important that the leader has administrative ability; "system" and "indicator" are together, which indicates that there should be some indicators to evaluate or construct the system.

Third, we will apply cluster analysis based on interviewees. Based on the word's similarity, we use cluster analysis toward all interviews. The results, including cluster figure and Pearson correlation coefficient matrix, are as below (Fig. 7.12 and Table 7.13).

According to the results above, generally speaking, all the interviews are similar, where the most similar pair is between Fan and Shi (0.704) and least similar pair is

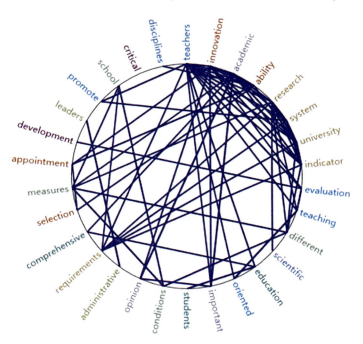

Fig. 7.10 Circle graph for correlation analysis of high-frequency words of CCNU interviews

Table 7.13 The Pearson correlation coefficient matrix based on interviews of CCNU

	CCNU-Fan	CCNU-Li	CCNU-Ren	CCNU-Shi	CCNU-Tu
CCNU-Fan	1	0.525	0.513	0.704	0.509
CCNU-Li	0.525	1	0.632	0.630	0.513
CCNU-Ren	0.513	0.632	1	0.567	0.542
CCNU-Shi	0.704	0.630	0.567	1	0.617
CCNU-Tu	0.509	0.513	0.542	0.617	1

between Fan and Tu (0.509). For the other interviewees, Li's interview is closest to Ren's (0.632) while is furthest to Tu's (0.509); Ren's interview is furthest to Fan's (0.513); Shi's interview is furthest to Ren's (0.567) and Tu's interview is closest to Shi's (0.617). This can also be observed from the figure of cluster analysis.

7.4.2 For East China Normal University (ECNU)

First, we take all seven interviews from ECNU as a whole and do the high-frequency word analysis. The result is as shown in Table 7.14.

7.4 Analysis by Universities

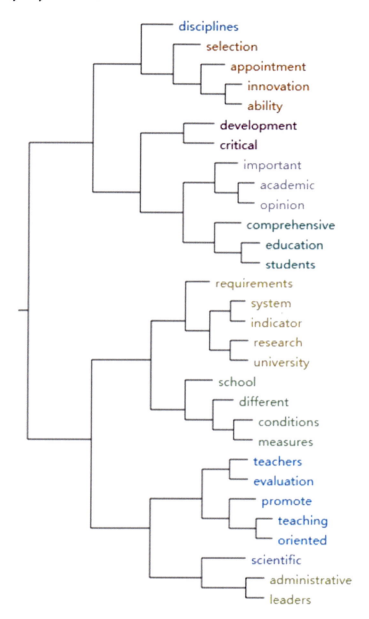

Fig. 7.11 Tree graph for correlation analysis of high-frequency words of CCNU interviews

Fig. 7.12 Cluster analysis for interviews of CCNU

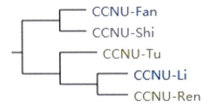

Table 7.14 The summary of high-frequency words in ECNU interviews

Word	Length	Amount of occurrence	Weighted percentage (%)
Teacher	7	149	4.63
Innovation	10	112	3.48
Academic	8	89	2.77
University	10	81	2.52

Fig. 7.13 The high-frequency-word cloud based on interviews of ECNU

Straightforwardly, we can see the high-frequency-word cloud as shown in the picture below (Fig. 7.13).

According to the analysis result above, we can observe that "Teacher" is the most frequent word (4.63%), which is slightly different from the result of comprehensive analysis. Moreover, there is no word whose amount of occurrence exceeds 150. Of course, these words are highly related to the innovation and reform of teachers in higher education, which is the topic of interviews'.

7.4 Analysis by Universities

Table 7.15 The coverage percentage of high-frequency words in each interview of ECNU

	Teacher (%)	Innovation (%)	Academic (%)	University (%)
ECNU-Ding	2.73	2.21	1.34	1.62
ECNU-Liu	2.88	3.84	1.55	1.05
ECNU-Pang	1.97	1.68	1.95	2.52
ECNU-Wu	1.71	5.17	0.00	0.97
ECNU-Yan	1.22	2.40	2.05	4.20
ECNU-Ye	2.18	1.73	1.38	1.51
ECNU-Yu	2.65	2.79	3.16	1.16

Table 7.16 The highest and lowest coverage percentage of each high-frequency words in each interview of ECNU

Key word	Interviewee	Highest coverage percentage (%)	Interviewee	Lowest coverage percentage (%)
Teacher	ECNU-Liu	2.88	ECNU-Yan	1.22
Innovation	ECNU-Wu	5.17	ECNU-Pang	1.68
Academic	ECNU-Yu	3.16	ECNU-Wu	0.00
University	ECNU-Yan	4.20	ECNU-Wu	0.97

Then, based on the high-frequency words we obtained above, we endeavor to get the coverage percentage of these words in each interview. The coverage percentage for each high-frequency word is summarized in Table 7.15.

According to the tables above, for the analysis of high-frequency word coverage percentage, for each interview, we can summarize the information of each high-frequency word in Table 7.16.

Second, we apply correlation analysis for high-frequency words in the following statement. Similarly, in this case, we use spherical graph to observe the correlation between the high-frequency words. Since there are too many words, we only select 30 notional words, as shown in Figs. 7.14, 7.15, 7.16, and 7.17.

According to the figures above, similarly, we can observe that in whole, the high-frequency words can be divided into two groups and almost every word has connection with another word. However, based on the terminal of the tree, we can obtain some basic ideas about these interviews, which embodies the situation of ECNU. For example, we can observe that "teachers" and "research" are together, as well as "articles", which indicates that the teachers in higher education should do some research and articles can measure the research performance of the researcher; "evaluation" and "mechanism" are together, which implies that there should be some useful evaluation mechanism in the innovation and reform of higher education.

Third, we will apply cluster analysis based on interviewees. Based on the word's similarity, we use cluster analysis toward all interviews. The results, including clus-

Fig. 7.14 3D clustering graph for correlation analysis of high-frequency words of ECNU interviews

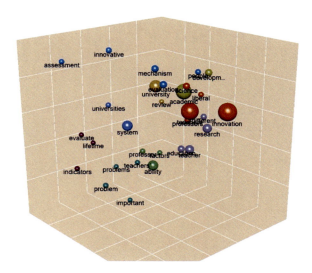

Table 7.17 The Pearson correlation coefficient matrix based on interviews of ECNU

	ECNU-Ding	ECNU-Liu	ECNU-Pang	ECNU-Wu	ECNU-Yan	ECNU-Ye	ECNU-Yu
ECNU-Ding	1	0.545	0.437	0.308	0.409	0.437	0.448
ECNU-Liu	0.545	1	0.516	0.454	0.404	0.448	0.588
ECNU-Pang	0.437	0.516	1	0.349	0.472	0.482	0.508
ECNU-Wu	0.308	0.454	0.349	1	0.323	0.457	0.375
ECNU-Yan	0.409	0.404	0.472	0.323	1	0.478	0.467
ECNU-Ye	0.437	0.448	0.482	0.457	0.478	1	0.484
ECNU-Yu	0.448	0.588	0.508	0.375	0.467	0.484	1

ter figure and Pearson correlation coefficient matrix, are as below (Fig. 7.18 and Table 7.17).

According to the results above, generally speaking, the interviews are not similar though these interviews are from the same university. We can observe that the most similar pair is between Liu and Yu (0.588) and least similar pair is between Ding and Wu (0.308), which indicates that these interviewees have different opinions and ideas even in the same question. For the other interviewees, we can observe that Wu's has significantly smaller Pearson correlation coefficient with other interviews

7.4 Analysis by Universities

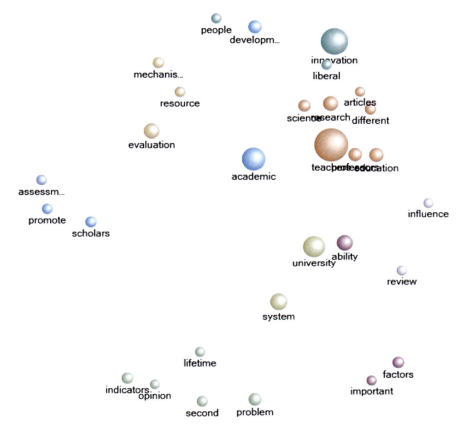

Fig. 7.15 2D clustering graph for correlation analysis of high-frequency words of ECNU interviews

which indicates that Wu's ideas and opinions are significantly different from the other interviewees'. Moreover, Ding's interview is closest to Liu's (0.545); Liu's interview is furthest to Yan's (0.404); Pang's interview is closest to Liu's (0.516) and furthest to Wu's (0.349); Wu's interview is closest to Ye's (0.457); Ye's interview is closest to Yu's (0.484) and furthest to Ding's (0.437) and Yu's interview is furthest to Wu's (0.375). This can also be observed from the figure of cluster analysis.

7.4.3 For Northeast Normal University (NENU)

First, we take all five interviews from NENU as a whole and do the high-frequency word analysis. The result is as shown in Table 7.18.

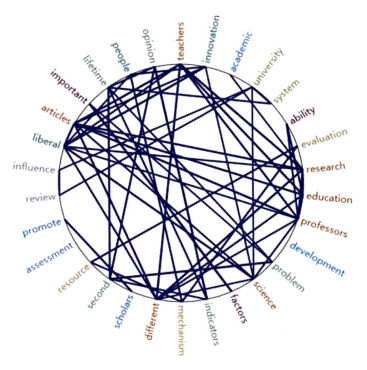

Fig. 7.16 Circle graph for correlation analysis of high-frequency words of ECNU interviews

Table 7.18 The summary of high-frequency words in NENU interviews

Word	Length	Amount of occurrence	Weighted percentage (%)
Teacher	7	108	4.44
Innovation	10	95	3.90

Straightforwardly, we can see the high-frequency-word cloud as shown in the picture below (Fig. 7.19).

According to the analysis result above, we can observe that "Teacher" is the most frequent word (4.44%), which is slightly different from the result of comprehensive analysis. Moreover, only one word, i.e., "Innovation" has occurred more than 80 times. That is to say, in these interviewees, their ideas and opinions are relatively separating comparing with the other universities even though they are all from NENU.

Then, based on the high-frequency words we obtained above, we endeavor to get the coverage percentage of these words in each interview. Note that for the group analysis, we take the university as the whole population. So, the result will be slightly different from the result of comprehensive analysis. The coverage percentage for each high-frequency word is summarized in Table 7.19.

7.4 Analysis by Universities

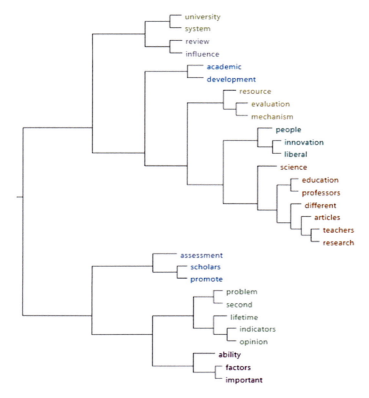

Fig. 7.17 Tree graph for correlation analysis of high-frequency words of ECNU interviews

Fig. 7.18 Cluster analysis for interviews of ECNU

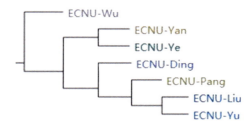

Table 7.19 The coverage percentage of high-frequency words in each interview of NENU

	Teacher (%)	Innovation (%)
NENU-Liu	2.29	3.87
NENU-Gao	1.97	3.26
NENU-Jin	2.28	3.17
NENU-Ma	1.07	2.43
NENU-Shi	1.97	4.11
NENU-Zhang	2.15	0.97

Fig. 7.19 The high-frequency-word cloud based on interviews of NENU

Table 7.20 The highest and lowest coverage percentage of each high-frequency words in each interview of NENU

Key word	Interviewee	Highest coverage percentage	Interviewee	Lowest coverage percentage
Teacher	NENU-Liu	2.29	NENU-Ma	1.07
Innovation	NENU-Shi	4.01	NENU-Zhang	0.97

According to the tables above, for the analysis of high-frequency word coverage percentage, for each interview, we can summarize the information of each high-frequency word in Table 7.20.

Second, we apply correlation analysis for high-frequency words in the following statement. Similarly, in this case, we use spherical graph to observe the correlation between the high-frequency words. Since there are too many words, we only select 30 notional words, as shown in Figs. 7.20, 7.21, 7.22, and 7.23.

According to the figures above, similarly, we can observe that in whole, the high-frequency words can be divided into two groups and almost every word has connection with another word. That is to say, although their topic is relatively separating, it still contains a lot of information and each of the information point can be connected. However, based on the terminal of the tree, we can obtain some basic ideas about these interviews, which embodies the situation of NENU. For example, we can observe that "education" and "assessment" are together, which indicates that there should be some assessment in higher education; "system" and "promote" are together, which implies the system in higher education should be promoted.

7.4 Analysis by Universities

Fig. 7.20 3D clustering graph for correlation analysis of high-frequency words of NENU interviews

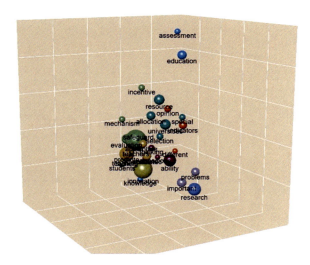

Table 7.21 The Pearson correlation coefficient matrix based on interviews of NENU

	NENU-Liu	NENU-Gao	NENU-Jin	NENU-Ma	NENU-Shi	NENU-Zhang
NENU-Liu	1	0.451	0.388	0.392	0.540	0.522
NENU-Gao	0.451	1	0.413	0.374	0.395	0.310
NENU-Jin	0.388	0.413	1	0.272	0.318	0.291
NENU-Ma	0.392	0.374	0.272	1	0.408	0.198
NENU-Shi	0.540	0.395	0.318	0.408	1	0.214
NENU-Zhang	0.522	0.310	0.291	0.198	0.214	1

Third, we will apply cluster analysis based on interviewees. Based on the word's similarity, we use cluster analysis toward all interviews. The results, including cluster figure and Pearson correlation coefficient matrix are as below (Fig. 7.24 and Table 7.21).

According to the results above, generally speaking, the interviews are so far away though these interviews are all from NENU. We can observe that the most similar pair is between Liu and Shi (0.540), which is with a relatively low Pearson correlation coefficient and least similar pair is between Ma and Zhang (0.198), whose Pearson correlation coefficient indicates that there is only weak correlation between these two interviews. The result indicates that these interviewees have quite different opinions and ideas even in the same question. For the other interviewees, we can observe that Liu's interview is closest to Zhang's (0.522) and furthest to Jin's (0.388); Gao's interview is closest to Liu's (0.451) and furthest to Zhang's (0.310); Jin's interview is closest to Gao's (0.413) and furthest to Ma's (0.272); Ma's interview is closest

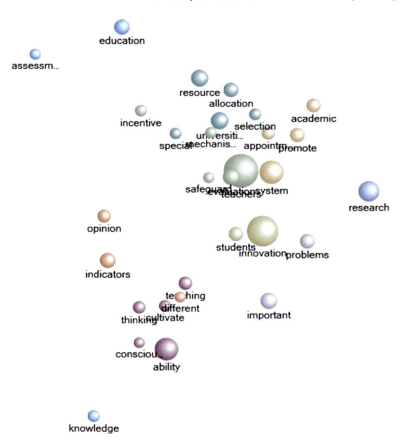

Fig. 7.21 2D clustering graph for correlation analysis of high-frequency words of NENU interviews

to Shi's (0.408) and Shi's interview is furthest to Zhang's (0.214). This can also be observed from the figure of cluster analysis.

7.4.4 For Shaanxi Normal University (SSNU)

First, we take all eight interviews from SSNU as a whole and do the high-frequency word analysis. The result is as shown Table 7.22.

Straightforwardly, we can see the high-frequency-word cloud as shown in the picture below (Fig. 7.25).

According to the analysis result above, we can observe that "Innovation" is the most frequent word (4.48%), which is almost identical to the result of comprehensive analysis. Moreover, the words whose the amount of occurrence exceed

7.4 Analysis by Universities

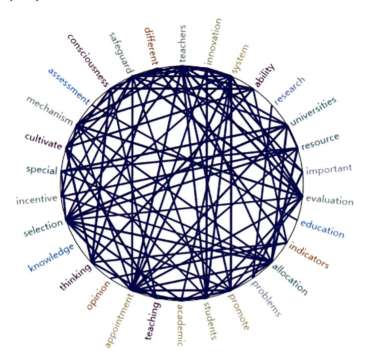

Fig. 7.22 Circle graph for correlation analysis of high-frequency words of NENU interviews

Table 7.22 The summary of high-frequency words in SNNU interviews

Word	Length	Amount of occurrence	Weighted percentage (%)
Innovation	10	373	4.48
Teacher	7	350	4.20
Ability	7	252	3.03
Academic	8	235	2.82
Research	8	152	1.83
University	10	152	1.83
System	6	151	1.81
Evaluation	10	124	1.49
Mechanism	9	88	1.06
Promotion	9	86	1.03
Teaching	8	82	0.98

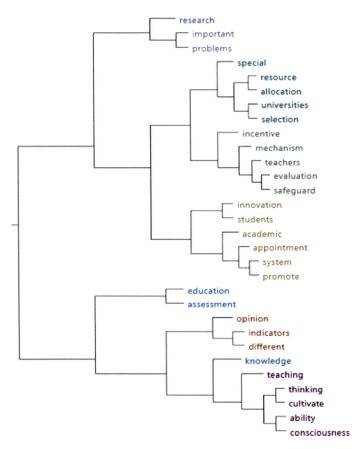

Fig. 7.23 Tree graph for correlation analysis of high-frequency words of NENU interviews

Fig. 7.24 Cluster analysis for interviews of NENU

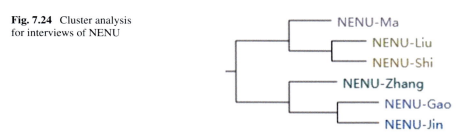

7.4 Analysis by Universities

Fig. 7.25 The high-frequency-word cloud based on interviews of SNNU

150 are "Teacher" (4.20%), "Ability" (3.03%), "Academic" (2.82%), "Research" (1.83%), "University" (1.83%), and "System" (1.81%). There is no doubt that these words are highly related to the innovation and reform of teachers in higher education, which is the topic of interviews'.

Then, based on the high-frequency words we obtained above, we endeavor to get the coverage percentage of these words in each interview. Note that for the group analysis, we take the university as the whole population. So, the result will be slightly different from the result of comprehensive analysis. The coverage percentage for each high-frequency word is summarized in Tables 7.23 and 7.24.

According to the tables above, for the analysis of high-frequency word coverage percentage, for each interview, we can summarize the information of each high-frequency word in Table 7.25.

Second, we apply a correlation analysis for high-frequency words in the following statement. Similarly, in this case, we use spherical graph to observe the correlation between the high-frequency words. Since there are too many words, we only select 30 notional words, as shown in Figs. 7.26, 7.27, 7.28, and 7.29.

According to the figures above, similarly, we can observe that in whole, the high-frequency words can be divided into three groups and almost every word has connection with another word, especially for the high-frequency words. However, based on the terminal of the tree, we can obtain some basic ideas about these interviews, which embodies the situation of SNNU. For example, we can observe that "innovative" and "teachers" are together, which indicates that the teachers should be innovative or innovation is a kind of requirement for the teachers in SSNU; "ability" and "aca-

194 7 Analysis of Interviews of Chinese Faculty Development

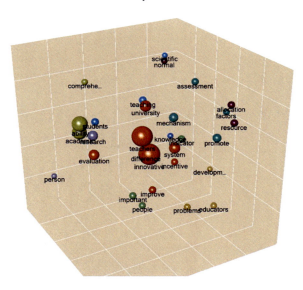

Fig. 7.26 3D clustering graph for correlation analysis of high-frequency words of SNNU interviews

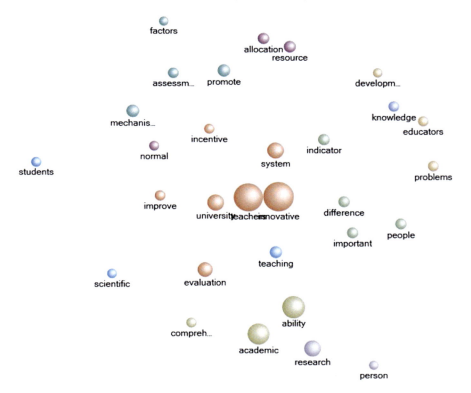

Fig. 7.27 2D clustering graph for correlation analysis of high-frequency words of SNNU interviews

7.4 Analysis by Universities

Table 7.23 The coverage percentage of high-frequency words in each interview of SNNU (Word 1–7)

	Innovation (%)	Teacher (%)	Ability (%)	Academic (%)	Research (%)	University (%)	System (%)
SNNU-Hao	3.75	1.79	0.78	1.52	1.32	0.81	0.87
SNNU-Chen	3.04	1.61	2.68	3.88	2.85	1.71	0.54
SNNU-Fang	2.80	1.86	2.39	1.94	2.37	1.12	0.56
SNNU-Huo	2.67	3.11	1.65	2.40	0.55	1.79	0.77
SNNU-Li	6.66	3.55	0.54	1.08	0.46	1.88	1.31
SNNU-Ma	4.15	2.56	0.94	0.88	1.10	1.73	1.17
SNNU-Wang	2.64	2.46	2.29	0.67	0.43	1.14	0.92
SNNU-You	3.42	1.33	3.29	2.22	0.17	2.74	1.28

Table 7.24 The coverage percentage of high-frequency words in each interview of SNNU (Word 8–11)

	Evaluation (%)	Mechanism (%)	Promotion (%)	Teaching (%)
SNNU-Hao	0.82	0.20	0.39	0.62
SNNU-Chen	1.12	0.12	0.00	1.09
SNNU-Fang	1.55	0.34	0.00	0.00
SNNU-Huo	0.61	1.73	0.64	0.24
SNNU-Li	1.88	1.04	1.25	1.09
SNNU-Ma	0.49	0.77	1.07	0.78
SNNU-Wang	0.97	1.37	0.99	0.94
SNNU-You	2.14	0.96	1.18	0.51

demic" are together, which implies that the researchers should have activities in academic contribution.

Third, we will apply cluster analysis based on interviewees. Based on the word's similarity, we use cluster analysis toward all interviews. The results, including cluster figure and Pearson correlation coefficient matrix, are as below (Fig. 7.30 and Table 7.26).

According to the results above, generally speaking, all the interviews are similar in medium degree, that is to say, they have common topic, but the details are different. The most similar pair is between Chen and Fang (0.746) and least similar pair is between Li and Fang (0.467). For the other interviewees, Hao's interview is closest

Table 7.25 The highest and lowest coverage percentage of each high-frequency words in each interview of SNNU

Key word	Interviewee	Highest coverage percentage (%)	Interviewee	Lowest coverage percentage (%)
Innovation	SNNU-Li	6.66	SNNU-Wang	2.64
Teacher	SNNU-Li	3.55	SNNU-You	1.33
Ability	SNNU-You	3.29	SNNU-Li	0.54
Academic	SNNU-Chen	3.88	SNNU-Wang	0.67
Research	SNNU-Chen	2.85	SNNU-You	0.17
University	SNNU-You	2.74	SNNU-Hao	0.81
System	SNNU-Li	1.31	SNNU-Chen	0.54
Evaluation	SNNU-You	2.14	SNNU-Ma	0.49
Mechanism	SNNU-Huo	1.73	SNNU-Chen	0.12
Promotion	SNNU-Li	1.25	SNNU-Chen; SNNU-Fang	0.00
Teaching	SNNU-Chen; SNNU-Li	1.09	SNNU-Fang	0.00

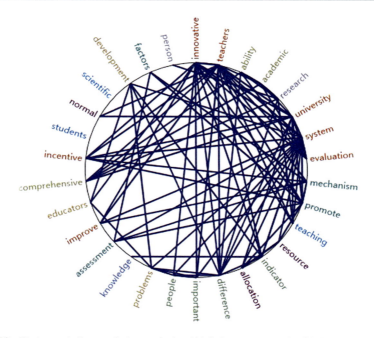

Fig. 7.28 Circle graph for correlation analysis of high-frequency words of SNNU interviews

7.4 Analysis by Universities

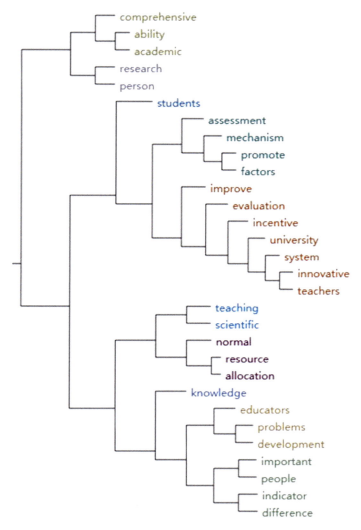

Fig. 7.29 Tree graph for correlation analysis of high-frequency words of SNNU interviews

to Ma's (0.660) while is furthest to Huo's (0.551); Chen's interview is furthest to Li's (0.487); Huo's interview is closest to You's (0.653) and furthest to Hao's (0.551); Li's interview is closest to Ma's (0.729); Ma's interview is furthest to Chen's (0.559); Wang's interview is furthest to Fang's (0.526) and You's interview is closest to Wang's (0.667). This can also be observed from the figure of cluster analysis.

Fig. 7.30 Cluster analysis for interviews of SNNU

Table 7.26 The Pearson correlation coefficient matrix based on interviews of SNNU

	SNNU-Hao	SNNU-Chen	SNNU-Fang	SNNU-Huo	SNNU-Li	SNNU-Ma	SNNU-Wang	SNNU-You
SNNU-Hao	1	0.595	0.565	0.551	0.619	0.660	0.557	0.579
SNNU-Chen	0.595	1	0.746	0.621	0.487	0.559	0.532	0.656
SNNU-Fang	0.565	0.746	1	0.586	0.467	0.546	0.526	0.596
SNNU-Huo	0.551	0.621	0.586	1	0.637	0.622	0.609	0.653
SNNU-Li	0.619	0.487	0.467	0.637	1	0.729	0.598	0.586
SNNU-Ma	0.660	0.559	0.546	0.622	0.729	1	0.661	0.666
SNNU-Wang	0.557	0.532	0.526	0.609	0.598	0.661	1	0.667
SNNU-You	0.579	0.656	0.596	0.653	0.586	0.666	0.667	1

7.4.5 For Southwest University (SWU)

First, we take all nine interviews from SWU as a whole and apply the high-frequency word analysis. The result is Table 7.27.

Straightforwardly, we can see the high-frequency-word cloud as shown in the picture below (Fig. 7.31).

According to the analysis result above, we can observe that "Innovation" is the most frequent word (4.65%), which is almost identical to the result of comprehensive analysis. Moreover, the words whose the amount of occurrence exceed 150 are "Teacher" (3.81%) and "Ability" (3.39%). There is no doubt that these words are highly related to the innovation and reform of teachers in higher education, which is the topic of interviews'.

7.4 Analysis by Universities

Table 7.27 The summary of high-frequency words in SWU interviews

Word	Length	Amount of occurrence	Weighted percentage (%)
Innovation	10	232	4.65
Teacher	7	190	3.81
Ability	7	169	3.39
Academic	8	134	2.69
University	10	116	2.33
Evaluation	10	114	2.29
System	6	94	1.88

Fig. 7.31 The high-frequency-word cloud based on interviews of SWU

Then, based on the high-frequency words we obtained above, we endeavor to get the coverage percentage of these words in each interview. Note that for the group analysis, we take the university as the whole population. So, the result will be slightly different from the result of comprehensive analysis. The coverage percentage for each high-frequency word is summarized in Table 7.28.

According to the tables above, for the analysis of high-frequency word coverage percentage, for each interview, we can summarize the information of each high-frequency word in Table 7.29.

Second, we apply correlation analysis for high-frequency words in the following statement. Similarly, in this case, we use spherical graph to observe the correlation between the high-frequency words. Since there are too many words, we only select 30 notional words, as shown in Figs 7.32, 7.33, 7.34, and 7.35.

Table 7.28 The coverage percentage of high-frequency words in each interview of SWU

	Innovation (%)	Teacher (%)	Ability (%)	Academic (%)	University (%)	Evaluation (%)	System (%)
SWU-Chen	4.20	2.46	1.71	2.32	1.74	1.57	1.19
SWU-Huang	3.25	1.52	1.66	2.49	1.57	2.68	1.02
SWU-Jin	3.43	1.86	2.68	1.45	2.71	1.53	1.33
SWU-Liu, G	3.04	1.43	3.69	1.56	1.95	1.56	0.68
SWU-Liu, M	2.57	2.32	1.37	2.16	1.64	1.78	0.71
SWU-Song	4.67	2.18	2.60	1.49	2.83	1.63	2.09
SWU-Zhang	4.10	1.54	1.29	1.65	1.26	1.26	0.45
SWU-Zhou	4.37	1.72	1.57	0.48	1.30	1.42	0.56
SWU-Zhu	3.39	1.37	0.93	1.30	3.36	1.80	0.74

Table 7.29 The highest and lowest coverage percentage of each high-frequency words in each interview of SWU

Key word	Interviewee	Highest coverage percentage (%)	Interviewee	Lowest coverage percentage (%)
Innovation	SWU-Song	4.67	SWU-Liu, M	2.57
Teacher	SWU-Chen	2.46	SWU-Zhu	1.37
Ability	SWU-Liu, G	3.69	SWU-Zhu	0.93
Academic	SWU-Huang	2.49	SWU-Zhou	0.48
University	SWU-Zhu	3.36	SWU-Zhang	1.26
Evaluation	SWU-Huang	2.68	SWU-Zhang	1.26
System	SWU-Song	2.09	SWU-Zhang	0.45

7.4 Analysis by Universities

Fig. 7.32 3D clustering graph for correlation analysis of high-frequency words of SWU interviews

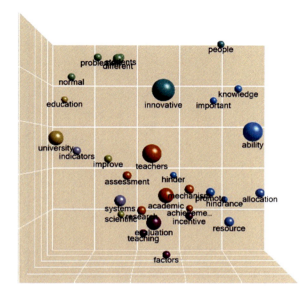

According to the figures above, similarly, we can observe that in whole, the high-frequency words can be divided into three groups and but the connection between the pairwise words are scarce, which indicates that the topics are relatively separating. However, based on the terminal of the tree, we can obtain some basic ideas about these interviews, which embodies the situation of SWU. For example, we can observe that "academic" and "research" are together, as well as the "assessment", which indicates that the research is kind of assessment of academic achievement and there is no doubt that assessment is quite vital in the academic research.

Third, we will apply cluster analysis based on interviewees. Based on the word's similarity, we use cluster analysis toward all interviews. The results, including cluster figure and Pearson correlation coefficient matrix, are as below (Fig. 7.36 and Table 7.30).

According to the results above, generally speaking, since all the Pearson correlation coefficients are larger than 0.50, we can draw the conclusion that all the interviews are quite similar, which indicates that the interviewees had the same opinions and ideas toward the same question. More specifically, the most similar pair is between Chen's and Huang's (0.778) and least similar pair is between Zhou's and Liu, M's (0.520). Note that Zhou's interview has a relatively small Pearson correlated coefficient with other interviews comparing with other interviewees, which implies that Zhou's ideas and opinions are slightly different from the other interviewees in SWU. This can also be observed from the figure of cluster analysis.

Table 7.30 The Pearson correlation coefficient matrix based on interviews of SWU

	SWU-Chen	SWU-Huang	SWU-Jin	SWU-Liu, G	SWU-Liu, M	SWU-Song	SWU-Zhang	SWU-Zhou	SWU-Zhu
SWU-Chen	1	0.778	0.708	0.650	0.674	0.698	0.702	0.576	0.669
SWU-Huang	0.778	1	0.711	0.659	0.684	0.662	0.692	0.576	0.663
SWU-Jin	0.708	0.711	1	0.693	0.612	0.680	0.664	0.604	0.631
SWU-Liu, G	0.650	0.659	0.693	1	0.677	0.675	0.635	0.571	0.581
SWU-Liu, M	0.674	0.684	0.612	0.677	1	0.611	0.623	0.520	0.572
SWU-Song	0.698	0.662	0.680	0.675	0.611	1	0.656	0.601	0.639
SWU-Zhang	0.702	0.692	0.664	0.635	0.623	0.656	1	0.643	0.641
SWU-Zhou	0.576	0.576	0.604	0.571	0.520	0.601	0.643	1	0.571
SWU-Zhu	0.669	0.663	0.631	0.581	0.572	0.639	0.641	0.571	1

7.4 Analysis by Universities   203

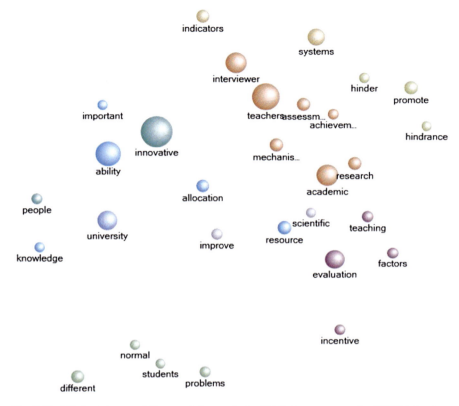

Fig. 7.33 2D clustering graph for correlation analysis of high-frequency words of SWU interviews

7.4.6 *For Other Universities (PKU, BNU, SJTU, and HUST)*

There are five interviewees are from four different universities. It does not make sense to summarize the common key words because their background is totally different and there might not be common sense among them. However, we can see how different they are based on the Pearson correlation coefficient matrix. The results, including cluster figure and Pearson correlation coefficient matrix, are as below (Fig. 7.37 and Table 7.31).

According to the results above, we can observe that their interviews are not similar. The most similar pair is between Liu's from PKU and Liu's from SJTU (0.535) and least similar pair is between Liu's from SJTU and Zhang's from BNU (0.259). This indicates that researchers from different universities may have totally different opinions and ideas.

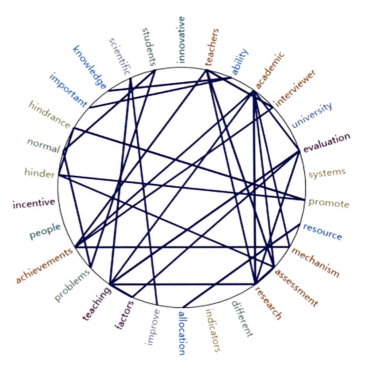

Fig. 7.34 Circle graph for correlation analysis of high-frequency words of SWU interviews

Table 7.31 The Pearson correlation coefficient matrix based on interviews of PKU, BNU, SJTU, and HUST

	HUST-Liu	HUST-Zhang	PKU-Liu	SJTU-Liu	BNU-Zhang
HUST-Liu	1	0.492	0.494	0.368	0.398
HUST-Zhang	0.492	1	0.523	0.524	0.496
PKU-Liu	0.494	0.523	1	0.535	0.391
SJTU-Liu	0.368	0.524	0.535	1	0.259
BNU-Zhang	0.398	0.496	0.391	0.259	1

7.4.7 Conclusion of Group Analysis

Based on all the outputs above, we can observe that the result is generally similar to the result of comprehensive analysis, that is to say, the high-frequency words are generally identical, and they occurred in different interviews with different proportions, which we can get the corresponding key points of the interview. It also indicates that with different positions, it is possible that the ideas and opinions can be different toward the same question.

7.4 Analysis by Universities

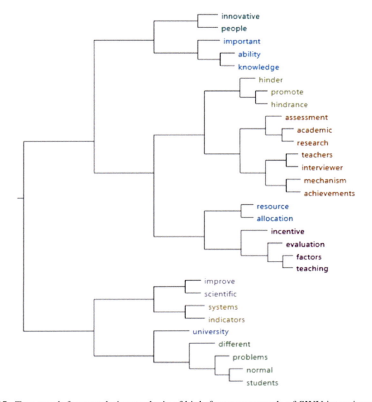

Fig. 7.35 Tree graph for correlation analysis of high-frequency words of SWU interviews

Fig. 7.36 Cluster analyses for interviews of SWU

Fig. 7.37 Cluster analysis for interviews of PKU, BNU, SJTU, and HUST

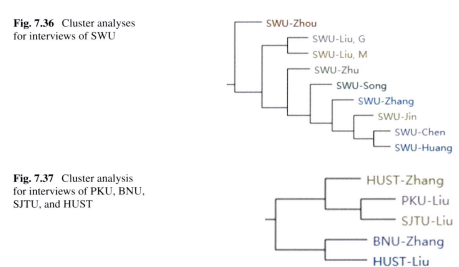

Chapter 8
Faculty Development at Chinese Context: Conclusion, Strategies, and Implications

This chapter concentrates on exploring faculty development at Chinese context from conclusion, remark, and implication perspectives. Along with the analyses result from previous chapter, this chapter is fundamentally subject to offer explanations and illustrations to examine the complexity of constructing faculty development at Chinese context. The conclusion, remarks, and implication are proposed to epitomize faculty development with Chinese characteristics.

8.1 Conclusions on Faculty Development at Chinese Context

The conclusions and strategies on faculty development at Chinese context are summarized into several major findings, including resource allocation mechanism and obstacles of resource allocation mechanism.

8.1.1 Resource Allocation Mechanism

In Chinese higher education context, faculty development is deeply embedded in the "resource allocation mechanism". In Chinese context, faculty resources serve as the most important resources in Chinese colleges and universities. The quality and responsibility of faculty are associated with the excellent degree of all aspects of the university (Yang, 2000, 2002, 2011; Zhao, 2009). It affects the academic activities of the university, the quality of the students as a whole, the excellent achievements of teaching itself and the academic. Universities' faculty is always considered not only the special resources that can be controlled, used, and managed by their universities, but also serve as the creator and the disseminator of the knowledge and the creator of the talent product. In other words, the standard of resource allocation of universities faculty is the embodiment of the maximization of the value of resources. The faculty from colleges and universities are expected to make full use of their abilities and make the greatest contribution to the development of their universities or colleges. Faculty efforts are inherently associated with the development of Chinese universities and colleges (Lin & Wei, 2016; Liu, 2018; Pang, 2012).

8.1.2 Obstacles of Resource Allocation Mechanism

The Chinese faculty members have the general characteristics of human resources: dominance, initiative, dynamism, intelligence, regeneration, and sociality. Besides, the resources of universities' faculty also have their own basic characteristics: first is the difficult measurement of the labor value of university's faculty. Faculty do not directly participate in the economic activities, in this sense, they provide a "service", which makes their labor value difficult to quantify; second is the work of faculty in colleges and universities has greater subjective initiative; third is the richness of faculty' resources in colleges and universities; fourth is the high academic qualifications and strong professionalism of college faculty; and fifth is the gradual diversification of the role of faculty in colleges and universities. As a whole, faculty, as a kind of high-grade human resources, have great scarcity in terms of their basic quality requirements, cultivation costs, or market supply conditions, which is a very scarce resource. From the macro-market supply situation, the qualified faculty resources are still facing a certain degree of the shortage in current stage. At present, there are many unreasonable aspects of the faculty resource allocation mechanism in universities, which hinders the development of teachers' creativity.

The "project system" restricts the academic innovation of faculty
In recent years, the implementation of "project system" in the allocation of the faculty resources has brought a lot of negative effects. The Chinese government uses the centralized funding allocation system to mobilize and control Chinese universities' faculty members' academic research topic and content. In other words, Chinese central government has allocated academic research funds for the project research area and assigned faculty member to study on specific research topic. So, a lot of inefficient and boring research subjects came out and these projects lead to the serious damage of the academic autonomy and the academic ecology, as well as the serious erosion of the logic of the academic field. Such a system is also more limited than encouragement for faculty's academic creativity.

Faculty immobility hinders the flexibility of faculty resources
The defects of the division of labor system and the rigidity of the system hinder the flexibility and optimal allocation of faculty resources. As a public institution, a university is a public ownership system. As a faculty member, everyone holds an "iron rice bowl" as the status of faculty. As a faculty member, there is no survival of the fittest. This rigid and lack of incentive mechanism is lack of incentive effect. This division arrangement hinders the optimal allocation of resources. The plan

configuration is still the main way. At present, the talent flow and talent exchange in current Chinese colleges and universities have developed rapidly, but in general, the most of the faculty members in Chinese colleges and universities have not yet entered the international intellectual market. The mechanism of faculty resource allocation is considered as a kind of compulsion.

"Familization" phenomenon of the university is particularly prominent
Currently, the management system of Chinese universities is not comprehensive and reasonable, especially under the current personnel management system, the "family-oriented" university has led to the emergence of the phenomenon of "inbreeding" in many Chinese colleges and universities. Academic innovation is embedded in the academic freedom and academic justice. The academic freedom is associated with the flow of faculty and students. The academic "Inbreeding" phenomenon inevitably leads to the destruction of the academic freedom and the decline of academic innovation, which related to the serious academic corruption and bureaucracy. The university "family" is a process of homogeneity, in fact, which makes the university academic edge structure too single, prompting the prevalence of inbreeding in colleges and universities, strangling the atmosphere of academic innovation, making scientific ideas rigid, restricting the construction of the subject, affecting the quality of higher education, and increasing the conversion cost of the research results.

8.2 Strategies on Faculty Development at Chinese Context: Resource Allocation Mechanism

8.2.1 Flexible Management

According to the characteristics of the faculty members, there existed different types of resource management mechanisms accordingly. Take the example of East China Normal University, they take senior professors as the wealth of the development of their university, they provide a variety of preferential treatment, good service to these experts and scholars; for middle-aged faculty members, the school encouraged and forced them to "go out", let them go out of their university to strive for more sufficient resources, the university will not give them any favorable conditions. Because they think that, if the middle-aged faculty members could do well, they can "grab" back outside, because "grab it" shows that their academic status has an impact on the academia. In order to prove their academic strength, middle-aged faculty members are required to strive for their own academic status in the country; for the young faculty members, their universities or colleges should provide more additional support to their professional academic development. Prof. Z President of East China Normal University, said that

> The young faculty members are like unearthed relics. We have to pick up the soil and let them unearthed quickly. So I say all the preferential policies are aimed at supporting young

faculty members to enhance their academic achievements and reputations. I will not aim at providing more resources to your middle-aged faculty members and senior faculty members, because the young faculty members are the future hope of the academic world.

Hence, the policy of flexible management has provided different mechanisms to each different stage faculty members in their academic field. It is conducive to inspiring different-staged faculty members' academic innovation by protecting, encouraging middle-aged teachers, and respecting senior teachers.

"Academic leaders" as department administrative leader
Many school leaders and experts suggested that assigning the academic leader, as the department's leadership, is a favorable factor for improving teachers' innovative ability. On the one hand, academic leaders have a strong academic insight and can grasp the direction of the development of the department. They have academic judgment and can accurately grasp the project subjects of the department; on the other hand, the academy is able to make a good grasp. The department leaders often participate in various academic seminars, which can open academic horizons. To some extent, it is beneficial to their academic development. Academic leaders are leading academics, relying on strong academic strength and leadership, and can organize a larger team. This is very important for the growth of the faculty of the entire department. Academic leaders should be leaders of colleges and departments, so that the whole faculty can concentrate on learning and enhance their creativity.

Team-bundled development
Team-bundled development is the process of the joint development of all young- and middle-aged faculty members in the process of completing tasks based on project tasks. Such as a project, the senior professors mainly provide the consultancy services, a wide range of resources, middle-aged teachers are mainly promoted, organized youth teachers to discuss together, provide experience methods, asked young faculty practice, so that in a project, the whole team can be developed at different age stages of faculty.

Transforming from scholar to administers
The vast majority of education experts and executives believe that academic researchers do a great deal of influence on their academic research, but some experts point out that scholars can do administrative work after the "peak" of creativity, and that many people have a peak in their academic career and the most creative stage of creativity. There may not be many breakthroughs, but the academic insight and judgment of these scholars are impossible for other people. Therefore, it is good for them to do administrative and school management, to give full play to their broad vision and resources, and to help the progress of the whole school.

Upgrading basic resources

Upgrading basic resources mainly involve to improving faculty's working conditions and academic research conditions. Maslow's hierarchy of needs theory also points out that only when people meet the most basic needs can people strive to pursue higher level needs. At present, young teachers are mainly for leadership, for older teachers, few opportunities to independently undertake the project, and in the process of research, there will be a lot of problems. Therefore, on the one hand, the government and schools should provide more policy tendencies for young teachers, to stimulate their creativity as a major event, and on the other hand, to encourage the departments to give young teachers funds and resources support, and to encourage senior professors to give guidance to young teachers.

8.2.2 Faculty Selection and Recruitment Mechanism

Historically speaking, current Chinese faculty selection and recruitment mechanism could be traced back to the end of the Qing Dynasty, which was initially embodied in the terms of address, conditions of employment, and remuneration for faculty practice by the Beijing Normal University. After a long history of the faculty recruitment mechanism development, Chinese higher education institutions have gradually established the four-level professional title evaluation system and entitled "professors, associate professors, lecturers and assistants." In 1986, the State Education Committee issued the Trial Regulations on the Higher Education Institutions' Faculty and clearly stipulated the faculty's duties, conditions of appointment, qualification evaluation, appointment, and appointment of faculty at all levels in Chinese Colleges and universities. This regulation breaks the regulations based on the provision of the power to appoint, judge, and dismiss the faculty and making a fair competition according to the academic level and working ability. As a result, the selection and recruitment mechanism of university faculty from "commentary" to "Recruitment" has entered a new stage of deepening the "teacher engagement system". Chinese current domestic faculty selection and recruitment mechanism is considered as a principle system of the combination of responsibilities, rights, and obligations of both universities and faculty. The faculty selection and recruitment mechanism includes the employment contract, recruitment process, appointment management, dismissal cause, income, and dispute treatment. The faculty selection and recruitment mechanism is considered as the incentive of the faculty engagement, which determines the mobility and quality of faculty, and guides the professional development of faculty. The academic profession has some special features, such as inquiry, autonomy, and discipline. How to improve the selection and recruitment mechanism for this special team is an important subject that we have to consider in the process of improving the appointment system of teachers and the construction of innovative teachers in our country.

Obstacles of Faculty Selection and Recruitment Mechanism
Interference of administrative power

As a social organization, the Chinese university is an organized social unit, which is subject to the rules of formal organization, and therefore has a certain hierarchy. In contemporary China, the degree of the marketization of colleges and universities is relatively lower than Western context and most of the Chinese colleges and universities adopt the "principal responsibility system under the leadership of the Party committee." By this logic, the administrative power within Chinese universities and colleges is definitely stronger than academic power. Along with such a special system, the interference of administrative power is very serious in Chinese universities' faculty recruitment mechanism. For example, a number of recruitment committees are made up of the administrators rather than academic professionals and the recruitment results of the professors' review of scholar are sent to the department for review and the final appointment resolution by the executive leader. The negative consequences are twofold: one is that the administrative personnel is lack of the professional knowledge and often offer inaccurate judgment and evaluation; two is that the administrative way tends to examine the number of faculty's articles that is published by the applicant or the grade of publication. It is not a qualitative evaluation of the academic innovation of the article itself, which is not only a biased evaluation standard but also a negative guide to the teachers' weight of academic achievements.

The deception of academic achievements

Although the approach of evaluating faculty's academic innovation based on the academic achievements is reasonable, there still existed some misunderstanding. The interviewee argued that,

> Some academic achievements or academic outcomes, even published in high level journals, could not represent faculty's high level of academic innovation. For example, in the context of Chinese academia, as we known, some academic achievements and outcomes with the title of national major research topics and national grand support project are much more easier to be published in Chinese authoritative academic journals, but the faculty own academic innovation may not necessarily high (Prof. C).

Similarly, some interviewee also expressed their agreement on the phenomenon of deception of academic achievements, which do not reflect the faculty's academic innovation and academic achievements.

> Many task-based research of faculty could not reflect faculty's academic interest and academic innovation in their own research. Therefore, if we do not make an in-depth analysis and objective evaluation of faculty's academic achievements, it is very difficult to really identify the level of academic innovation of faculty. This could also be considered as one implicit deception of academic achievement and academic innovation (Prof. Zhou)

The evaluation method hinders faculty's academic innovation

In contemporary Chinese higher education system, both the teaching assessment and academic research assessment adopt the quantitative evaluation method. The measurement of scientific research results greatly erased the academic innovation of faculty.

First of all, emphasizing on the number of papers and the grade of the journal assessment made faculty members produce a large number of low-level and low-quality papers in order to complete the assigned research task; Secondly, the evaluation methods of the number of papers and journals made faculty give up their research interests and pursue the so-called "research hot spots" to meet the requirements of the Chinese academic journals. This not only leads to some basic problems, which seem to be very important, but also the research interest and academic enthusiasm of faculty - the motive force of academic innovation. Once research becomes a task and the faculty academic innovation would be difficult to achieve; thirdly, focusing on the examination method of journal level, which enables some faculty to publish articles in foreign periodicals. This leads to faculty's research closely following the trend of foreign academic research, and indifferent to China's local problems, which hinders our academic innovation and development (Prof. Huang).

The short period of evaluation is considered as another barrier to stimulate faculty's academic innovation. The examination cycle of 1 year's evaluation is contrary to the principle of academic research.

> "Academic work is inquiring, and the process of knowledge exploration is uncertain. In fact, the enthusiasm, no matter how sincere and profound it reaches, can't compare with a result anywhere. Therefore, it is not an effective way to measure the effectiveness of professional scholars in specific period, especially for the creative work. Academic output, especially high quality academic output requires a long time preparation and flexible external environment. A short period of assessment for faculty is constantly on the run, stifling the academic innovation force. In addition, too frequent examination will also stimulate the emergence of academic plagiarism. (Prof. Huang)

8.2.3 Strategies on Faculty Selection and Recruitment Mechanism

Improving strategies based on the evaluation mechanism of faculty development. First of all, the assessment of faculty academic innovation should transfer from the quantitative-oriented method to quality-oriented method. The number of single papers and the grade standard of journals seriously restrict the exertion of faculty's academic innovation and undermine the pure academic environment. The assessment mechanism should be changed from simple quantity pursuit to quality and teaching level.

Second, the implementation of classification assessment should be adjusted and changed the assessment cycle and assessment design as soon as possible, and carry out classified assessment. Based on the characteristics of subjects and individual differences of faculty, we should give full consideration to the principle of scientific research and classify the design of assessment cycle and assessment form.

Third, the exit mechanism construction is beneficial to encourage faculty's academic innovation. In the relevant laws and regulations of Chinese university appointment system, all the regulations should be implemented in the system. However, due to the influence of traditional ideas and the backward personnel security system, faculty members who are dismissed are facing many difficulties. The "employment system" of faculty in colleges and universities in China is actually a "lifelong recruitment system". In fact, the degree of marketization of Chinese universities is relatively low and the exit mechanism is basically "empty talk". The system of appointment is a system of tenure. A serious lack of exit mechanism is an important factor affecting faculty academic innovation. In addition, the lack of exit mechanism has made the existing faculty member lack competitiveness and gradually lost the power of academic innovation. The lack of exit mechanism leads to the normal flow of faculty, the negative atmosphere, and academic discipline.

First of all, improve the personnel supporting system. One of the important reasons why the exit mechanism is difficult to be implemented is that the registration system of China's household registration, archives, and social security system is still relatively backward. In addition, by the influence of the social environment, teachers will face a lot of trouble after they are dismissed. Improving the personnel supporting system and reducing the risk of dismissing teachers are the primary tasks of implementing the exit mechanism.

In order to deal with this problem, Chinese universities and colleges should establish a reasonable procedure for faculty dismissal or resignation. We have established strict regulations and regular procedures for faculty' exports, and set up a scientific appointment system of "able persons and mediocre persons." Again, the combination of regular appointment and tenure appointment is considered as an effective approach to promote faculty's academic innovation. The tenure track system has played an important role in maintaining academic freedom, ensuring occupational safety, and attracting outstanding talents, and has guaranteed the quality of higher education to a certain extent. Colleges and universities in China can learn the mode of foreign universities and colleges and universities. At the same time, the majority of the senior posts are employed for life, while the regular appointment is carried out for most teachers, that is, the combination of regular appointment and lifelong appointment.

The academic incentive mechanism
The faculty's academic innovation is mainly reflected in the innovative academic achievements. Therefore, the current academic incentive mechanism influences faculty academic innovation outcome. Chinese academic incentive mechanism mainly includes some types: bonus, subsidy, title promotion, scientific research funds, honorary titles, administrative posts, and some research guarantee conditions for academic innovation research activities, such as wages, housing, working conditions, atmosphere, and so on. The Chinese academic incentive mechanism is to stimulate faculty's innovation spirit to improve their academic innovation competency or improve the guarantee conditions for the academic innovation of faculty. But in reality, many incentive academic mechanisms do not produce the corresponding incentive effect. At the same time, the improvement of innovative research ability and the creation of innovative research results have its inherent special laws, closely related to individual interest, curiosity, academic belief, and academic spirit, and the external incentive mechanism can have limited effect and influence on it, and more need a kind of internal needs and motivation. Therefore, both external incentive

measures and intrinsic academic purport play an important role to promote faculty academic innovation.

External incentive mechanism

The external incentives include the basic guarantee conditions of wages, salaries, housing, and working conditions.

> The establishment of the incentive mechanism for Chinese university faculty is important and we should construct the establishment of incentive mechanism for University faculty academic innovation. Good salary and stable living environment are the most basic life support for faculty to engage in innovative academic activities. It can make college teachers do not have to run for a living and live a decent life, so that they can wholeheartedly learn and do research (Prof. Wu)

In addition, working conditions as the external incentives include the equipment, facilities, equipment, and books needed for academic research. For innovation in science, experimental equipment and conditions are particularly important. These conditions are indispensable resources for college teachers to carry out innovative research. For innovation in the field of liberal arts, book resources are also very important for faculty to improve their academic innovation. Relaxed academic cultural environment also provides inevitable external incentive to stimulate faculty to enhance their academic innovation. It contains two aspects: one aspect is the real autonomy for the academic researchers. When they create and think about the problems, they do not have to worry about whether such views will offend the interests of Chinese central government and other political power organization. Creating a loose, tolerant academic environment and free academic culture could change current status of faculty's academic attitudes and efforts. In other words, it is possible for the independent innovation to make scholars dare to criticize the existing educational system, thus triggering Chinese academic system reform or reconstruction, rather than defending this system. On the other hand, the examination mechanism should be loose and frequent. The quantitative assessment of the number of periodical papers, the number of books, and the number of scientific research projects, especially the time and energy of the academic researchers, makes them difficult to deal with all kinds of assessment. For the subject, many subjects have time constraints, and they are required to make problems within 1 or 2 years and report regularly. As we all know, a lot of research, especially the arts, needs to be modified and processed over a long period of time, and the inspiration should be involved for 2 or 3 years. However, most of the universities in China adopt this method of quantitative assessment and make the quantitative result, which linked to wages, allowances, and bonuses to a great extent. Hence, to some extent, some scholars call it "institutional impetuosity". The traction of this quantitative assessment mechanism decreases the faculty, especially young faculty's academic development in the long term.

Honors

There are many awards for rewarding the academic innovative work for faculty. For example, "the Yangtze River Scholar", "the Purple River Scholar", "the new century talent", etc., these honors are often the special products under the special historical conditions, which have played a very good incentive effect under the specific conditions at that time, but whether the conditions will be lost after the conditions are lost.

> As professor Liu said, "Changjiang Scholars" is a special product of Chinese academic system under the special historical conditions. At that time, the salary of college faculty was very low. In order to retain and attract some foreign and domestic scholars, it started such an honorary incentive system. Each person rewarded one hundred thousand. This is a special practice under special historical conditions. It is still necessary and useful. However, under normal circumstances, it will not play a great role. Will it be good to go on or not? Is it big or bad? It needs to be considered and measured.

The motivation of a scientist is likely to promote knowledge from a keen expectation, develop to a strong interest in gaining personal prestige, or even to deviate from the ideal of scientific research and the expectation of society for their role under certain conditions. Reputation and honor are often rewarded with innovative achievements in the early years of the researchers. When scholars get these honors, they become an identity, a title, and the accompanying income, interest, or a power resource. If we want to turn honor into an incentive factor for college teachers, we need to emphasize responsibilities after honor acquisition, including social responsibility and academic responsibility.

Bonus, allowance, and job title promotion
An important manifestation of academic innovative achievements is publishing articles in SCI, SSCI, or CSSCI and other journals. Many colleges and universities stipulate that a faculty is given a certain amount of bonus or an integral system to publish a high-quality article, or to publish an article in a periodical of a certain level, accumulating a certain score, and then giving the corresponding reward according to the annual integral. The intensity of awards is not uniform among colleges and universities, some of them are high and some are low. The publishing of articles and books determines the bonus, the amount of the allowance, and the promotion of professional titles. However, this kind of reward and assessment method is a "double-edged sword". It also inevitably brings some negative factors while encouraging college faculty to engage in academic research. It has directly led many people to publish articles in order to get bonuses and professional titles, making academic research very utilitarian purposes, focusing on the quantity rather than the quality.
Research funds

The universities' faculty has applied a variety of academic topics, such as the key topics, such as the Ministry of Education, general topics, youth projects, key team projects, or some horizontal projects, to obtain a certain number of research funds. These projects are designed to provide financial support and condition guarantee for the academic research innovation activities of university faculty, and promote the improvement of academic innovation ability of college faculty.

> It is necessary to analyze whether it can really promote the development of College Teachers' innovation ability. If the subject is fully applied in accordance with the interests of the individual, in the case of obtaining the support of scientific research, the teacher can be more qualified to do the research he wants to do. No doubt it can play a very good incentive effect.

8.2 Strategies on Faculty Development at Chinese Context … 217

However, if these subjects are completely under the circumstances, for example, according to the government, these studies would be hard to go deep and the innovation of the results will be discounted with the study of needs, not my wishes, or the abandonment of the historical and philosophical studies that you like.

Intrinsic academic interest, curiosity, and academic belief
Innovative academic activities are different from the nature of general work. The creation of important innovative results often originates from the intrinsic interest, curiosity, desire, and impulse of the researchers. Aristotle once said that, "there is a kind of knowledge that is known for life." In order to make the creation, innovation of utility under a certain pressure is difficult to produce innovative results of the real. Innovation is not a problem that money and interest can solve. On the contrary, many innovations are generated under extremely hard conditions. The scientific research work of the university teachers should also be exploratory and creative, so they should have the spirit of the scientific man itself. If it is purely based on the spirit of scientific people, researchers will not write papers or monographs with more quantity and quality, and their scientific research results, of course, have some degree of innovation.

> Scholars who really have academic innovation are often those who do not count on fame, fame, honor and power, especially in the field of Humanities and social sciences. These scholars often do not take part in the research topic. "Ten years wear a sword", with a kind of interest, academic belief and pursuit, academic spirit, meditation sit on the bench. With a long and continuous attention to a certain field of research, it will eventually produce innovative research results and produce masterpieces and generations. Only those with lofty spirit can create endless driving force.

As Professor Zhang of East China University of science and technology said,

> we should advocate the social atmosphere of academic and academic, or the individual value orientation of a scholar. It doesn't require any utilitarian purpose of scholarship. Let's not talk about how much an officer can earn through learning, and how much money he can earn through learning. To do knowledge is to learn knowledge, to understand the secrets of nature, to pursue and explore according to their academic interests and interests. If you want to do research for the purpose of winning the prize, it will not win the prize; if you take the purpose of gaining reputation, reputation, status and money to do academic, there will be academic corruption, academic falsification, academic bubble and so on.

Implications on faculty development at Chinese context

Overall speaking, the findings suggested that Chinese faculty has encountered tremendous barriers that limit their professional development at Chinese universities. The resource allocation mechanism, the faculty selection and recruitment mechanism, and the academic incentive mechanism are considered three major mechanisms that impede the development of faculty academic innovation. The implementation of "project system" in the allocation of the faculty resources has brought a lot of negative effects. The defects of the division of labor system and the rigidity of the system hinder the flexibility and optimal allocation of faculty resources. The management system of Chinese universities is not comprehensive and reasonable, especially under the current personnel management system, the "family-oriented" university has led to the emergence of the phenomenon of "inbreeding" in many Chinese colleges and universities. The interviewees proposed that providing flexible management, offering "academic leaders" as department administrative leader, build team-bundled development model, and upgrading basic education resources are essential to improve the advancement of faculty academic innovation. Findings also indicated that, in the faculty selection and recruitment mechanism, interference of administrative power, the deception of academic achievement, and the faculty academic evaluation hinder faculty members' academic innovation. In addition, findings also argued that, in the academic incentive mechanism, external incentive mechanism should be along with intrinsic academic interest, curiosity, and academic belief. The faculty members also suggested the urgency for Chinese universities and colleges to implement "fresh" mechanisms to promote faculty academic innovation.

Chinese faculty members have encountered tremendous tensions in order to enhance academic innovation contextually. In addition, current faculty selection and recruitment mechanism also provides negative influence on improving Chinese faculty academic innovation, such as the interference of the administrative power, the deception of academic achievements and the evaluation method. Moreover, the current academic incentive mechanism also offers disputable negative effects for advancing Chinese faculty's academic innovation, including external incentive mechanism and intrinsic academic interest, curiosity, and academic belief.

There existed several factors that influence the development of universities' faculty academic innovation. Chinese current social concept on "quick success and instant benefit" is not conducive to improve the academic innovation of universities' faculty. For example, in Chinese current academic evaluation, the quantity is not valued. The number of academic achievements is often overestimated in the evaluation process of the professional titles, academic awards, and recruitment of new faculty, but the quality of the results is not concerned. The Chinese current research projects pay attention to the practical application of the research quality. The notion of "official-oriented" academic evaluation still exists, which shows that people who have the potential for the academic innovation and make certain academic achievements tend to serve as administrative posts, which, to a certain extent, affects the further development of academic innovation. More seriously, the current Chinese university personnel system is not comprehensive, which is not conducive to the academic innovation of university faculty. There are no clear measures for improving the academic innovation, and the content of the university faculty personnel system is too formalized and there is a lack of the modern university personnel system. The economic pressure of young faculty is not beneficial to promote their academic innovation. For example, the economic pressure is a real problem for Chinese university faculty, especially for young faculty. Young faculty have just entered the job market and many years of study and pay need to get material rewards, and are faced with the pressure of the family, house, parents, and so on. But currently, the income of young faculty is not high, and it is difficult for them to apply for their job. So the economic pressure is relatively large. Therefore, many young faculty are busy with various social part-time jobs, diverting the energy of academic research, let alone academic innovation.

Along with the dilemmas on Chinese faculty member as previously illustrated, a series of the education reform should be undertaken to enhance Chinese faculty's academic innovation inherently. First, it is pivotal to create a stronger academic atmosphere for Chinese faculty. University is considered as the place of knowledge production and knowledge innovation. We believe that a strong academic atmosphere is a guarantee for improving academic innovation of university faculty. Both the government and universities should provide a strong atmosphere for the academic innovation of university faculty. This academic atmosphere includes the freedom of academic research, the freedom of academic cooperation, the freedom of academic criticism, and the freedom of academic publishing and the academic autonomy. Second, it is important to initiate the reform on university personnel system. The current personnel system of university faculty should be modified and perfected to adapt to the academic innovation of university faculty, especially the exertion of academic innovation. We believe that the establishment of modern university personnel system is essential to enhance academic innovation for Chinese faculty members. Third, providing a platform for the development of interdisciplinary knowledge also contributes to the improvement of faculty's academic innovation contextually. The development of interdisciplinary knowledge focuses on the knowledge basis for the academic innovation of the universities' faculty. Both the Chinese central government and national universities should provide sufficient opportunities and platforms for faculty member to actively engage in the development of the interdisciplinary knowledge of university faculty, which include the development of interdisciplinary cross-research platform, the academic exchanges and the academic cooperation among the universities' faculty, and the application of interdisciplinary research projects. The academic innovation evaluation as an evaluation system plays an important role in guiding academic innovation of China's universities' faculty. Innovation is uncertain, but it is not without direction. The notion of academic innovation, as a special approach of human innovation, has its specific connotation and direction. Therefore, the evaluation of the academic innovation ability has an important guiding role for the academic innovation of China's universities faculty. It has pointed out the direction for faculty to focus their ability and energy on their academic innovation, and is conducive to the formation of academic innovation value orientation of university faculty. Moreover, the evaluation of academic innovation as a reward and punishment system plays an important role in encouraging academic innovation of university teachers. The academic innovation of faculty is not a system itself, but once the academic innovation and evaluation are connected, it has an important incentive to the academic innovation of the university faculty.

References

Lin, J., & Wei, H. (2016). The international trend of university teacher development [J]. *University Education Management, 10*(01), 86–91(in Chinese).

Liu, Z. (2018). From the perspective of governance, organizational transformation of teacher development in American Research Universities: Path and reference [J]. *Modern Education Management* (03), 58–63 (in Chinese).

Pang, H. S. (2012). Research on the function and operation mechanism of the University Teacher Development Center [J]. *Journal of the National Institute of Educational Administration* (08): 60–65 + 33 (in Chinese).

Yang, R. (2000). Tensions between the global and the local: A comparative illustration of the reorganisation of China's higher education in the 1950s and 1990s. *Higher Education, 39*(3), 319–337.

Yang, R. (2002). *Third delight: Internationalization of higher education in China*. New York, NY: Routledge.

Yang, R. (2011). Self and the other in the confucian cultural context: Implications of China's higher education development for comparative studies. *International Review of Education, 57*(3–4), 337–355.

Zhao, Z. Z. (2009). Conceptualization of citizenship education in the. *Chinese Mainland Education Journal (Hong Kong)], 57*(1–2), 57–69.

Printed in the United States
By Bookmasters